Aussie
SOLDIER
Prisoners of War

Aussie SOLDIER
Prisoners of War

Denny Neave and Craig Smith

BIG SKY PUBLISHING

Big Sky Publishing Pty Ltd
17 Rilatt Street
Wavell Heights, QLD, 4012
Australia
Phone: (61 2) 9918 2168
Fax: (61 2) 9918 2396
Email: info@bigskypublishing.com.au
Web: www.bigskypublishing.com.au
Web: www.aussiesoldier.com.au

The National Library of Australia Cataloguing-in-Publication entry
Author: Neave, Denny, 1970
Title: Aussie Soldier Prisoners of War/Denny Neave, Craig Smith.
ISBN: 9780980325157 (pbk.)
Subjects: Prisoners of War--Australia.
Australia--History, Military--20th century.
Other authors/contributors:
Smith, Craig (Craig Edwin)
Dewey Number: 355.1120994

Senior Editor: Alistair Mival
Proofreading and edit: Diane Evans, Sharon Evans and Anna Kassulke
Cover and layout design: Think Productions
Typesetting by Think Productions
Printed in Australia by Ligare Pty Ltd

Cover photography courtesy Australian War Memorial
Main photo: AWM Negative Number E00985: Studio portrait of an unidentified First World War soldier in Australian service uniform, including greatcoat and slouch hat.

Photo insert: AWM Negative Number 11702: Singapore,1945. Members of the 2/18th Aust Infantry Battalion ex-prisoners of war of the Japanese, looking out of an opening in the wall of their native hut at the Changi Gaol.

This book is dedicated to all Australian prisoners of war and their families for all they endured during their service. They share a common bond: knowing what it is like to fight for freedom only to have it removed from them. And yet they never stopped fighting.

Bridge work, Burma-Thailand railway, Griffin, Murray. Pen and brush and brown ink, pencil, white gouache on paper

AWM Neg. ART25107

Contents

Acknowledgments

This instalment in the *Aussie Soldier* series was made possible thanks to many people. Firstly, and most importantly, to the soldiers, who gave up their time to fill out questionnaires and be interviewed. They shared some of their most treasured and personal memories with us, some of which were extremely difficult to recount. Both Craig and I were touched by the humanity and courage these soldiers exhibited. Their bodies may not be as they once were, but their minds are as sharp as they were sixty years ago. It was truly a privilege and honour to talk to them. To the family members of those soldiers who have passed away, thank you for sharing your loved ones' personal records. The pride you feel can now be shared with an entire nation. A complete list of contributors to *Aussie Soldier Prisoners of War* can be found at the end of the book.

To the organisations that do such a fantastic job preserving our heritage: The Australian War Memorial, the National Library of Australia, the State Library of South Australia, the State Library of Victoria, the Department of Veterans' Affairs, the Department of Defence and the Australians At War Film Archives have again provided invaluable resources and given permission for all the material we requested to be reproduced, including official records, personal records and photos. Your support, and that of your front line staff, is very much appreciated.

Military and unit associations again played a significant role in spreading the word and helping us locate contributors. The majority of these associations are run by volunteers who work tirelessly to keep their members informed and their units' histories alive. Included here is Bill Rudd, who has researched and built a fantastic website, 'AIF POW Freemen in Europe'. Your assistance in finding POWs who served in Europe is appreciated. To Lieutenant Colonel Peter Winstanley OAM RFD (retired), who has built a similar website that keeps the memories of the POWs under the Japanese alive. The site 'Prisoners of War of the Japanese 1942—1945' and your help in providing contacts, has also proven extremely valuable. To Olwyn Green OAM, thank you for sharing and allowing access to your interviews with the Korean veterans. To Paul Rea, author of *Voices from the Fortress*, thank you very much for writing the 'Epilogue' and the story of Walter Steilberg. Your uncovering of the truth of Terezín concentration camp and the Australian soldiers it held is commendable.

To the publishing fraternity for granting permission to reprint previously published material – your understanding and approval has meant that many memories can be resurrected. In particular, I would like to thank the following for their permissions: Don Wall Publishing for *The Heroes of F Force*. The Department of Veterans' Affairs for *Sandakan 1942—1945* and *Stolen Years: Australian prisoners of war*. The Australian Broadcasting Commission for extracts from interviews conducted on *Four Corners, Lateline* and *Compass*.

To our families for their patience and understanding during another year of research and writing. To Craig's family, Sheree and boys Andrew, Matthew, James and Daniel and to my family, Sharon, Ziggi and Jaz. We can now all have that Christmas break!

Finally to the team at Big Sky Publishing and others who have helped shape this book. To senior editor, Alistair Mival, and sub-editors Sharon Evans, Diane Evans and Anna Kassulke, we are grateful for your effort and patience in dotting those "I's" and crossing those "T's". And to Pat Kan and his crew at Think Productions, your layout, design and typesetting are once again spot on.

Introduction – A POWs History

Repatriated prisoners.
Their emaciated state
shows how brutally they
were treated by the
Japanese
H98.103/3437

Nearly 35,000 Australian service personnel were taken prisoner during the Boer War, World War 1, World War 2 and the Korean War. Surviving as a POW demanded extremes of courage, defiance and mateship from our servicemen and women. For many, their greatest victory would be to simply stay alive and make it home; this required as much strength of character as fighting on the front line. Those who survived to tell their tales of extreme suffering and hardship also carried with them the memories of those who died. The many moving stories about survivors and their comrades who never saw Australia again have become integral to our national identity.

As POWs are relatively few in number, their stories often take a back seat when it comes to tales about battles and conflict situations. Like most soldiers, former prisoners do not like reliving the horrors of war, so many locked their memories away in a vault that was rarely opened to others. Those who did share their often vivid and compelling accounts highlight the contradictions of war – the compassion and generosity on the one hand, and the cruelty, hate and indifference on the other.

It is in our national interest to preserve the memories of our POWs and recognise their importance for our short military history. We need to encourage the stories to be told. And we must listen, not out of morbid curiosity but to gain a better understanding of all the facets of our past. We must not allow the history books to go unchallenged in countries where horrific crimes against our soldiers were perpetrated. And we must continue to acknowledge and praise the work of external organisations such as the Red Cross because without their efforts so many more POWs would not have returned home.

This introduction is heavy on statistics and numeric comparisons of different conflicts. While it might seem dehumanising to talk about soldiers in terms of numbers and percentages, it is essential if we are to understand how the following chapters unfold and how the contributors' recollections have been used. There is, for example, a simple reason why most of the stories relate to WW2 experiences. More than 30,000 of the 35,000 Australian POWs or so mentioned at the start of this introduction were captured during that conflict. Approximately 200 were taken prisoner during the Boer War, 4,000 during WW1 and 30 in Korea.

The Boer War raged in South Africa from 1899 to 1902, and for the Australian contingents, the conflict was essentially of a guerrilla nature. Of a force of around 16,000 soldiers, about 200 were taken prisoner by the Boers, who preferred to strip captured soldiers of their arms before letting them go. It was in this war that the legend of Lieutenant Harry "Breaker" Morant was born. Morant and Lieutenant Peter Handcock were found guilty by the Colonial authorities of executing eight Boer POWs. Although they claimed to be following orders, it did not make their actions any more acceptable. While the trial smacked of a cover-up at the highest level – the facts indicated that Commander in Chief Lord Kitchener had ordered the execution of Boer commandos caught wearing British and Colonial khaki – Morant and Handcock's actions and their fate can be seen as a fore-runner to future approaches to war crimes involving POWs. On both sides of the wire, vulnerable prisoners have always been at the mercy of their captors.

In World War 1, the Germans captured 3,850 Australians on the Western Front in France and Belgium, many of them during the first battle of Bullecourt in April 1917. The Turks captured about 200 in the Sinai, Palestine and Gallipoli. Nearly 10 percent of the soldiers incarcerated by Germany died in a prison camp, primarily due to lack of food and other critical supplies. Allied blockades later in the war caused such a shortage in German food supplies that civilians suffered even more than Allied POWs who had access to Red Cross food parcels. Survival in the cruel Turkish camps was even harder and nearly 40 percent of POWs never made it home. By the end of the Great War approximately 395 prisoners had died in camps throughout Germany and Turkey.

Of the 30,000 plus Australians taken prisoner during World War 2, almost 8,000 were captured by the Germans and Italians after battles in Greece, Crete and El Alamein in North Africa. About three percent of them died before the war was over. Those captured in Greece endured long journeys to overcrowded transit camps before a difficult rail trip across occupied Europe. Those taken prisoner by the Italians were eventually handed over to the Germans who transported them by rail over the Alps to one of about 40 major camps spread throughout Germany. Officers were usually separated from their men and sent to Oflags (Offizierslager) while other ranks were sent to Stalags (Stammlagers or base camps). RAAF personnel went to Stalag Lufts and Navy personnel to Marlags.

While the Nazis generally adhered to the Geneva Conventions with respect to the treatment of Allied prisoners, many of their POWs had to battle severe cold without adequate clothing and supplies. Towards the end of the war some were forced to march in winter to evade the advancing Allied forces although they were unfit. Australian POWs frequently attempted to escape and nearly 600 were successful. Many who gained freedom rejoined the fight while others joined local resistance movements.

In the Pacific, about 22,000 Australian personnel were imprisoned by the Japanese, almost all following mass capitulations in Malaya, Singapore, Java, Burma, Timor Ambon and Rabaul. Tragically, more than 8,000 – a shocking 36 percent – did not survive. Many died of malnutrition, disease and overwork. Many more were simply murdered by their captors despite the Geneva Conventions. At Tol on New Britain 160 were killed, 110 were murdered at Parit Sulong in Malaya, more than 200 at Laha on Ambon, and 21 at Bangka Island. More than 2,500 Allied personnel died during the infamous 261 kilometre death marches from Sandakan to Ranau. These are just some of the better-known incidents because we have witnesses who survived to tell the tale.

The Japanese held most of their prisoners at Changi in Singapore. From there working parties – essentially slave labour – were sent to far-flung parts of the Asia Pacific region such as Burma, Thailand, Borneo and Japan. They were put to work repairing war-damaged infrastructures, mining, loading and unloading ships and construction. The most infamous of these projects was the 421 kilometre Burma-Thai railway. A combined Allied labour force of 61,000 prisoners and 180,000 indigenous and local labourers were forced to build what became known as the "Death Railway". About 16,000 POWs died during its construction, 2,815 of them Australian.

The camps' remote locations and the many Asian faces made it almost impossible for the Caucasian Australians to escape their hellish existence. Many tried but almost all were swiftly captured and executed. Eight men succeeded in Borneo, but only with the assistance of some Filipino-Chinese locals. Soldiers who were shipped from island to island in the Pacific also faced the threat of being torpedoed by Allied submarines. The Japanese policy was not to mark vessels carrying POWs so more than a thousand soldiers died in these "Hell Ships".

Thirty Australians were taken prisoner during the Korean War. Considering the extreme hardship they endured under North Korean and Chinese guard, it is perhaps surprising that all but one – William "Slim" Madden – survived the experience. The POWs were subject to forced marches, torture, inadequate diet, disease and a lack of medical supplies. The way the prisoners were treated varied considerably depending on when they were captured. Before and after the truce talks in July 1951 there was a marked improvement in their treatment, food and medical attention. Rank also played a part. Under their communist regimes, the Chinese and North Koreans believed that the lower a prisoner was in rank the more likely he was to be a victim of the capitalist hierarchy. The lower ranks were therefore more easily "educated" in the ways of communism.

No Australians were captured during the Vietnam War which was probably due to their methods of operation, avoidance of large-scale battles as well as the location of their major area of operations in Phuoc Tuy province. With the exception of Iraq and Afghanistan, more recent campaigns have been in less threatening environments, either as peacekeepers or acting as support and protection for United Nations personnel. In Iraq and Afghanistan, the site of several large-scale battles, Australia has been fortunate that no personnel have been taken prisoner. In these environments soldiers are more likely to be used as hostages for political or financial gain by radical idealists or fundamentalists.

History has seen many international attempts to define the "rules" of war and to regulate the conduct of individuals and countries doing battle. This took on a more formal form in the 19th century with a series of treaties and international agreements which addressed the "laws" of war, banned weapons and the treatment of POWs. These laws have evolved over time, with significant changes after WW1 and WW2.

The specifics of a number of these laws, including the Hague Conventions of 1899 and 1907, Geneva Protocol (1935), the United Nations Charter (1945) and the four Geneva Conventions, are interspersed throughout our soldiers' stories to provide a context for their experiences. Countries who signed these documents were expected to abide by the rules, although at the 1946 Nuremberg war crimes trials it was established that a country did not need to be a signatory to the Conventions to be bound by them. It was recognised that treaties like the Hague Conventions, which had been widely accepted by all civilised nations and which had been in effect for a reasonable period of time, could be interpreted as binding for all nations, not just those who signed the original treaty. Sadly, such laws often gave prisoners no protection and many suffered atrocious conditions and harsh treatment.

The co-author of this book, Craig Smith, recalls a defining moment in his early childhood when Leslie "Brick" Edmunds, who lived across the road in Seven Hills, Sydney, told him something that only resonated for him much later in life. A former POW who was captured at Crete in 1941, Edmunds would occasionally have a few drinks on the Smith family's front deck at weekends. One warm summer's day, Edmunds watched as the nine-year-old Smith threw dirt bombs at plastic soldiers entrenched in the flower bed. "Mate," he said eventually, "it is good to play soldiers.

It's not good to be one." Not understanding what he'd just been told, the child stopped for a second, then increased the ferocity of his attack. After researching hundreds of accounts of captivity, we can conclude that if there is one common thread for many prisoners of war it is that they experienced both the generosity and the hateful cruelty humans are capable of. War is a crucible for such extremes. Edmunds's soldiering had led him into that world and he had no desire to see anyone enter it again.

As with previous *Aussie Soldier* titles the style of this book is intentionally different from traditional works of military history. We choose not to bury the soldiers' names in the footnotes. Instead, the names appear alongside their own words. We also do not want to overwhelm readers with too much historical detail. Such books have their place but we have taken a different tack. Instead, we have two chapters, "The Battle Book" and "POW Camps", which can be used to reference the battles, campaigns and prison camps mentioned. They are only short summaries of the battles the contributors to this book were involved in and are by no means a complete history. Dates, figures and exact details of events are always a contentious issue given the time that has passed. We have endeavoured to verify the contributors' accounts to the best of our ability and have used the Australian War Memorial as the fall-back position on contentious information. We should also add that while *Aussie Soldier* is focused primarily on members of the Army, we are by no means devaluing the place in history held by the fine Air Force and Navy personnel who were also taken prisoner. It is simply that our skill-sets and contacts are based in the Army. Finally, we have intentionally not stated the rank of the soldiers whose stories are reproduced in the book, because in our eyes they are all equal.

The story of Australian POWs needs to be told again and again by as many voices as possible. These brave people are an integral part of our identity as Australians. Just as our national character was forged to some extent on one day at Gallipoli, so years of courage, defiance and mateship as a POW tests this character as much as a bayonet charge or a bombing run over enemy territory. *Aussie Soldier Prisoners of War* is the story of POWs told by those who experienced it. You will relive their capture, living conditions, escape attempts, punishments, humour, strength and — for some — the taste of freedom. We are privileged to be able to share this collection of reminiscences and experiences that should be treasured as part of our rich military history.

Denny Neave and Craig Smith
Sydney, February, 2009

Prologue
Mates from the Burma-Thai Railway

Working party on the
"Railway of Death"
Sketch by Fred Ransome Smith

You won't find Songkurai on any maps; it doesn't exist anymore. Its history is buried in the overgrown jungles of Northern Thailand, a place that has been forgotten, except by those who lived through its horrors. They will never forget. It lies some 13 kilometres south of the Three Pagodas Pass on the Burma-Thailand border.

In 1943 Songkurai was one of the many Japanese slave labour camps on the railway that was being built by Allied prisoners of war and conscripted indigenous labourers.

The senior officer of this camp was Lieutenant Colonel F.J. Dillon (later Brigadier), a regular soldier in the British Army. He was a magnificent man, revered by all who survived. Songkurai was reputably the worst camp of them all; its death toll was the highest. Songkurai was where Jim Birse saved my life.

Jim was a Scotsman, a Private in the Gordon Highlanders. On several occasions during the battles of the Malaya-Singapore campaign, the Gordons and Australians had been engaged in side-by-side actions. As a consequence, a great esprit-de-corps existed between the AIF and the Gordons.

I became very sick in this camp and was sent to the 'hospital hut'. It bore no resemblance to any hospital known today. There were no beds, medicine or sheets. The Hut was made of bamboo and attap. The framework was bamboo and the roof and sidings were attap — a thatch of dried coconut-palm fronds, effective if they were laid on close enough, but here the roof leaked like a sieve in the monsoon rains. The hut was probably 50 metres long and on each side a bamboo platform ran down its entire length, about knee-high above the ground. The platforms were two metres wide and were where the patients lay. Each patient's 'bed space' was barely two feet.

When someone died and the body was removed, a little more space was created for the survivors. My good fortune was being allocated a bed space next to Jim Birse. Jim told me that I had been semi-delirious when I arrived — I had cardiac beri beri, BT malaria, avitaminosis, dysentery and tropical ulcers on my legs and feet. I was indeed a very sick man — but all of us in the 'hospital hut' were in a similar condition. Jim stacked my small haversack and whatever else I had at the head end of my space on the platform.

The stench of that hut was beyond description. Dysentery patients were fouling their bed spaces, because they were unable to hold on until bamboo bed pans arrived. Tropical ulcers, some running from the knee to ankle and with maggots wriggling in the suppuration, stank to high heaven. In addition, the open trench latrine was about ten metres away and it overflowed with the help of monsoon torrents and spread the filth around an area of some twenty or more square metres.

Well, you might say, one could not live through this chaos. Of course, many did not – if your luck was with you, you survived. But if you were sent to the 'cholera hut' you did not. The bodies of the dead were cremated in bamboo fires and how the slaves kept up the supply of fuel to cremate the dead is beyond my comprehension.

Jim would wash me and clean me when I fouled myself. He emptied my bedpan. He was the greatest mate I could ever wish for.

Without a mate, you died.

Food was abysmally short. Our Japanese masters would supply the skeletons able to work on their railway with barely enough rice to keep the body and soul together. They believed that if you were not able to work, you were not worth feeding. Sick men had very little chance of recovering on this starvation diet. I couldn't even walk. I was totally dependent on Jim.

Jim would somehow scrounge some food and share it with me. On numerous occasions at night, in the pitch dark, he would creep out and into the Japanese kitchen, steal whatever he could find and bring it back to our hut and share it with me. Despite my imploring him not to take this dreadful risk – if caught he would lose his head – he said we would all probably die here anyway.

I remember one night he came back with four boiled potatoes. We had a feast. Now that is hard to imagine, but when one is starving – not just hungry – any food is manna from heaven, be it snake, lizard or rat.

That night we were talking about home, me about Sydney, and him about Inverurie. He had heard of Sydney but his hometown was lost on me. We talked about what we would do when we got back home, if we were so lucky.

Jim was expounding the magnificent qualities of Glen Grant whisky to me. 'Aye, it's sweeter than the mornin' dew,' he claimed. We made a pact that if we survived the war, the first thing he would do was share a bottle with me! I said, 'No, we will share two bottles – one each!'

At that time, I don't think I had ever tasted whisky. Beer, yes, and an occasional rum, but whisky was not on my menu. I am certain that Jim was ahead of me liquor-wise, even though we were close in age. I think I was one year older.

We both survived Songkurai. Eventually I was sent back to Kanburi with the Australian prisoners of war and Jim was sent somewhere else with the British POWs. There was no way that we could maintain contact. The Australians of F Force were sent back to Changi. After the Burma-Thailand Railway experience, Selerang Barracks, was wonderful, we felt we were 'home'.

Whatever happened to Jim Birse I didn't know, and there was no way of finding him. Eventually, the war ended and I came home but the 'Jim Birse' name was always in my mind. Of course, I had a great love for this man and it was a wonderful experience to have known him. So life went on and I married, and Jim became a memory from the other side of the world.

Thirty-five years later, in 1978, I took long service leave and took a round the world trip. We started in Honolulu, USA and then went on to England. We spent a week or so in London and then hired a car and toured around. Eventually we travelled into Scotland and called in to the Freemason's Grand Lodge of Scotland in Edinburgh. I had joined the Masons years earlier and the Grand Secretary of Scotland, a wonderful man named Stuart Falconer, made me very welcome.

We were chatting and I mentioned that I would like to find a man named Jim Birse who I had been very friendly with in a POW camp in Thailand during WW2. I knew he had come from the village of Inverurie, somewhere near Aberdeen, and that he had been a Private in the Gordon Highlanders in Malaya in 1940. I said I had no idea whether he was still alive.

Stuart Falconer picked up his telephone and spoke to the Adjutant of the Gordon's Regiment about my quest. (The Gordons have records of every person in the regiment for the past 250—275 years). Within 15 minutes, the adjutant phoned back to say that Jim Birse was still recorded as living at Inverurie in 1975!

I was given some contacts to look up when I reached the place, and so we set off and arrived two days later. By this time my most urgent mission was to find a ladies' hairdresser – my wife was adamant! We found a barber shop so I thought while I was there I may as well have a haircut also. Realising that the barbers deal with customers who are usually long term residents, I asked him how long he had been at Inverurie. He said 25 years. 'Do you happen to know a Jim Birse?' I asked. 'No, but I know a Bob Birse,' he replied. Thinking he could be a relative, I asked where I might find Bob. 'Oh he has the barber shop about 50 yards down the road,' he answered. I explained to him the reason for my enquiries and he wished me luck. When my wife, Olga, was finished, I paid the bill and we walked down to the next barber.

I felt a bit stupid going into a barber's shop straight after having a haircut, but a smallish bald man came quickly out from the back of the shop. He looked just as I remembered Jim, but was plumper. He said, 'Canna help ya?' I asked if he knew a Jim Birse, and whether he was still alive or was he (Bob) related to Jim. 'He is ma brother, and yes, he is still alive,' he replied. I then explained the reason for my questions. This made him excited and he asked if he could come with us 'to show me the way'. Gently, I said 'No', but thanked him for his help – this was a thing between just Jim and me. He understood, and promised not to phone his brother and spoil the surprise.

I found where he was living, bought two bottles of Glen Grant whisky at the local off-licence and drove to his house. I left Olga in the car with one bottle. I took the other and went up to the front door and rang the bell. The door had a centre panel of fluted glass, which was semi-opaque. I could see a figure but not clearly. A voice said, 'Ma hands are wet and I canna open door. I'm peelin' potatoes. Will ye go round the back?' So round the back I went where the door was the same but with a lever instead of a knob. He opened the door with his elbow. There he stood in an apron, with a potato in one hand and a knife in the other.

With one hand behind my back clutching a bottle, I said, 'Good day, Jim'. He stared at me for several seconds, until I said, 'Don't you know me?' I was a lot different from when he last saw me at Songkurai 35 years ago. Back then I weighed about 7½ stone (43 kilos) and was now 13 stone (82 kilos). He said, 'I feel I should, but I canna place you'. I said, 'I'm from Australia and I've got a bottle of Glen Grant for us!" Instantly the penny dropped! The potato and knife dropped and he just surged forward and grabbed me. We stood like that for what must have been a full minute – an unforgettable emotional minute – both with tears in our eyes. it was the greatest reunion I've ever known.

Jim's wife came home from work not long afterwards and all four of us went out for dinner. Olga and I stayed that night with Mr and

Mrs Jim Birse. There was very little Glen Grant left in the second bottle the next morning. In fact, Mrs Birse had to telephone Jim's boss to say he would not be at work that day, he was sick. But oh, what a memorable night!

It was the greatest reunion I've ever known.

Jim Birse died at home in September 2007.

Ken Gray
Ex-F Force
8th Australian Division

Chapter 1
Capture

" Prisoners of war are in the power of the hostile
government, but not of the individuals or formation
which captured them. They shall at all times be
humanely treated and protected, particularly against
acts of violence, from insults and from public
curiosity. Measures of reprisal against them are
forbidden."

Article 2, third Geneva Convention

Boer prisoner of
war camp, 1900

Chapter 1 – Capture

As children we are excited by games that involve hiding, chasing, escape, and avoiding capture. As young men and women we struggle to gain our independence from family or freedom from certain social norms. We are taught to defend our beliefs, to speak out and vigorously resist threats to our freedom. To submit to another person's will, voluntarily or under force, is not something that comes naturally to most. Surrender, capture or admission of defeat – emotional or physical – goes against the grain of our Australian temperament.

Our national anthem joyously reminds us that we are young and free. Since Federation, more than one million Australians have joined the armed forces to fight for that freedom. The irony is inescapable. By joining the armed forces, men and women surrender much of their personal freedom for the benefit of others and they also enter a profession that significantly increases their chances of being captured and becoming a prisoner of war. More than 34,000 Australians were incarcerated by the enemy between the Boer and Korean Wars. Others have been detained during conflicts and operations since then, but none were classified "prisoners of war" (POWs).

"We were gonna fight our last stand there. We shook hands with one another and all of a sudden they sent for the NCOs. Our NCO came back and said, 'I just got orders from Egypt to surrender. The orders were we must capitulate.' Then he said, 'What's the bloody word mean?'"

Servicemen and women dread capture. The fear of summary execution, the humiliation of capture and the demoralising experience of being at the mercy of the enemy are powerful reasons for that dread. But for many Australians, it was also the loss of independence and self-identity that we hold so precious.

There were many ways to be captured: it could be the outcome of a superior's command, as at Singapore and Crete; or chance, like getting lost on the Western Front; or the urge to save your mate's life, as happened to some in Korea. You could choose to surrender or you could be ordered or compelled. No surrender was easy to accept. Many POWs felt capture meant they had failed in their mission. They felt, often mistakenly, that they had let their mates and families down. This sense of personal pride helped many to survive their years of captivity and to develop a strong determination not to allow their incarcerators to break their spirit. It seems the majority of Aussie POWs would rather have kept fighting, but were forced by a lack of bombs, bullets or bully beef to surrender.

In 1941, Lansell West, a soldier from Victoria, was given no choice but to surrender after German paratroopers took control of the airfields on the island of Crete. The anger and resignation he felt was echoed by many Australians who faced a similar prospect of internment. His battalion had moved to the beach at night ready for evacuation. He recalls:

"'The rear guard's here! The rear guard's here, with us.' They all jumped and panicked, trying to force their way onto the barge. The colonel said, 'Don't let anybody in.' He says, 'Shoot 'em if they try to break or force their way in.' The first batch of battalion's headquarters went onto the barge and the colonel was with them. When the Navy announced they weren't coming back for any more, he said, 'I'll stay with my battalion.' He came back, and climbed up on the rock, and said, 'The Navy's not coming back for any more today.' Colonel Walker said, 'What I propose to do is hide in the hills and try to hold them off during the day, and we'll signal to the Navy at night to pick us up.' He didn't realise at this stage that the Navy wasn't coming back at all. They had suffered too many losses. He said, 'Now, if there's any man here that doesn't want to be in that, he can fall out.' The blokes said, 'If it's good enough for you, sir, it's good enough for us.' 'Right,' he said, 'let's get moving. Get organised.'"

Lansell and many others were ready to stay and fight: "We were gonna fight our last stand there. We shook hands with one another and all of a sudden they sent for the NCOs. Our NCO came back and said, 'I just got orders from Egypt to surrender. The orders were we must capitulate.' Then he said, 'What's the bloody word mean?' We didn't even know what 'capitulate' meant. It was an insult to the blokes we had seen die. To be sold out like that! Not given any choice, like a mob of sheep. And, anyway, we were working out what we'd do. You were just so disheartened that they would do that to you. I've never forgiven our Army for that."

The capitulation order for Crete, dated 31st May, 1941 read:

"From: Major General Weston, Royal Marines.

To: Colonel Colvin.

In view of the following facts:

A. My orders direct me to give preference in evacuation to fighting troops. This has rendered the active garrison below that which is necessary for resistance.

B. No rations are left this Saturday night; most of the troops are too weak, owing to shortage of food and heavy strain, to organise further resistance.

C. The wireless will give out in a few hours and the risk of waiting for instructions from Middle East command cannot be accepted, as this will leave the officer in charge without guidance as to his course of action.

D. THERE IS NO FURTHER POSSIBILITY OF EVACUATION.

I therefore direct you to collect such senior officers as are available in the early hours of tomorrow morning and transmit these orders to the senior of them. "THESE ORDERS DIRECT THIS OFFICER TO MAKE CONTACT WITH THE ENEMY AND CAPITULATE."

Signed: E. Weston, Major-General RM."

"Some bloke acted as an interpreter there and the German commander said, I would like to compliment you on your fight, you all fought well and bravely. We respect you for that."

Other soldiers from Crete remember how their part in the war ended.

"A couple of hours after dark, troops in a hurry ran past on the track, being urged to go faster. 'Hurry or we'll miss the boat,' I heard as they stumbled past on the stony track in the darkness. This Australian rearguard had been promised that they would be evacuated if they could hold till darkness and break contact with their opponents. They

reached the beach after midnight, after forcing their way through the line-up on the beach. Colonel Theo Walker and his batman boarded a landing barge and on asking when the next barge was expected was informed that this would be the last for the night, because the ships had to be well out to sea by dawn to have any chance of getting through to Egypt. Theo said he would not leave his men after what they had been through together and went ashore to surrender with the other troops. The start of another day, 1st June, 1941, opened with the roar of dozens of planes heading south to overtake the escaping ships and then it was not long before signal smoke flares were sent curving into the sky from down below us. Unknown to us, the Germans had arrived and set up a wireless control post. Soon orders to surrender, after piling up all weapons, came through. I hid my revolver and bayonet knife amongst stonework in a shed and straggled down with the others, to form into a column under guard and begin the long climb back over the White Mountains to the north coast, to be a guest of the Nazis."
Ron Lister, Crete, 1941

"This is where you really felt vulnerable and not too happy looking down the barrel of this gun. At this moment you waited with a sick feeling. You are not able to say goodbye to your family. But once we were checked out by the German officer, NCOs were ordered to march back up over the ridge and marched about 50 miles to a prison compound. This consisted of a barbed wire fence, a few tents – not enough to accommodate all prisoners – an open latrine pit which was about 12-foot long, with forks both ends for a pole to sit on. Just make sure you kept your balance."
Rick Hunter, Crete, 1941

"We just flopped down among all the other blokes who were already there, and the German commander, he stood up. Some bloke acted as an interpreter there and the German commander said, 'I would like to compliment you on your fight, you all fought well and bravely. We respect you for that.' Our own bloody leaders didn't respect us too much."
Lansell West, Crete, 1941

For many who were able to board the ships that were evacuating soldiers from Crete their fate was the same as those who missed the boat, and for others it was worse as many ships were sunk at sea by the Luftwaffe. Malcolm Webster was evacuated from Heraklion in Crete by the British destroyer *HMS Hereward*. His evacuation was short-lived as the ship was sunk in the Kaso Straits. Malcolm drifted at sea for over five hours without a life jacket, before being picked up by an Italian torpedo boat and taken prisoner. The tragedy is that on this ship alone over 300 other soldiers drowned or were killed in the torpedo and bombing explosion. Another four ships were hit or destroyed, bringing the casualty and fatality rate to over 1,000. For many missing, the evacuation boats off Crete could have saved their lives, however they faced years of torment as POWs.

"Well, from what my friends have told me, they were utterly disgusted. My little mate, he threw down his rifle. He says, 'You're a lot of mongrel so-and-sos. I want to fight. What do you want to give it away for?' 'It's orders.' Zipper said, 'Bugger the orders. Give us a machinegun. I'll fix a few of them."

The surrender at Singapore and Java transpired not because soldiers where overwhelmed in battle but as an attempt by command to prevent considerable loss of military and civilian lives. The 8th Division's defence of Malaya and Singapore had been outstanding considering the lack of supply lines, food and water. On Java, soldiers faced the impossible task of resisting a vastly superior force. We recognise now that these surrenders resulted in a prisoner fatality rate greater than 30 percent as the enemy worked them to death without pity or remorse. For many, the initial surrender seemed surreal. Days could pass before a Japanese soldier was seen. In February 1942, Ray Wheeler had barely set foot in Singapore before he was told he had to surrender.

"We were holding a salient, the AIF had a perimeter to defend and we were about two or three hours from headquarters," he recalled. "There were three of us at that time. A runner came through and said, 'You have got to report back to headquarters.' We knew something was on because the noise had stopped. There was only a little bit of scattered small arms fire that we ever heard and we came back and we got back to Tanglin Hill where the headquarters was. An officer we didn't know, an English officer, came forward and said, 'You chaps have just arrived in and I have got to tell you, you are now prisoners of war of the Japanese. You will not destroy your weapons, you will not attempt to escape, and that is an order.' I wrapped my gun butt around a rubber tree and smashed it, put the firing pin in the gas port in the rifle and snapped it off. And we had an ammunition truck which had the mortar bombs and all that on it. The driver and myself put a couple of hand grenades and a note on the steering wheel: 'Don't drive this. You'll blow up.' First time they pressed the brake, they'd go up. That's what we did with our weapons."

The reality is that without the soldiers sacrificing their freedom, tens of thousands of civilians would have died. But that didn't make it any easier. Ray Wheeler was one of nearly 15,000 Australians captured when Singapore fell. His reaction was typical of his comrades, many of whom had their own stories too.

"After lunch, rumour had it that we had asked for a cessation of fire at 4pm while a parley took place. This rumour was the only correct one we heard and the ceasefire order was given. Singapore had taken a terrific battering that day. Water and sanitation were disrupted while the dead were lying around in thousands. All essential services with the exception of the electric light had been blown kite high. At 20.00 hours that night, and things were now deathly quiet, all arms in our building were collected, the men marched out with their gear; an official announcement was made that the island had accepted unconditional surrender and we must consider ourselves prisoners of war."
Jack O'Donnell, Singapore, 1942

"We are now prisoners of war of the Japanese, although strictly speaking under the Geneva Convention, of which the Japanese are signatories to the sections concerned, we should not be so. We are now awaiting the future to find out what is in store for us. During the morning the Japanese entered the city of Singapore. Very few came in and then mainly officers and a few patrols. Our own military police were still patrolling the city, keeping order among the civilian population and stopping any looting that they could find."
Gerard Harvey Veitch, Singapore, 1942

"About two days before the surrender I had assisted to prevent the Japs breaking through our battalion lines by firing the last of my bombs, about probably 70 or 80 into them, from a situation that I had behind a bit of an embankment. We just assumed that we were set now. They weren't going to be able to dislodge us and we had some vague feeling in the back of our minds that right behind us was going to be a big force to support us. Then when we got the message about our surrender."
Fred Hodel, Singapore, 1942

1942 Allied map
of Singapore

*Fred Skeels, Spud Murphy
& Jack Thorpe in Manila*

"Well, from what my friends have told me, they were utterly disgusted. My little mate, he threw down his rifle. He says, 'You're a lot of mongrel so-and-sos. I want to fight. What do you want to give it away for?' 'It's orders.' Zipper said, 'Bugger the orders. Give us a machinegun. I'll fix a few of them.' It was that intense feeling that you've done your job, but there's still more to do. We had force in the perimeter, I believe near the gardens and palace, and we could have held off quite a while there. We had our artillery there with us, machineguns, and battalions. Okay, Japs would have come round both sides and come in the back. We'd have got killed but we could have held them another couple of days, I'd say."
Ray Brown, Singapore, 1942

"With the cessation of bombing, machinegun attacks from the air, and not having to be continuously on the run, we experienced feelings of both disappointment and relief. It was good to have a sleep and await further instructions, which were not long in coming. We were ordered to put all our rifles and other arms in a tennis court near our final position. Although the unit was less than three hundred men it was amazing just how much gear was stacked on the grass. Rows of .303 rifles, bayonets, pouches of ammunition and hand grenades were all laid out for handing over to the enemy. Parting with our rifles was like saying goodbye to an old friend and some had their firing pins removed so they were useless – but that action was very unofficial. We had been taught to depend on them for our defence, look after them and get to know their idiosyncrasies. Now they had to go. It made me realise we were captives with a very doubtful future, although at that stage no Japanese guards had appeared. Many of us decided to retain some items that might be useful later and I got hold of a small pair of multi-grips and kept quite a good pocket-knife which I still have. Both items were invaluable in the months to come."
Gordon Nelson, Singapore, 1942

"We figured they wouldn't even get across. I mean, we'd been brainwashed. Singapore was a fortress. There's four lines Pinky Evans, an English soldier wrote and it goes: 'Singapore, mighty fortress, guardian of the east, the Japanese didn't think so, they took it in a week'. I always remember we were all in our beds at that time in the ward, and in came this squad of Japs, this is our first experience of being prisoners of war and we're crouched down in our beds, thinking. 'Hello, this is it; I wonder whether they're nasties.' And they came along. They left one of their fellows

near the door and he had his back turned to us at first, and we're watching him. Then he turned round. Well, I never! I'll be blowed; it was Quasimodo with a hair lip instead of a hump. The poor fellow, he was so ugly and I thought, *They can't all be like this*. Oh, he was ugly and bow-legged– not that he could help that – but it was a dreadful impression to put on a young bloke right from the start. But he turned out all right. They left us alone. They took anything like money or watches from us, but they didn't kill us."
Bill Young, Singapore, 1942

"We were now prisoners of the Japanese, a turn of events that we never thought likely. Being wounded and death was a possibility, but a prisoner of war - no!"

"The 10th Australian General Hospital, together with 2/10th Field Ambulance, were sent to St Andrews Cathedral and, opposite this, the Adelphi hospital to prepare to receive wounded. Between the cathedral and hospital we had some 430 wounded. On 12th February, 1942 our remaining 65 Australian Army Nursing Service sisters left to board the Vyner Brooke for evacuation to Australia. The vessel was attacked by Japanese planes and sunk. Twelve of the nurses drowned and 22 reached the shores of Bangka Island only to be shot by the Japanese. On 15th February an eerie silence fell upon us. The sound of artillery and mortar fire ceased and only the moans of severely wounded could now be heard. The war was over for us. We were now prisoners of the Japanese, a turn of events that we never thought likely. Being wounded and death was a possibility, but a prisoner of war – no!"
Bill Flowers, Singapore, 1942

After three weeks' vigorous but fruitless resistance, and despite the reluctance of Brigade Commander Arthur Blackburn VC CMG CBE ED, the Allied forces surrendered on 9th March, 1942. Jack Thorpe was among those on Java to surrender. He admired Blackburn, who also saw service in WW1, and trusted him to make the right decision. Jack Thorpe recalls, "After several days on the beachhead it became clear that though Australia was aware of our plight, there was no hope of rescue. We also learned that the Dutch, whom we had come to assist, had capitulated. So there we were, stuck in the jungle with our backs to the sea, no means of escape and food fast running out. With no other option, Brigadier

Blackburn had to drive into the nearest town in a vehicle flying a white flag. His intention was to try and negotiate a conditional surrender with the Japanese commander of the area. Under the terms of a conditional surrender, a soldier can be returned to his country of origin or stay on as a civilian. We hoped to go home. But the Japanese would have none of that; it was surrender at once or be wiped out. The Dutch had already surrendered and so all the Japs on the island could be sent to get us. Since we had no food we really had no alternative but to agree to an unconditional surrender. Although we were to have a terrible time as prisoners of war, I think that Brigadier Blackburn, who was a great soldier and who had won a VC in WW1, did the right thing in surrendering. At least that way some of us were able to survive."

While Aussie soldiers in Singapore resented the surrender order, in Java the tactical situation was clear. The soldiers believed that more men would have died if they had fought on.

"Brigadier Blackburn told us to toss all rifles, ammunition and grenades in the river. Then Blackburn told us to cram as many men as we could onto each truck and push the empty trucks over the edge of the cliff into the river below. Each of the trucks had three gallon cans on the running board with their contents written on the outside, with the first letter bigger than the rest – WATER PETROL OIL being the correct order. As we were pushing it over I noticed one of the trucks had a can in the wrong order – PETROL OIL WATER – POW."
Jack Thorpe, Java, 1942

"That evening companies were called together and told by Brigadier Blackburn that the Dutch had unconditionally surrendered and as we were under their command that included us. He told us it was very little use going to the beach, as quite a lot of people had been trying to get away for the last week. All arms and ammo had to be stacked on a truck and taken to the Japs on the 10th. We naturally destroyed as much as possible. Most of the trucks and staff cars were pushed over cliffs and a very few rifles or Brens were sent in complete. Grenades and ammo were thrown in all directions. We had a lot of trouble turning the few trucks we had left, as the road was very wet and slippery. It was pouring with rain practically the whole time."
Alfred Burkitt, Java, 1942

"We were marched through the town, obviously for propaganda purposes, but the Greeks (mainly women, as the men were still at the front) lined the streets and applauded us and shouted, 'Thank you'. Some tried to touch us, but were beaten heavily."

The Greek campaign was a painful defeat. The Australians faced an almost impossible task when they landed there in March 1941. The Germans had a significant armour advantage, as well as air superiority. A withdrawal to Crete and Egypt was called by mid-April. On Anzac Day 1941, Aussies and Kiwis, exhausted but with their heads held high, were holding off the enemy or embarking for the next battles. However a number of these delay positions saw large numbers of Australians negotiating surrender in the face of superior German numbers and firepower. Two prisoners of this campaign detail their experiences.

"After capturing a large number of Germans in Larissa we were escorting them back to Athens and put them on a waiting ship. After they were aboard we marched off and their ship sailed. On our way back we were picked up by a mixed convoy and told the Germans had broken through the lines and we were going to Kalamata. We lost a lot on this convoy through German Stukas dive-bombing us. As soon as we arrived, news came that the Germans were approaching Kalamata. Our ANZAC mates, the New Zealanders, charged them whilst we provided covering fire. We held them for a couple of days. A carload of high-ranking German officers met with Brigadier Parrington, our British commanding officer. The Germans had massed troops and artillery and intended using their air force if we did not surrender, so we were ordered to remove bolts from our rifles and throw them into the sea. We were marched through the town, obviously for propaganda purposes, but the Greeks (mainly women, as the men were still at the front) lined the streets and applauded us and shouted, 'Thank you'. Some tried to touch us, but were beaten heavily. Something to remember. They suffered terribly under the Occupation with starvation and disease. We POWs had nothing but admiration for their spirit. However, we were about to have our own spirit tested."
Stan McDonald, Greece, 1941

"Later in the night, and after one small boat had reached the shore, it became clear that the Navy would not be embarking the 8,000 troops who were anxiously waiting for them. This situation was partly due to the uncertainty of the presence of four bombs or mines that were seen to be dropped near the pier and had not exploded. There were wounded and their stretcher-bearers, some hundreds of soldiers from base sub-area, 100 Indian mule drivers and about 2,400 British troops, mainly from depot units. Only 70 of the New Zealand and Australian infantrymen had arms. They launched their attack to retake the pier at 20.15 hours. It was this attack that captured the two field guns. They were supported by another group of NZ troops. The local commander of British forces, Brigadier Parrington, judged that although he had momentary control of the situation on the ground, he had no supplies or ammunition with which to continue his resistance. He therefore opened negotiations with the German commander for a ceasefire. The result was our surrender took effect at 05.30 hours, 29th April.

"We moved further into an open field where the officers were separated from the other ranks and two machineguns were set up, one at each end of this group. There was some concern for a short time as to the intentions of our captors, as rumours had been voiced earlier of massacres of some prisoners in France by German troops after the cessation of fighting in 1940. It was also uncertain whether they would exact some sort of revenge for the heavy casualties they had suffered in the previous night's fighting for the pier in Kalamata. However, our captors in this particular incident fought their war with strict regard to the Geneva Convention and to the rules of war – much to our relief. In due course, despite having had no further food that day for lunch or tea, we slept well in the field under the stars."
John Crooks, Greece, 1941

The vast majority of Aussie POWs came from a mass surrender or capitulation order. Many individuals also fell into the enemy's hands when they were separated from their main force or wounded in battle. Others were fighting for their lives and were simply overwhelmed, which was something that happened to Frank Daff in Pretoria during the Boer War. On May 29, 1900, Daff and a comrade were taken prisoner by the Boers, a few miles from a place called Boksburg, as they travelled from Kroonstad to Pretoria. At dusk, about 200 Boers came upon them very suddenly. No shots were fired. Daff later wrote, "We had our hands up pretty smartly."

"Eventually their guide thought he had found the right spot, but they were surprised to hear German voices. They had blundered past the German first line."

Some soldiers were simply geographically embarrassed and stumbled into enemy hands. Private Bill Manly was collecting wounded Australian soldiers from the battlefield in 1916 as a member of the 13th Australian Field Ambulance at the dressing station in Pozières Woods on the Somme. When the call came to pick up four wounded soldiers, he set off into 'no man's land' with 15 comrades, including his brother James. They were carrying stretchers and white flags. Shells began to land around them in ever greater numbers. Darkness was falling and finding their way was becoming harder by the minute. Eventually their guide thought he had found the right spot, but they were surprised to hear German voices. They had blundered past the German first line. "Ah, come Englander," was the order. Being unarmed they had no alternative but to obey, and so they entered the German trenches at gun point. It was the start of a stretch of captivity which was to last for 15 months.

With a typical Aussie disregard for authority, Eric Donnelly disobeyed an order to withdraw, so he could try and save his mate. One of 30 Australians taken prisoner in 1953 during the Korean War, Donnelly was ordered by his platoon commander to pull back when his patrol was ambushed by Chinese PLA troops. But Donnelly was resolved to go back and help his mate, Peter.

"I only took two paces to my right when a bullet smashed into my right leg causing me to spin around like a ballet dancer pirouetting in the snow. I crashed to the ground alongside Peter, losing my grip on the Owen gun as I spun around. I called out, 'I've been hit.' And a mate of mine from Tasmania, Gordon Welles, yelled out, 'Blue's been hit. I am going to get him.' Lieutenant Bousfield screamed out, 'Don't be a bloody fool. Down the hill.' Gordon got to within two yards of me but then decided to obey Bousfield's command. He went down the hill as ordered. In the months to come I was to replay this scene many times in my mind's eye. At first I was bitter, thinking I had been deserted by my comrades. Over time I came to realise that Brian (Bousfield) did the only thing possible, as he had the responsibility for getting us all out. If I

German paratroopers landing at Crete, 1941, photo looks to have been edited for propaganda purposes

Surrender table at the Ford Motor factory.
Lieutenant General A.E. Percival, surrenders
unconditionally all Commonwealth Forces
on Singapore Island. 15th February 1942

AWM Neg. 127903

had obeyed his order to get down the hill and regroup, instead of trying to get Peter White out, I may not have been shot. Who knows? The reality now was that the patrol had withdrawn down the hill and Peter and I were left to our fate. Peter mercifully died a few minutes later, so my attempt to get him out would not have succeeded anyhow. I could hear the patrol fighting its way back across the valley. I tried to crawl down the hill in the direction that we came but I could not move my legs. A nerve in my leg or spine must have snapped, because I had no feeling from the waist down. I started to think I had lost both legs.

"I looked up towards the enemy trench line and saw a Chinese soldier carrying a burp gun. He was crouched down and heading to where I was lying. He prodded me a couple of times to make sure I did not pose a threat to him. Then he reached down and grabbed me by my right leg. Up to then I could not feel it. As he exerted pressure on my leg, a shaft of pain went right through my body. I let out the most spine-chilling scream of agony that would have shocked the most stout-hearted. The Chinese soldier was no exception. He dropped my leg. Just then another shell came thundering into our position. The Chinese soldier scurried back to his trench line for protection while a couple of more shells crashed in. Shortly there was another break in the shelling and the enemy soldier once again ventured to where Peter and I were lying. This time he grabbed me by my hair and started towing me like a toboggan through the snow on my back. I was able to assist by pushing with my hands. Anything to get away from horror of the 25-pounders. He towed me the 15 yards or so up to his trench and then let me go over the edge. I remember being in freefall and then blacking out."

"At dawn came my 'Waterloo'. As soon as it became light, the enemy made a series of sharp attacks on both flank and front and through overwhelming numbers we were forced to retire."

Other soldiers share their recollections about the moment the war was over for them:

"At dawn came my 'Waterloo'. As soon as it became light, the enemy made a series of sharp attacks on both flank and front and through overwhelming numbers we were forced to retire. I received a wound in my left arm which temporarily knocked me

out. Recovering in a few minutes, I bound up the wound, which was bleeding profusely, and snatching up my rifle, went into the fight again. Turks seemed to be everywhere, both living and dead. Beside me were Sergeant Drysdale and Trooper McColl of my regiment and we seemed to be the only three Britishers among hundreds of the enemy. We had taken a position behind a small sand hill and a glance around showed that, being on the extreme right flank, we had been separated from our squadron and were cut off. The Turks rushed on us with fixed bayonets and after a sharp scuffle we were overpowered."
George Handsley, Romani, 1916

"You evidently hear the last second of the shell that hits you, or is close to you, because what you do is crouch down under the wall nearest the enemy. Of course, no trouble at all, the whole wall just rolls over you. I was thrown away like a rag doll, and the bloody swale just rolled over on top of me. I was buried up to the shoulders. I had no chance of ever freeing myself. It was the Germans who dug me out. They carried me out on a stretcher."
Jim Wheeler, Bullecourt, 1917

"I got hit late in the afternoon of 31 May, 1941. A couple of Germans came down shooting and I don't know exactly – even today – how it happened, but the shooting hit the rocks behind which I was hiding and it was like being hit by a sandblast. I fell off these rocks and went down over a slight cliff and got wounded. It tore part of my forehead away and ear, and when I came to I'd been bandaged by Germans and I was a prisoner of war."
Keith Hooper, Crete, 1941

"On July 26 we launched a night attack in one of the first battles of Alamein. We reached our objective – Myteriya or Ruin Bridge – and were able to fill a couple of sandbags to cover a shallow sangar on the rock. We took many prisoners, but while the anti-tank and transport were crossing the minefield an 88mm got busy, lighting up the narrow path cleared. Some vehicles tried to go around the obstacles – and hit mines – so only six out of 16 guns made it and few trucks. Come dawn on 27 July, a British tank unit was to join us. The minefields beat them and some 40 panzers came instead, wiped out the anti-tank guns and routed us out of our holes. A mortar-laden truck tried to make a run for it. It was hit and burned a few yards from where Jack Fitzharding and I were huddled under our sandbags, unable to move for exploding mortar bombs. As explosions eased, Jack crawled out from the sheltered

end of our L-shaped slit and said, '****!' I hurriedly joined him and faced a German half-track aiming a 3-pounder and a machinegun at us, as an NCO called, 'Come out, Aussie.' We didn't argue. We walked off in our shorts, shirt and tin hat."
Ray Middleton, El Alamein, 1942

"We had been fighting the Germans in Crete for a bit and I had not gone to the toilet for a while. During a lull at night I was about to drop my strides when the sergeant whispered, 'Bullshit Edmunds, I am not going to have you shit in the position. Do it out there.' [He pointed] to a small gully near our platoon position. I dutifully crawled past the gunner and found a very discreet hidey hole. Being a bit modest, I moved just out of sight of the Bren gun. After making a scrape, I took my pants off to do my business. As I sat crouched there, with a .303 next to me, I heard the distinctive click of a Mauser being cocked and [saw] a Kraut pointing his rifle at me with a bloody big grin on his ugly face. 'Halten Soldaten! Hände Hoch.' He paused and then said a phrase in English that I would hear in my head over and over again: 'For you, the war is over.' Quickest shit in my entire life!"
Leslie "Brick" Edmunds, Crete, 1941

"I arrived in the village of Tolos as a straggler left behind on field security duty. I was advised by locals that our troops were being evacuated. However, by the time I arrived, the enemy ground troops were only a few kilometres away and so the evacuation from Tolos was over. I went along the beach and grabbed a dinghy with three other Australians. I had a map and we decided our best chance was to head for Crete. With enemy patrol boats keeping the coastline under surveillance we could only travel by night and lay-up by day to rest. We made it to Cape Maleas and thought that may be our last sleep on the Greek mainland. Given our weary state, our sleep must have been sound. It took the rudest of awakenings to rouse us. Strange voices yelling around us and a kick to the ribs had me sitting up in a nightmarish daze. 'Oop, oop, oop, hands oop,' a voice roared. We had been captured by a boat patrol. They offered us cigarettes. Our captors were not personally ill-disposed toward us. The German officer in charge told us in broken English, 'For you, der var iss ofer'. It was frustrating to learn that we were somewhat unlucky in our capture as the two German patrol boats patrolling in opposite directions had arranged a meeting place to exchange reports. The agreed rendezvous? Cape Malea, of course. Our captors came ashore onto our beach."
Ralph Churches, Greece, 1941

"During the night of 16th July, 1942 our company went on a fighting patrol, on orders to knock out several field pieces (heavy artillery guns), harass the enemy, take a position and hold it. All was achieved except the positions. Someone got their wires crossed and the positions we took were about 1,200 yards forward of where we should have been. It was dark; there was full action throughout the night. It was not until daylight that we realised the mistake, but it was too late. We found ourselves staring at a squadron of German tanks of the 21st Armoured Division."
William Hoffman, El Alamein, 1942

"I could have cried to look at them so cold and still. They had been so brave in the morning, so strong, but in the evening a few hours later they were dead, and we had not hated them nor they us."

An unnamed Boer prisoner recounts the capture of nine Australians in 1900. His story was published in London's *Daily Mail* and later in the Melbourne *Argus*. Maybe the Boer exaggerated the events of the capture to make a good impression. The fact that eight of the nine Australians captured were wounded indicates they had fought as hard as he claimed. The Australians were conducting a delaying defence to allow British forces to withdraw when their officer commanding ordered a counter attack.

"Our field cornet gave the order to cease firing and called on them to throw down their rifles or die. Then one of the big officers, a great rough-looking man with a voice like a bull, roared out, 'Forward Australia! No surrender!' These were the last words he ever uttered, for a man on my right put a bullet clean between his eyes and he fell forward, dead. We found later that his name was Major Eddy, of the Victorian Rifles. He was as brave as a lion, but a Mauser bullet will stop the bravest. His men dashed at the rocks like wolves; it was awful to see them. They smashed at our heads with clubbed rifles or thrust their rifles up against us through the rocks and fired. One after another their leaders fell. The second big man went down early, but he was not killed. He was shot through the groin, but not dangerously. His name was Captain McInerney.

Chapter 1 – Capture

"There was another one, a little man named Lieutenant Roberts; he was shot through the heart. Some of the others I forget. The men would not throw down their rifles; they fought like furies. One man I saw climbed right onto the rocky ledge where big Jan Aldrecht was stationed. Just as he got there, a bullet took him and he staggered and dropped his rifle. Big Jan jumped forward to catch him before he toppled over the ledge, but the Australian struck Jan in the mouth with his clenched fist and [he] fell over into the ravine below and was killed.

"We killed and wounded an awful lot of them, but some got away; they fought their way out. I saw a long row of their dead and wounded laid out on the slope of a farmhouse that evening – they were all young men, fine big fellows. I could have cried to look at them so cold and still. They had been so brave in the morning, so strong, but in the evening a few hours later they were dead, and we had not hated them nor they us."
Boer prisoner, South Africa, 1900

Another prisoner of the Boers, Trooper Hal Harnett, realised it was hard to keep fighting with no horse, no weapon and a lot of Boers pointing weapons at you. He sent this letter to his father to explain how he was captured while covering withdrawing forces:

"The bullets were coming like hail, many of them were explosives and cracking just like a stock whip. Captain Thompson and Sergeant Major Arnold were beside me, the latter at last said, 'I think we had better retire or we'll be captured.' The captain thought so too, so we made for the horses.

"I was the last to leave the stone wall with Bill Cameron; the others all seemed to go in a bunch for the horses, but Cameron and I waited a moment then made a dash. I ran to where I left my mare – she was not there. The Carbineers were galloping away like mad through our horses. A general stampede was the result. I could get no horses, so I started to run away. I ran some distance – bullets all the while buzzing and hissing round, but never a one touched me.

"At last I came to a gutter and jumped into it and hid. I was there for about 15 minutes, perhaps, it seemed ages, when I heard Boers jabbering quite close. One young chap came up and took my rifle, bandolier and revolver. I then saw escape was useless, so I went up to Doyle who was hit slightly on the thigh and then Dick Meecham called me and asked for assistance. He was shot in the back and out through the neck. I dressed him up a bit, as well as I could.

"Boers were now round us in scores – the commandant came up, saluted and asked how we were. Wilkinson and MacDonald then appeared and all 13 of us – bar Meecham, who could not travel – marched about eight miles to the lager."

"I was completely blind in my right eye, and could scarcely see out of my left eye. We wandered about for days in no man's land, hiding during the daytime and trying to find our way back to our trenches at night."

After WW1, the Australian Defence Department set up an inquiry into the treatment of Australian prisoners of war by the Germans. The report How Germans treated Australian Prisoners of War was published in 1919. To protect soldiers' identities, those interviewed were made anonymous. Their stories show the spirit of the Australian soldiers who fought until overcome.

"We repelled an attack by the Germans at Villers-Bretonneux on, or about, 20th April, 1918. I was out collecting rifles between our lines and those of the enemy; and must have got too far from our lines and close to a German outpost, for suddenly there was a burst of machinegun and rifle fire and my mate was shot through the head and killed. I was knocked just below the left shoulder and disabled; the bullet shattering my arm. I was picked up by a small party of Germans."
Unnamed Private, France, 1918

"As I stumbled into this shell-hole I received another wound in the left side from a bullet. We lay in that shell-hole till dark. I was completely blind in my right eye, and could scarcely see out of my left eye. We wandered about for days in no man's land, hiding during the daytime and trying to find our way back to our trenches at night. The ground was muddy, and covered with an unyielding undergrowth of thistles, which cruelly lacerated our hands whilst attempting to crawl through. We could hear Germans talking on every side of us. We advanced in this painful fashion for about 300 yards. We heard a large party of Germans approaching along

what I took to be some sort of communication trench. The enemy party set to work to deepen the trench, which lay just a few yards in front of us. After they had been working for an hour – perhaps a little less – our artillery suddenly opened fire upon them. A German officer and two German soldiers immediately jumped into the shell-hole in which we were hiding. That ended it. At first the Germans were just as amazed and dumbfounded as we were, but as soon as the German officer realised how matters stood, I and my two comrades became his prisoners of war."
Unnamed Officer, France, 1916

"Sergeant M-- was lying on the bottom of the trench seriously wounded, and before retiring Lieutenant H-- called for volunteers to carry him out. Another man and I carried him along the trench for about 100 yards, when I was hit by a lump of shrapnel on the shoulder (left). I was completely disabled. I lay there for about an hour when I was picked up by a German officer and carried by him into a dug-out in the German lines, and handed over to the German AMC men. The last I saw of Sergeant M--, he was crawling along the trench on his hands and knees and being assisted by other men."
Unnamed Private, France, 1918

Pilots of the Australian Flying Corps were part of the AIF in WW1, the equivalent of today's Australian Army Aviation Corps (the RAAF was not formed until 1921). Lieutenant LH Smith was engaging a second German aircraft in Palestine after successfully destroying a first when:

"About 1,000 feet from the ground they fired everything they had about the place. Gordon was hit through the head. One bullet passed me hurriedly, but in passing hit me a severe blow on the cheek bone, rendering me unconscious. This proved a blessing in disguise. One is strapped into a cockpit by a belt and straps, with sufficient length to allow one to move about. As we dived to earth our plane turned on its back, I fell out, then as it straightened out again for the final plunge I was suspended to the side of the plane. The terrific force of the crash plunged the engine right through my cockpit. You will now realise had I been in the cockpit my chances were not so good. The details of the crash were given to me by several German officers who had witnessed the scene. This crash was also witnessed by our other plane who returned home and reported us both killed.

"I regained my senses in the early hours of the following morning. I found myself in a bell tent, and on looking out soon realised where I was. Without giving the position much thought, I bolted from the tent towards the Dead Sea, approximately 40 miles away. I did not realise that the Arabs in this locality are particularly dangerous, and wouldn't hesitate to cut one's throat. Unbeknown to me a sentry had been placed to guard me, and after running only about twenty yards I found myself face to face with a deadly looking bayonet. He screamed for help and spoke to me in Turkish.

"Not understanding the language I thought he meant me to return to the tent. I looked again at the bayonet and walked back. I did not sleep the balance of the night, and noticed the guard had been reinforced. I could not understand why I was there and felt very sick and sorry. Later the next day I was escorted to see all the damage done. There was our plane and the German plane both smashed to pieces, also both German pilots and my good friend of many flights. I can never forget this dreadful sight and for the first time I realised what must have happened. All three officers were buried with full military honours at Kitrine."
L.H. Smith, Palestine, 1917

Sometimes Aussie soldiers were taken prisoner after giving up their arms outside a general order to surrender or after being overwhelmed in combat. There were many reasons behind such a decision. Sometimes continuing to fight was futile. Sometimes they were the victims of a surprise enemy action. The decision could be made in a split second or debated at length between soldiers. When given the order to surrender, some Australians fought to avoid capture and others tried to escape to fight another day.

In Greece during WW2 the orders were given to withdraw. When evacuations began many who were left stranded looked for every possible means of escape. Doug Nix recalls, "We were waiting for the tides to change to be able to get away before light, but with all the bombing raids going on they just didn't return. We were given the order to just get away from the problem as quickly as possible. I can remember commandeering a New Zealand officer's car; it was like a Hummer with a wooden compartment on the back. Three or four of us got in it and went down to the end of the road. It was about a mile south of the Kalamata and the Peloponnese,

POW Camp, Langensalza, 1917

PRG1300_15_6

Allies surrendering to the
Japanese, 1942

and that was it. We grabbed a type of boat, a barge, rowing-boat thing and tried to row away. We had the idea of sailing to Crete, because we knew blokes were going there, but we only got a couple of miles offshore before being blown out of the water. We drifted back onto the beach and got up in a cave. One bloke was wounded with shrapnel from being in the water. We took off down the track to the village to get some food and as I walked around the corner there was this German standing in the middle of the track with an automatic weapon pointed at us. He was telling me to halt and stand still and not move. He grumbled away in German at me and I didn't understand. I was just watching. Behind him came an officer, and he asked us in perfect English who we were. We told him and said we had a couple of wounded up in the cave. He says, 'Well, we'll send some medical staff up there,' which they did later on. He said to us, 'Don't worry about it, for you the war is over.'"

"We saw an Australian ambulance come around the corner off the street at Megara and we thought we would get out, only to find it was driven by German paratroopers. They said, 'For you, the war is over. Get in the back.'"

Other soldiers in Crete and Greece, who tried to flee when their withdrawal turned sour, told similar stories.

"Corporal Tommy Jones, Private 'Pinshead' Brown and I were waiting under an olive tree at Megara, about halfway between Athens and Corinth on Anzac Day, 1941. We were waiting for our turn to withdraw via a launch boat that was taking 55 people at a time out to a destroyer. We were the next 55 to go when a landline got caught in the propeller of the boat. That was it for us. We missed the boat as it was leaving at 4am. We were told to make our way over to Corinth Bridge by 4pm as it was going to be blown. A number of blokes decided they were going to make the swim to the destroyer. It was night and we could not see a lot but we could hear gurgling sounds. Browny took off his overcoat and swam out. We did not think he made it, but found out years later he did get away. Lots of people drowned trying to get to the destroyer. We made our way to the canal by foot as Tommy had bullet wounds in his upper leg. We walked for six hours. German planes would tow in gliders that landed with motor bikes and machineguns. Then

the paratroopers dropped. The sky was filled with them. They were dropping in trees and telephone wires and everywhere just in front of us. So we had to turn around and go back. We were machine-gunned by a German plane on the way, but did not get hit. So at 4pm after 12 hours of walking we were back where we started. We saw an Australian ambulance come around the corner off the street at Megara and we thought we would get out, only to find it was driven by German paratroopers. They said, 'For you, the war is over. Get in the back.'"
Alfred Stone, Greece, 1941

"Our colonel told us to go with him or head for the hills. There were 18 of us who spent the first night in a cave. The next day, three of us wandered off starving, hungry, on blistered feet to try and find a boat after seeing some of our boys catch a lift on a barge to Libya. We spotted a small boat pulling into an inlet and I went to ask them for a ride. A young man slowly walked towards me and tapped me on my shoulder. I told him I didn't have any cigs and he took a pistol from inside his shirt and poked it deep into my stomach. I got a hell of a shock. These blokes dressed and looked like Poms. We were rounded up and marched off to join other men from our battalion."
Les Manning, Crete, 1941

"I was just out there having a little bit of a look around and there were tanks in front of us. And I thought, You bloody beauty. Then I thought, Bloody hell, they've got black crosses on them."

Doug Lefevre and John Hawkes were both captured on Ruin Ridge with the 2/28th Battalion during the first battle of El Alamein. Jack Calder was captured fighting with the 2/32nd Battalion. In all cases the men realised that a .303 bullet could not stop a panzerkampfwagen and they decided, quite correctly, that they should surrender. Lefevre explains, "First of all we began firing at them with our rifles and Brens, but we may as well have been shooting at the moon because they just kept coming – on and on. And one by one they picked us off and one by one they took us prisoners. However, being on the right flank we were one of the last to be picked up. I took off my watch which was a present from my wife when I left and buried it in a tobacco tin in the desert. I thought, *Well, the Germans are not going to get it if I can't have it.*"

"I was just out there having a little bit of a look around and there were tanks in front of us. And I thought, *You bloody beauty*. Then I thought, *Bloody hell, they've got black crosses on them*. And then there were some anti-tank guns in front of us, 6-pounder anti-tank guns. These blokes were shooting at these tanks. They were engaging them. Then from behind me a blooming machinegun comes up and it shot all those blooming anti-tank gunners and I looked back and there's tanks behind me with black crosses on them too. Bloody hell! Then it was on. The tanks came up and if you didn't get out of your hole they dug you in. They just came out and said, 'Out, out' and the gun they pointed at you looked as though it was a foot in diameter. This great big gunner just said, 'You, out.' And I got out. I thought, *If I bend down and pick up that Tommy gun would he reckon I'm going to have a shot at him?*. And I thought, *Oh my God, I don't know. These Germans might think that*. So I didn't, and I left my pack behind so I had nothing. I had my tin hat. I had my first field aid dressing in my shirt and these shorts that I had cut right off, and boots and socks. That's all I had. No water bottle, not a bloody thing and, by gee, I was a poor prisoner."
John Hawkes, El Alamein, 1942

"The company found it had overshot the front allotted to it by about 1,000 yards. All our supporting arms, medium machineguns and anti-tank guns were back 1,000 yards behind us. All we had were our .303 Lee Enfield rifles and three Boyes anti-tank rifles. As the dawn began to break, we found we were in a perilous position. We were on an exposed flat plain of ground and the men were unable to dig in, as the area we occupied was mostly rock. Enemy armoured vehicles of various types had taken positions on three sides of us and at about 07.00 a German officer, through a loudspeaker system, called on us to surrender. As there was no response from any of our officers, the Germans commenced to attack our position with small arms fire. There was no way we could fight our way out of the situation and as we began to take casualties, our company commander, Captain Keith Forwood, reluctantly surrendered to the German force at about 07.30."
Jack Calder, El Alamein, 1942

Being caught flat-footed by the enemy often gave soldiers no choice but to surrender. Resistance could be suicide. An embarrassed Aussie soldier was sometimes left to lament his lack of judgement, the enemy's sheer cunning or just plain bad luck. Often he had years in a prison camp to contemplate precisely how it happened. This is what Doug Crawford, who was captured in Greece in 1941, discovered.

"I was driving the lead vehicle. I came upon what I thought was our troops. I had my two motorcyclists out in front to spring the trap, but the road was being blocked by what I thought was Greek soldiers, retreating back behind the next defensive line. In fact, they were captured. I didn't know, I didn't see. So they slowed us up considerably. My driver, who was sitting where I should have been, was shot with a revolver. The machineguns had opened up on the convoy and I surrendered, smartly. I don't really recall what happened. I mean, there was just no option at that moment. The options would have been thought on reconnaissance before. But I had no idea at that stage that the front had collapsed."

"We didn't talk among ourselves. It was quite silent. We were drained of emotion. There were no tears. Perhaps I was thinking, How can anything as terrible as this be happening in such a beautiful place?"

It is expected that war be conducted according to certain humanitarian rules, outlined by the Geneva Convention. Sadly, some combatants and nations do not recognise these rules so atrocities occur, such as the murder of opponents who are unarmed or have surrendered. Australian nurse, Vivian Bullwinkel, was evacuating Singapore with wounded and a contingent of 65 nurses when their ship *Vyner Brooke* was sunk. About 150 survivors, including Bullwinkel and 21 other nurses, made it ashore at Radji Beach on Bangka Island. The decision was made to surrender to the Japanese soldiers, who killed the men before making the nurses wade into the sea. They then machine-gunned the nurses in the back. Bullwinkel was struck by a bullet and pretended to be dead until the Japanese left. She hid with a wounded British private for 12 days before deciding to surrender once again. This time they were taken captive. Her recollection of that shocking massacre makes for terrible reading.

"After a time...I can't remember how long...the chief engineer came back with a party of about 15 Japanese. The chief engineer told them, 'This is the party and we want to be taken prisoner.' But the Japanese officer brushed him aside and had a conference with his men. Then the British soldiers were told to get up and they were taken around a small point out of sight. We were left sitting on the sand. There was no sound or anything. Then the Japanese who had gone with the men came back wiping their bayonets…we just looked at each other. We didn't feel any emotion. I think by this time we were feeling shock on top of everything else. The Japanese stood in front of us and indicated that we should go into the sea. And we walked into the sea with our backs to them. We knew what was going to happen, but all I can remember thinking was: 'I am sorry Mother will never know what has happened to me but it will be nice to see Dad again.'

"We didn't talk among ourselves. It was quite silent. We were drained of emotion. There were no tears. Perhaps I was thinking, *How can anything as terrible as this be happening in such a beautiful place?* I'm not sure I heard the shooting…yes, I think I did hear a *rat-tat-tat* and I suppose it was a machinegun. I got hit. The force of the bullet, together with the waves, knocked me off my feet. I just lay there, swallowing a tremendous amount of saltwater until I was violently ill. And, after a while it sort of penetrated that I wasn't dying right there and then. I thought *I'd better stay low until I couldn't stay low any longer*. The waves brought me right into the shallow water.

"Finally, when I did sit up and look around, there was nothing. The Japanese had gone and none of the girls were to be seen… nothing. It's a bit hard to say, but I think it might have been just after midday. I started to shiver and all I wanted to do was get up into that jungle and lie down. So I got up and walked across the beach and lay down just off a track that led to the nearest village. Whether I passed out or not, I don't know…but I know that I woke up on one occasion and it was pitch dark."

After surrendering a second time to a different group of Japanese soldiers, Bullwinkel was treated reasonably. But her story forces us to consider just how many Aussie soldiers who surrendered were shot on the spot? A German soldier in a trench in 1917 takes an Australian prisoner after losing three comrades just minutes before. What does he do? A Boer soldier captures a member of the New South Wales contingent in 1900 after losing his family in a concentration camp. What does he do? There is no one else around. Do they pull the trigger as our own "Breaker" Morant did to his Boer prisoners? If no one survives to tell the tale then the soldier who lies dead in a faraway land somewhere, whether shot or executed, is recorded as MIA (missing in action) or KIA (killed in action). We must pause to remember those who surrendered and were summarily executed. We must also praise those who survived years of hell at the hands of their captors and who returned home to share their stories.

When you surrender to an enemy, your future is in his hands.

Chapter 2
Processing

" No physical or mental torture, nor any other form of coercion, may be inflicted on prisoners of war to secure from them information of any kind whatever. Prisoners of war who refuse to answer may not be threatened, insulted or exposed to unpleasant or disadvantageous treatment of any kind."

Article 17, third Geneva Convention

Les Manning and mates outside Stalag 13C, 1942

The world has a long history of rules and regulations that define the conduct of individuals and countries at war to prevent maltreatment. The numerous documents, treaties, protocols, Conventions and laws are detailed and complex. The treaty that relates specifically to the treatment of individuals in a war situation is known as the Geneva Convention. Initially this international treaty was developed to protect soldiers who were wounded on the battlefield as well as the medics who tended to them. Over the years, however, the Convention has been expanded to refer to all those caught up in conflicts, but not taking an active part in fighting. Unfortunately, it was not until after the Second World War that all four Conventions were fully ratified and signed by the majority of countries throughout the world. The Germans agreed to be bound by the 1929 revision of the Geneva Convention and Japan to elements of the 1907 Hague Convention when they entered WW2 so they were expected to treat POWs in a humane manner.

For some soldiers the initial fear and threat of execution dissipated once they had time to reflect on their capture. Others remained shell-shocked. But for all POWs, the most pressing question was: what will happen next? The answers were as different as the individuals and the environment they found themselves in.

" This left all of us with only our shirts, shorts, boots and socks. The officers were removed and taken off in trucks to a rear area and were not seen again until the end of the war in 1945 in England."

Generally, if the process accorded with the Geneva Convention, ranks would be separated, individuals questioned about their personal details and identity cards provided. Searches would be carried out and all weapons and military equipment confiscated. Personal effects, protective equipment such as helmets and gas masks, food and water would not be taken away. The POWs would then be evacuated to camps far from the combat zone. The evacuations were expected to be conducted humanely and in conditions that resembled their captors'. Each POW was to have sufficient food, water and clothing as well as medical attention if required. Naturally, whilst they provided these minimum requirements, the expectation amongst captors was that the prisoners would cooperate. Failure to do so meant certain privileges could be withdrawn or restricted.

Unfortunately, the harsh reality for many prisoners was that not all aspects of the Convention were adhered to. Murray McDonald tells us the story of how he was captured by the Germans in Greece.

"The first thing the Germans did was strip all the men of arms and equipment, including water bottles and haversacks that contained our iron rations (bully beef and hard biscuits)," he recalls. "This left all of us with only our shirts, shorts, boots and socks. The officers were removed and taken off in trucks to a rear area and were not seen again until the end of the war in 1945 in England. We were then taken to the back of the German lines where we began a long march to the first in a series of POW camps."

"With no food, and drinking from the creeks, we became gaunt, shambling creatures whose own parents would not have recognised them"

For many POWs, the next phase involved marching, more marching and even more marching as they were led on a torturous journey from camp to camp towards what would be their new home for the remainder of the war. Others were shunted from train to train, with drawn out spells of marching in between. Most found the travel conditions extremely uncomfortable, regardless of the mode of transportation. Hardship was the only constant during years of captivity. Murray McDonald recollects what happened following his capture in Greece.

"We were eventually put on a train from Kalamata for an unknown destination. Conditions on the train weren't too bad as it was a passenger train. However, sections of the line had been destroyed to slow the German advance or had been bombed by the Germans to shatter our defensive positions. This was in the Peloponnese – rugged mountain country – so we were forced to march over valleys and mountaintops for days, rejoining a train until we came across the next bombed-out section, where we would have to march again. Rifle butts were used on those who dropped to the rear of the march."

Evacuations from the combat zone, where many had been captured, often took weeks or even months. Many of the Allied prisoners in the European theatre during WW2 continually shifted camps as the Axis war effort slowly faltered and the battlefront moved closer to

Germany. Travel by foot, boat or train took an immense toll on the POWs' physical condition wherever they were.

"With no food, and drinking from the creeks, we became gaunt, shambling creatures whose own parents would not have recognised them," recalls Murray McDonald. "We made it to our first destination at Corinth where some food was provided: a large cauldron of cabbage soup each day. After a week we were to repeat the marches and occasional train ride to Salonika. After a few weeks there we were told we were going by train to a camp in Austria. Although we were in no fit state to give three cheers, the thought of a train ride seemed promising. But we were herded into cattle carts, 60 to each, doors locked and one small window per cart. Lying down was difficult and those wounded were given priority. Once daily, in open country, we were allowed out to use the side of the line as a toilet. Many of the already ill were now desperately sick so we were glad to reach Wolfsberg, in Austria. As we staggered and crawled through the gates of the prison camp, one of the German officers remarked in English that he would send a message to the authorities stating that if he ever received prisoners in such a state he would personally see that the offenders were severely punished. He was a colonel and seemed to be speaking with sincerity."

"We left Africa unshaven, unwashed, unfed, in tattered clothes, covered in lice and weighing approx 6-7 stone."

Other prisoners recounted stories just as disturbing as McDonald's.

"The prisoner-holding compound at Skenes was a stinking hellhole and most of the men were lousy with one illness or another. The old barracks were filthy, lice and flea-infested ruins and we suffered dysentery and leg infections from the biting bastards. Some men lost their battle there. If we had stayed much longer we would have all died of unnatural causes. Eventually we were loaded up and sent to Athens where we watched the poor Jews getting a hell of a time at the end of the Jerry's rifle butts. This is when we started to see the cruel side to them. Soon it was our turn to be herded onto railway cattle trucks by screeching Huns and their rifle butts. Our journey took seven hellish days with no food or medicine before arriving at a large camp outside Hammelburg. The men were a pitiful sight. We were shown the showers and felt lucky to have got out alive after seeing the ceiling covered with suspicious-looking

nozzles. When our rags were confiscated and fumigated, one bloke had left a spud in his pocket and it was half-cooked when he got it back. We were numbered and my coat was stamped 'KG' which meant 'POW' in German."
Les Manning, Crete, 1941

"When we were handed over to the Italians, the German Officer actually apologised saying 'I am sorry my orders are to hand you over to the Italians, as all POW's taken in North Africa are to be handed over to Italy.' So on 17th July the Italians began to march us behind their lines. We were held in transit camps for weeks before heading to Italy. We left Africa unshaven, unwashed, unfed, in tattered clothes, covered in lice and weighing approx 6-7 stone (I had weighed 12 stone prior to capture). The ship was a very ordinary piece of machinery and we were put in the hold below deck. I do not know how many men there were in the hold, but there was no room to lie down, only sit or stand. The hold was full of men with dysentery and there were only 44-gallon drums to service the lot. Naturally, they filled quickly and began to spill with the rolling of the ship. This horrible filthy trip lasted several days, again with no food or water."
William Hoffman, El Alamein, 1942

"One of the first things the Germans did was to separate the officers from other troops. The officers, who could not be put to work under the Geneva Convention (that laid down conditions governing the treatment of prisoners of war), were transported by plane to Athens. There we were paraded through the streets to expressions of sorrow from the local population and dropped off at a railway siding south of the city. Boarding Orient Express-type carriages with a piece of raw fish and a couple of thick biscuits, we travelled to Gravia where we detrained to march 40 miles over the Braillos Pass before reboarding a train. The food we were given was to last us for five days."
Ron Lister, Crete, 1941

"It was around 17.00 before we were all placed in a barbed wire enclosure at an old British Army POW camp, possibly El Duda, which was previously used as a staging camp for captured Italian and German soldiers. The German officer in charge of our guard detail advised us we were being handed over to the Italian Army, as all POWs taken in North Africa were the responsibility of the Italians as that was their territory. I was ordered to bring a detail of men to a shed outside the camp where we were given some

Italian aluminium drinking dixies which held about half a pint of fluid. At this stage there were 75 men in the group. Some had to go to hospital with wounds received that morning. I was issued with seventy-five 100-gram tins of Italian bully beef of a doubtful vintage. It wasn't easy trying to sleep that first night in captivity. The whole camp was full of fleas the size of flies and we were still hungry and thirsty despite the earlier tins of food and the drums of water. The next morning we were pushed onto the open trucks like sheep; the guards were very free with their use of rifle butts if you didn't squeeze in further. Anyone complaining got hit with a rifle butt around the head or body, so everyone learned to keep their mouths shut."
Jack Calder, El Alamein, 1942

" They were starving us, we could hardly walk and if you stepped out at night you were shot"

"He took us down and put us in the compound with a few thousand other blokes. They took everything of value from you, your watches, even wedding rings (they were gold). They didn't hesitate to take anything if they could get the opportunity. They used them to barter with and buy things. They separated officers and NCOs. They didn't realise Australians thought for themselves and that they didn't need an officer to lead them. If an Aussie wanted to go and do something, he went and did it, and that was his attitude. The Germans thought they were doing the right thing but they were wrong, because by separating us the ordinary private had a chance to do what he wanted."
Doug Nix, Greece, 1941

"After one month as a prisoner of war on Crete, we marched 15 miles to Suda Bay, kept going all night, got on a German boat heading for Greece this time as prisoners of war. Sailed again to Salonica. We stayed in a concentration camp that was hell for over a month. They were starving us, we could hardly walk and if you stepped out at night you were shot, they shot a few of the boys. We then left Saloncia for Germany by train in cattle trucks. We passed through Yugoslavia, Bulgaria and Austria before arriving at Bavaria in South Germany. On the way 20 of the boys escaped. I was too weak. The Jerry guards grabbed six of us and said because of the others escaping they were going to shoot us. They lined us up in

the middle of the night in Belgrade Yugoslavia, but they fired over our heads. I thought it was my last day."
Lindley Ashby, Crete, 1941

In Singapore, Malaya and Java, the situation was different. The Japanese had not taken prisoners in earlier battles in the Asia Pacific campaign. Now they had to deal with over 80,000 men, including more than 22,000 Australians. Working out the logistics of processing such a vast amount of people took time. The Japanese were very disorganised and early on the prisoners virtually looked after themselves. This was not a blessing as they often had to provide their own sanitation, food and water as Walter Holding recalls: "On the Tuesday morning they decided we had to march out to Selarang Barracks, which was in the Changi area. When that march started there were close to 80,000 troops – Australian, British and Indian – on the road to Changi so it was a pretty busy road. We carried what we had. We had a bit of stuff with us but not much. When we arrived we were put into private houses in the area. Robert Barracks, which was a bit further out, was turned into a hospital because we had quite a lot of casualties. Our engineers erected the barbed wire fences around the perimeter of the camp. Our own barbed wire was used. We settled into our quarters and then we just sat around. We did not know what to do. It was a bloody terrible set up – or so it seemed at the time."

" By now a lot of the men were suffering from dysentery and it was not unusual to cop a good splash, day or night, because there was only one toilet bucket in the corner of the cell."

The prisoners were becoming tense. News was spreading of Japanese atrocities inflicted upon surrendering and captured troops. Within the first two weeks of surrender more than 500 Allied soldiers were killed outside the battle. Jack Thorpe, who surrendered in Java, recalls his fears: "We'd been told they didn't take prisoners, they shot them instead. And we had seen their barbarity against our own earlier."

Thorpe also describes how he was processed. "We shifted that afternoon to a tea plantation where we stayed for several days until

Private
Reginald
Lindley
captured at
Crete, 1941

POWs after
processing on
the march to
Stalag Luft 1

they took us by train back to Batavia. We all went to different parts of the city. I was taken to the jail section on the wharf where 30 of us were put in one cell. It was so small you could not lie down. All you could do was sit down with your knees bent up and under your chin. By now a lot of the men were suffering from dysentery and it was not unusual to cop a good splash, day or night, because there was only one toilet bucket in the corner of the cell. The stench was terrible. There was only one window in the cell to provide fresh air and light and that was high up near the roof. Food was rice pushed through the door in a bucket. Our drinking water was also in a bucket, which often ran out so we could not get any more until the next day. We were in the bloody cell for about 10 days and nobody spoke. The only noise made was by somebody with dysentery who would let a loud fart go and then laugh out aloud.

" After the Jap guards had counted us, we were given our POW numbers - mine was 5168. Each number was printed on a piece of white cloth and had to be worn over the heart so the Jap guards had the best possible target."

"On the eleventh day the Japanese guards came around. They opened up the cell door and told us to get on the truck that was nearby. Well, we were like a lot of zombies. After all that time crammed in together our legs would not work. The truck was only 30 yards away but it took us about half an hour to get there. Getting onto the back of the truck was a problem too, with the bloody Jap guards bashing us with their rifle butts. Eventually we were all on the truck and taken to a camp that had been the HQ of a Dutch bicycle battalion on the outskirts of the city. By the look of it, the rest of the Australians on Java were there as well.

"After the Jap guards had counted us, we were given our POW numbers – mine was 5168. Each number was printed on a piece of white cloth and had to be worn over the heart so the Jap guards had the best possible target. Then we were dismissed and shown to our huts. Ours was the first on the left as you entered the compound. The first on the right was the guards' quarters. The Japanese at this time seemed hell-bent on trying to break our spirits. During the day, if a Jap walked within your sight, you had to bow low and remain there until he'd walked past. If you didn't, you got bashed, usually with a rifle butt. At night, about every two hours, they would enter the huts and call you to attention. Anyone who was not standing at the end of his bed when the guard walked through got the end of a rifle butt in the face. It was nerve-racking and terrible. If you tried to wake your mate up and the Jap saw you, you both got a bloody hiding. It was a no-win situation. I got into the habit of sleeping with one foot on the floor."

" The Japanese were overwhelmed by our sheer numbers. But once they realised they had a huge supply of slave labour, they very quickly decided what to do with us."

Other prisoners captured during the fall of Singapore and the Pacific region had similar stories about the early days of being detained.

"After a couple of days we received orders from our own command that we were to move to the former British Army's Selarang Barracks about 30 kilometres from our surrender location. We were allowed to take only what we could carry ourselves – the clothes we had in our packs, two army blankets and anything else we might be able to scrounge. I had managed to get a couple of tins of fruit and, of course, our water bottles were full. Flying from buildings, were hundreds of their white flags with a large red blob in the middle (the hated 'poached egg'). We were not allowed to talk to the mostly Chinese locals who crowded the footpaths to watch our misery. Some were sympathetic but others hated the British and showed it by jeering and laughing. The guards were everywhere and prevented any sort of communication with the sympathisers."
Gordon Nelson, Singapore, 1942

"After we marched into Changi on 17th February 1942, we did not see much of the Japanese for some days. Our own officers supervised us and ensured some semblance of order and discipline was kept. You could say that the Japanese were indifferent to us at this early stage, insofar as they made no attempt to supply any food, or in fact anything at all. We had to subsist on the stores we had with us. At this point, the Japanese were overwhelmed by our sheer numbers. But once they realised they had a huge supply of slave labour, they very quickly decided what to do with us."
Willoby "Bill" Wharton, Singapore, 1942

"The march dragged wearily on all afternoon and by evening we were tired out, with the weight of our packs and enervating heat.

Along the route we noticed that nearly every second house and shop displayed a Japanese flag, many of them home-made and obviously prepared for the occasion. Poor devils. They probably thought that a Jap flag would save them from any ill-treatment at the hands of their new masters. From shops and houses, the native population, mostly Chinese and Tamils, came out in force to watch the spectacle of the conquered white army marching towards its place of imprisonment. Alas for the prestige of the white man in the East. Most of the Asiatics stared at us with interest. Some seemed contemptuous, but a few of them openly expressed their sympathy and came out with buckets of drinking water and cups to offer us much-needed relief from our thirst. This handful of people earned our lasting gratitude and one felt that they regarded our misfortune as a passing phase, and that they would be ready to welcome the white man back again when the temporary reign of the little yellow men had ended."
Ray Wheeler, Singapore, 1942

"In the late afternoon things got very quiet, although some of the troops got a bit out of hand and started a bit of looting, especially of army trucks, with the result that there were quite a number of troops who were getting round in officers caps and Sam Browne belts."

"Well, for the first fortnight we never saw a Jap and then all of a sudden the Japs turned up and everyone packed his gear and we were put on a train and brought to a camp called Bicycle Camp and we still lived on our own rations."
Roydon Cornford, Java, 1942

"In the late afternoon things got very quiet, although some of the troops got a bit out of hand and started a bit of looting, especially of army trucks, with the result that there were quite a number of troops who were getting round in officers caps and Sam Browne belts. Some of the troops broke into a shop in North Bridge Road and took beer and other stuff. I had to break about a dozen bottles of beer and some other bottles of liquor which had been taken from some men at the gate. They were watching the operation and seemed to be in two minds as to whether to mob me or not, but apparently reason still held sway with some of them and they

quietened the remainder. The worst elements in the mob were some of the 2/3rd MAC drivers who had already something to drink and were well keyed-up."
Gerard Harvey Veitch, Singapore, 1942

"We never saw a Jap for about two days, only in the distance, and we were scrounging around looking for food and this Jap officer came out of the side of the road. He spoke good English and wanted to talk. He told us we weren't going to be too welcome by the Japanese army. And he told us to get back to where we were supposed to be. We weren't that far away, only a few hundred yards. From then on we started to see more and more of them. I think it was about the 16th or 18th February, somewhere around then, that we were marched out to Changi. We had to march through the city for everyone to see and it was an eye-opener. The amount of civilians, you could believe the stories they told us. They surrendered because of the death to the civilian population. The city was in ruins. There were large blocks where a building had been completely demolished and packed with bodies ten deep. Every now and then a big truck would go past with the remains of people on it. When you got out of the city into the suburbs heading towards Selarang, you would find great big pits dug and quick-limed. Bodies were just thrown willy-nilly into these pits."
Ray Wheeler, Singapore, 1942

"A lot of men were wounded and quite a lot of Japanese were killed. They found a lot of their flags and put them on the ground. It was the first time I had seen that big red-ball flag. The pilots eventually saw it and flew away. I had been wounded, but not very badly. I was put in a Bren gun-carrier and they took us to a place. I can't think of the name at the minute. We were unloaded and they let us lie there. They burned all their dead there – hundreds of them. We were then taken down near the sea. We had to make our own huts and everything. After a while I got very sick. I got malaria and dysentery and was put into a so-called hospital. All you got to eat was a bit of crummy old rice that you couldn't eat."
John Prosser, Timor, 1942

From 1929 onwards, the Geneva Convention stated that name, rank and serial number were the only thing POWs were required to provide if they were captured. Of course, the enemy always wanted

Heinrich Himmler inspects a POW camp in Germany. He committed suicide before being tried for war crimes

A typical POWs room
German camp

more information so they could increase their pool of intelligence. Sometimes the enemy wanted to know a prisoner's unit or previous job. Even such small amounts of information could be useful. But not all POWs were interrogated. Often simply searching through a prisoner's personal effects was enough to assist the enemy. In isolation, information obtained by search or interrogation may have appeared meaningless. However, when it was combined with other sources and accounts from other prisoners, the enemy was able to construct a very accurate picture of the enemy.

"The Japanese were trying to get information relating to military installations in Australia but none of the officers broke. They'd been strapped to chairs and bashed with pieces of wood and metal, burned with cigarette lighters, and so on."

Often captors were not interested in the information a prisoner could provide. Many were more intent on playing with his mind and trying to break him down – to destroy his spirit and will to fight or escape. Regardless of whether the purpose was to gather intelligence or to break spirits, violence, tricks and intimidation were used. Soldiers are trained to deny the enemy information if they are captured and to manipulate and falsify information that is divulged. While this may seem possible during training, it is hard to maintain such discipline under torture and when the human body and mind are at breaking point. The Geneva Convention states that a person may be interrogated provided their human rights are retained. Article 17 reads: "No physical or mental torture, nor any other form of coercion, may be inflicted on prisoners of war to secure from them information of any kind whatever. Prisoners of war who refuse to answer may not be threatened, insulted or exposed to unpleasant or disadvantageous treatment of any kind."

Sadly, however, some interrogation tactics were far from acceptable in terms of the Convention. Jack Thorpe was captured by the Japanese in Java and he paints a vivid picture of the inhumane treatment suffered by many at the hands of their captors.

"The Japanese were trying to get information relating to military installations in Australia but none of the officers broke. They'd been strapped to chairs and bashed with pieces of wood and metal, burned with cigarette lighters, and so on. Colonel Williams of the 2/2

Pioneers, and possibly others, had then been subjected to the often fatal water treatment, whereby water was poured into a man's body via his nostrils. None of these tactics had worked. We'd thought all this had finished when one day the guards came along and called out for 5168 to go the Jap HQ. That was me. I was marched into a room and stood in front of a Japanese officer sitting at a table. He asked for my name and where I came from. We'd been given orders by our officers that if we were called up for interrogation we were to tell them where we came from, but nothing more. It was important they didn't find out our civilian occupations, so they were unable to benefit from any of our skills. So I told him that I was Jack Thorpe from Armidale. He then asked me how far Armidale was from Perth. I told him 50 miles. 'Was there a rail line from Perth?' I said no. 'Was the road from Perth dual or four carriage?' I said single. 'How many bridges were there between Perth and Armidale?' I said none. Then he asked me how many men there were in the division of Australians on Java. I said I didn't know because I'd only been on one ship. 'How many ships were there?' I didn't know. He very casually got up, took a folder from the table and started to walk towards me. He stopped about two feet away, lifted his right hand and gave me such an almighty whack across the face that I was completely stunned for a moment. He pulled a Shell Oil road map out of the folder and told me I was telling lies. He told me it was fatal to tell lies to the Japanese Imperial Army and I would be severely punished. After many more whacks around the head he let me go."

At the outbreak of the Korean War in 1949, most nations had signed the Geneva Convention. However, two notable non-signatories to this document were the USA and the People's Republic of China. The USA and North Korea declared they would abide by these Conventions at the outbreak of the war. Then in 1950 when they joined the war, China finally declared it would do the same. Later it became clear that North Korea and China had not adhered to the Convention. They tried to void their responsibilities by declaring POWs war criminals, and as such they were not entitled to the safety net of the Geneva Convention. It was a flawed argument. Even if some POWs had committed war crimes, they were still to be treated humanely. Soldiers who break specific provisions of the laws of war lose the protections POWs are entitled to, but only after facing a tribunal. At that point they become unlawful combatants. Regardless of their status – POW or unlawful combatant – a person must still be treated with a specific degree of compassion.

"Captain Phil Greville of 1RAR was captured together with Private Denis Condon on the evening of 22/23rd August, 1952. He was kept in solitary confinement under severe interrogation for 90 days"

Only a small number of Australian soldiers were taken prisoner during the Korean War, but the treatment they received was severe. Eric Donnelly, who was captured after he was wounded, recalls: "A Chinese officer came over to my stretcher and spoke to me in perfect English. He asked who I was. I gave him the card we had been instructed to supply should we fall into enemy hands which gave name, number and rank. He told me it would be difficult to get medical treatment until I told the People's Liberation Army the truth. He said I would be going to school when I was better. I asked him what he meant, but he would not expand."

After being moved from the frontline to an interrogation centre, the torture of sleep deprivation and lack of medical treatment began for Eric Donnelly. "After travelling all night, we ended up in a cage with a very low ceiling. This room or cage was about ten feet square and the ceiling was about three feet from the floor. This stopped you from standing up but you could sit or squat on your haunches. As I was in a horizontal position, it didn't affect me too much. In the cage with George Smith and myself were three South Korean soldiers who looked as if they had been there for some time. This was an interrogation centre. English-speaking Chinese or Korean soldiers would come in at all hours of the day or night to question me. The questions were of a general nature and were always followed with the threat that I would not get medical treatment unless I told the truth. A typical question might be: 'Where did your grandmother go to school when she was a little girl?' If you told them you didn't know, they would get very upset and say: 'You must tell us the truth. You will not get medical treatment until you tell the truth.' The easy way out seemed to be to make things up. I would make up a fictitious story and tell them she had attended such and such a school which they would duly note down in their little notebooks. All the time I was in this centre I was in extreme pain from the injuries to my leg, mouth and back. Sleep was very hard to get and whenever I did fall asleep from sheer exhaustion, I was shaken violently and then asked further questions. Because I was making up answers to a lot of the questions, I often gave the wrong ones when they repeated their questions. They would scream out, with their eyes bulging out of their heads and their faces a matter of inches from my face: 'You have lied to us. You will not get medical treatment'."

Donnelly's experience wasn't unique, as another Australian Korean War Veteran, Ron Cashman, describes: "Captain Phil Greville of 1RAR was captured together with Private Denis Condon on the evening of 22/23rd August, 1952. He was kept in solitary confinement under severe interrogation for 90 days, first at a field interrogation centre where he was kept in a packing case, into which were also eventually packed a South Korean soldier and a civilian. His next incarceration was at the 'Caves' where he was put in a small lean-to attached to the side of a Korean house. A number of other POWs under intensive interrogation were kept in similar accommodation. He was forced to sit to attention all day unless he was under interrogation."

Cashman also details the capture and interrogation of another officer, Lieutenant Charlie Yacopetti, a 3RAR platoon commander.

"On 25th May, 1953, Lieutenant Charlie Yacopetti was leading a patrol near Hill 355 when it was attacked by two groups of Chinese. Yacopetti was hit in both the arms and legs and his right ankle was badly shattered. He lost consciousness and was captured. For about a month he was held at the frontline, being interrogated up to eight hours a day. He was promised medical treatment provided he gave information. He was eventually sent north to the 'Caves' where he had his wounds dressed for the first time."

" They brought out a party of soldiers and lined them up in front of us. They loaded their rifles and asked us to give them the information they required."

Often officers and non-commissioned officers would be separated and interrogated to gain immediate tactical advantage. They were searched for information, weapons and any item that would contribute to battlefield intelligence. Sometimes they were beaten into submission. On other occasions they were given a hot meal and drink. Interrogation tactics are many and varied and they have evolved and changed from conflict to conflict. Nonetheless, tactics did always involve a disregard for an individual's liberties and human rights.

Chapter 2 – Processing

"They brought out a party of soldiers and lined them up in front of us. They loaded their rifles and asked us to give them the information they required. We still refused crying out to them to shoot away. I believe they would have carried out their purpose had it not been for a German officer, who spoke a few words rapidly in Turkish and gave them the order to 'imshi' (go away)."
George Handsley, Romani, 1916

"The German sergeant tried very hard to get some information from me concerning the disposition and movements of our troops. I did not answer his questions. He said he would make me. I told him I did not think he could. He produced a map and when I told him to put it away he became angry. I was feeling sick and weak from loss of blood at the time. The hospital was one the Germans had captured from us during their advance. I was the only wounded Australian there. Under the circumstances the treatment and medical attention were good. The medical officers visited the wards daily and I received the same food and treatment as the German wounded."
Anonymous soldier, France, 1918

"During the interrogation he'd seemed very concerned about how many Australians might be on Java, which I think indicated that they had indeed got a terrible hiding at Buitenzorg. He seemed set on the idea that there was a full division of troops – that is 18,000 men – whereas, in fact, there'd only been 2,000. Happily, he left the camp at the end of the interrogations and we never saw him again."
Jack Thorpe, Java, 1942

" I noticed his hand was shaking. I looked up into his face and thought, My God, this bloke is more frightened than I am. And that's saying something."

"He looked up and said in excellent English, 'Stand to attention in front of *superior* officer.' Well, as I didn't know he was an officer and I certainly didn't think he was superior, I still remained at ease. So he snapped that I was to stand to attention. I thought, *Well, I might as well do the right thing*. So I stood to attention. The Italian spotted my collar badge and he said: 'Which regiment is this?' And, of course, we had been drilled to give only your name, rank and number. So I said, 'LeFevre, WX5933, Lance Corporal.' He said, 'I didn't ask you that.' He said, 'Which regiment does this come from?' I said, 'I don't know. I picked it up in the desert.' So he got out of the chair and grabbed this Beretta and stood in front of me – he was about a foot taller – and he pressed it against my forehead. I noticed his hand was shaking. I looked up into his face and thought, *My God, this bloke is more frightened than I am*. And that's saying something. He said, 'If you don't tell me I'll shoot you.' And I thought: *Why doesn't the cavalry come or the Air Force; why doesn't somebody come?*

"Anyway, somebody did come in. It was a German officer and he was dressed in an Afrika Korps uniform. He came in and said in English, 'What is going on here?' The Italian spoke in German and the German officer said, 'Put the gun away and sit down. What's the problem?' I thought, *here's a mate*, and I said, 'Well, Sir, this officer has asked me where this badge came from and I don't know.' The German picked up the belt and looked at it. He went outside through the back door. He was gone for about a minute and he came back and put the belt on the table and said, '10th Light Horse, Western Australian Cavalry Regiment, now disbanded.' I thought, *My God, he knows more than I do*, because I didn't know the 10th Light Horse had been disbanded. And to add insult to injury, he said: 'It's now probably the 10th Armoured Unit and it is based in north-west Australia,' which is something that we didn't know. So then he said, 'Let the boy go.' So I plucked up courage and I asked: 'Can I have my belt back, Sir?' The Italian officer answers, 'No you can't.' So I said, 'I can't run around with my pants hanging down.' So the German went out and came back with a piece of twine, which I tied around my pants. I wore it for the next six weeks to stop my pants from falling down."
Doug LeFevre, El Alamein, 1942

Apart from intelligence gathering, the enemy had other tasks to perform while processing prisoners. Those who were wounded required treatment. Sometimes the captors did not have the necessary medical provisions; on other occassions it was simply not provided, or used to try and extract more information from someone or to take revenge. Richard Armstrong still bears strong resentment towards his captors after an event that happened to helpless Australian soldiers. Three battalions, the 2/29th, the 2/30th and the 2/19th, were regrouping after ferocious battles with the Japanese in January 1942 at Gemas, Muar and Parit Sulong Bridge.

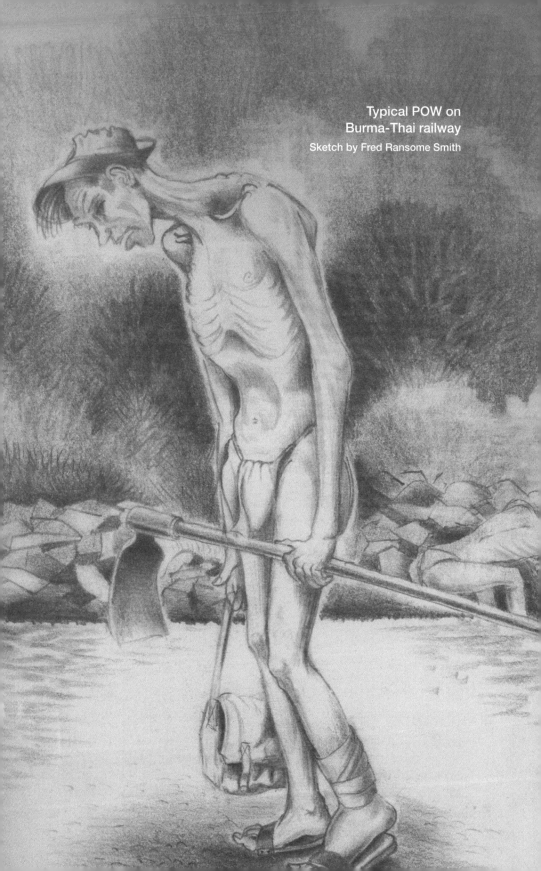

Typical POW on
Burma-Thai railway
Sketch by Fred Ransome Smith

"Having made their victims helpless, these little yellow butchers - here I use the term 'yellow' to describe their cowardice and not their skin colour - proceeded to bayonet and behead the victims before pouring petrol over them and setting them alight."

Armstrong recalls: "It was here at Parit Sulong Bridge (that) the Japanese committed one of their early major atrocities of murder and brutality against unarmed prisoners. Our ambulances were left to their tender mercies, and with the ambulances were 137 wounded men, including 11 Indian troops. The Japanese tied their hands behind their backs. To do this effectively, the Japanese tied both thumbs together with wire or fishing line. Having made their victims helpless, these little yellow butchers – here I use the term 'yellow' to describe their cowardice and not their skin colour – proceeded to bayonet and behead the victims before pouring petrol over them and setting them alight. Many of these victims of Japanese atrocity were not dead when they were set alight but actually burned to death. It appears the reason for this act of wilful murder was because the fit men of the two battalions, the 2/19th and the 2/29th, refused to surrender to the Japanese. As an act of spite the Japanese murdered about 138 helpless men. Here, as with our unarmed nursing sisters on the beach of Bangka Island, the Japanese made a mistake and without their knowing it one man escaped to live and tell of his horrific experience, as did Sister Vivian Bullwinkel on Bangka Beach. The sole survivor was Lieutenant Ben Hackney of the 2/29th Battalion. When the Japanese left the scene of their crime, Ben Hackney crawled away into the jungle and with the help of some Chinese civilians was eventually smuggled into Changi following the surrender of Singapore."

We can gain some encouragement from the fact that a lot of enemy soldiers were more inclined to show mercy than to kill wounded POWs. The experiences of wounded prisoners varied from campaign to campaign, captor to captor and ranged from compassion to horror.

"I arrived there (at the German dressing station) more dead than alive, and my wound was dressed by a German doctor who did not waste any sympathy on me because I was Australian. He

wanted to know why we Australians had come over to fight against Germany. I told him we were there to assist the nation to which we belonged. I remained there that night and slept on an old bed of blankets. Next morning I was taken to Wavrin by ambulance wagon and placed in hospital. It was a hospital for German wounded and besides myself there were three Australians and one Englishman. We were treated exactly the same as the German wounded and the food we got was wholesome, but not too plentiful. The hospital staff consisted of German doctors, a German matron, and AMC orderlies. Our wounds were dressed regularly, and, on the whole, the treatment meted out to us was fair, very fair. I remained there for one month and was then moved to Douai."
Anonymous soldier, France, 1916

"They bandaged my wound and helped me to a village called Revenshaw. There my shattered arm was dressed and strapped in a wire frame. I was not ill-treated in any way. I remained there for five days and received good medical treatment and attention. I was taken thence (after my leg was amputated) to Valenciennes, where I lay in hospital for about a fortnight. At the time there were very few Australian prisoners of war there. The treatment we received was very good. The German doctors and German nursing sisters were both skilled and attentive. The food, too, was good, as it was supplied in the main by French civilians."
Anonymous soldier, France, 1918

"The Japanese had no respect for our enormous number of wounded, some with horrific injuries. Once they were all hospitalised in Changi, our magnificent medical officers began the task of mending the men. However, the task wasn't that easy. We all know that once you lose a lot of blood you need vitamins to help your body regain its vitality, and our medical officers had not one single item to help our wounded survive their traumatic injuries."
Don McLaren, Singapore, 1942

"At Muar, there was about 200 of our chaps of the battalions and the artillery that were wounded and the Allies couldn't get in to break them out. So Colonel Charles Anderson, who was in charge of the 2nd/19th Battalion where he won the Victoria Cross for that establishment there told his chaps to make their own way out, because they couldn't do anything. So they broke out and those who were wounded, there was a couple of hundred of them and an officer in charge of them asked the Japs could they help these

wounded. The Japs refused. They just machine-gunned them, set fire to them with petrol and burnt them, and then just emptied them into graves."
Cyril Gilbert, Singapore, 1942

The Geneva Convention and organisations like the United Nations and the International Red Cross and Crescent outline the basic tenets of processing prisoners and their entitlements. While many countries either signed up, or stated they would ratify or abide by these laws, many have found it difficult to control their people over the years. They either could not cope with the volume of prisoners or simply reneged on their commitment. A POW's experiences early in his captivity would shape his attitudes towards the captors for the duration. Those who had been processed now had to think what they would do next – escape or survive. For those in European POW camps, escape was always on their mind. But in Asia, it was a vastly different story.

POW at Stalag 18A

Stalag Luft soccer field

Chapter 3
Daily Life

"The basic daily food rations shall be sufficient in quantity, quality and variety to keep prisoners of war in good health and to prevent loss of weight or the development of nutritional deficiencies. Account shall also be taken of the habitual diet of the prisoners."

Article 26, third Geneva Convention

Contents of a Red Cross care package

The POWs' daily experiences varied depending upon the captors, the country they were in and how the war was progressing. Some prisoners had few major complaints apart from the fact they were incarcerated, whereas others suffered extreme hardship and appalling treatment.

Regardless of the campaign, captors or country, there invariably came a point when Australian POWs had to deal with inadequate, food, quarters, clothing, work or medical treatment. Although many of us are familiar with the fact that large numbers of Australian prisoners suffered at the hands of the Japanese and the Germans, we should also be mindful of the experiences of a lesser number of POWs who were held by the Boers, Turks, Italians, North Koreans and Chinese.

Prisoners of war always had a vast amount of time to kill. Some camps provided opportunities to work, rest and even play. Prisoners of diverse backgrounds brought with them different skills and talents which often resulted in education through association. For the majority, more often than not the work was hard and the hours long, and it was made all the more taxing when they were fighting illness, starvation, poor shelter and sub-standard clothing. Many simply did not have the energy to play, so their downtime was spent conserving energy in order to survive.

" There was even heating and hot water that we later discovered was provided by steam from the mine. As POWs we'd never seen quarters like these before and could hardly believe the luxury of it all."

According to Article 25 of the Geneva Convention, accommodation for POWs should be dry and have adequate heating and lighting. POWs forced to work on the Burma-Thai Railway had to live in makeshift huts made of bamboo and thatched roofs. Jack Thorpe remembers: "Our living quarters were bamboo huts with 'attap' roofs and an open doorway at each end. There were sleeping platforms of roughly-trimmed bamboo slats running down each side where we POWs slept crammed together like sardines. The dirt floor was continuously flooded during the monsoon season and it was just as muddy inside our quarters as it was outside – but nothing inside the huts was dry anyway."

Tom Pledger was struck by how little protection the huts provided. "When the sun was shining you could lie on your bed and watch it from sunrise to sunset and it was never out of your vision so you can just imagine what it was like when it was raining."

When some of the prisoners were moved to Japan to work in the coal mines they initially thought their accommodation was luxurious. "There was a proper guardhouse, a mess room, shower and washing facilities, and there were proper toilets at the end of each hut, which only slept 10," recalls Jack Thorpe. "There was even heating and hot water that we later discovered was provided by steam from the mine. As POWs we'd never seen quarters like these before and could hardly believe the luxury of it all. True, the hot water and heating was often turned off, or broke down, and you needed a mate to help you shower. He'd have to bash the shower-head with a broom to break up the ice and stop it reforming while you did your best to wash off the dust and grime from the coal mine – without soap, of course. But on that first day we knew nothing about this so we thought we'd struck it lucky with our quarters at least."

According to Ron Lister, a good roof overhead made little difference in the brutal German winter. "Washing facilities in winter were scarce as most of the water pipes froze up. With typical German inconsistency, they ordered that only the colonels would take a weekly hot shower; the exception being anyone who presented himself to the German doctor with proof that he was infested with lice. He, together with his room-mates, would then be entitled to a hot shower at some future date –any time up to a month later."

Bill Flowers was at Changi where he worked in the hospital. He frequently grumbled about the primitive living conditions, but it was not until a soldier from F Force was sent back to Changi sick that Flowers realised their camp was in fact tolerable. "Thank God, I'm home," the soldier told him. Flowers thought: "Such a comment described the hell that the fellow had endured and gave one food for thought that Changi POW camp conditions were much more bearable, although less food for thought and more food for the stomach would have been readily accepted."

Article 26 of the Geneva Convention requires that daily food rations be sufficient in quantity, quality and variety to keep prisoners in good health and prevent weight loss or the development of nutritional deficiencies. If prisoners are required to work then the Convention insists that additional rations be provided as necessary. Food was a frequent topic of conversation amongst POWs regardless of where, or when, prisoners were incarcerated; it was also a major source of either anticipation or disappointment.

It appears that only in the Boer War was food close to plentiful for POWs. This was due primarily because money was sent out from Britain to supplement prisoners rations, including the Australians'. Often funds were raised by local groups, such as women's auxiliaries. Seen through the prism of two World Wars and more recent conflicts involving terrorists and insurgents, the civility of the Boers in allowing this money through to prisoners seems remarkable. Harold Harnett, who was captured in South Africa in 1900, certainly wasn't too happy with his lot, but was able to supplement his rations with the money he received. "The rations consisted of one small loaf of bread daily; sugar, coffee and one pound of beef was issued only on Wednesdays. Occasionally I bought some pork and fruit etc. Things are awfully dear."

"For 15 weary months we had been forced by starvation and hardship to submit to humiliation and indignities. We were allowed barely sufficient food to keep body and soul together."

The 4,000 prisoners of the Great War were few compared to a total of 61,000 killed and 155,000 wounded. These Australians, who were captured while fighting, still experienced hardship as POWs especially in terms of severe food shortages. The British blockade reduced German supplies to their own troops, and consequently POWs had even less to eat. Many would have perished without Red Cross parcels. Germany had agreed that a non-working POW was to receive 2,000 calories a day, a working one 2,500 a day and a heavy worker 2,850 a day. This was agreed to at a time when the average German was consuming 1,000 calories a day. The German government did not fulfil their obligations according to the Conventions as an unidentified soldier recalls.

"For dinner: water and a few pieces of mangelwurst. For tea we received another dish of the same or a drink of tea. That was our first day's food. A number of French prisoners were already receiving parcels from home and would share some of their German rations with us. We soon became weak and exhausted.

The wiry men held out best of all. When the parcels were in regular succession, we were better fed and clothed than the average Hun. On one occasion we had cleaned out a treacle tin. A workman came along and licked it with his tongue. We began to realise that Germany and her people really were hungry and depressed."

Others recall similar food shortages:

"For 15 weary months we had been forced by starvation and hardship to submit to humiliation and indignities. We were allowed barely sufficient food to keep body and soul together, and were forced to gather weeds and herbs for sustenance. We were gaunt, unwashed, unshaven and devoured by vermin; knowing practically nothing of what was going on beyond our barbed-wire enclosures and seemingly dead to the world. For all we knew we were being mourned as dead. Would we ever see our loved ones again?"
Tommy Taylor, Bullecourt, 1917

"The ration was of the slenderest. One litre of the poorest kind of vegetable soup, a small piece of black bread, and sometimes when we got it lucky, a piece of sausage about the size of your thumb. Without exaggeration, a prisoner's ration in Germany was never at any time more than just enough to keep body and soul together, and it was also no better than pig food. We cooked up anything we could find, including stinging nettle leaves, wild turnip leaves, and mouldy old mangolds out of musty cellars and devoured them thankfully. Later we were given meat, which we called sea-lion. All fat was taken from it and the remainder, beastly-looking stuff, quite black and full of salt, was dished out to us. At first, although we were starving, none of us could eat it, but in the long run we were glad enough to tackle it and we were to see the time in the bitter northern German winter when we actually looked forward to 'sea-lion day' for a satisfying feed. The bread at this time was evidently made of sweepings for it was full of oat husks and very gritty, but we ate that too, and were very glad to get it."
Justin Dawson, France, 1917

"The Germans put us in a fort at Lille. They never gave us anything. We may have had a slice of bread a day and a pot of soup, nothing else. We were building dugouts, huts, carrying and loading shells. We had one slice of bread in the morning and at lunchtime a pot of soup, which was more or less like water."
Horace Ganson, France, 1917

"When we reached the prison camp we were given a bath and our heads were shaved again. We were then placed in a small room called the 'quarantine room' for 14 days. At this period of our imprisonment our food consisted of a small loaf of bread daily and a half pint of boiled wheat twice daily."
George Handsley, Romani, 1916

"Food seemed to be the centre of our thoughts, our lives, and our morale was affected by it more than by any other single factor."

In the Japanese camps during World War Two the food was scarce, bland and lacked substance. Prisoners who worked did not receive extra rations. If a POW was sick and unable to "provide service to the Emperor" their rations were halved. This strategy did not help any of the POWs regain their "good" health. Soldiers in the larger camps could buy food with the pay they earned for working. In the remote camps in Thailand and Burma, where more than 30 percent of men perished, there were no such luxuries. Food meant survival.

Rice became the POWs' staple diet and for many, whether they liked it or not, if they had not been given it for three years they would not have lived to tell their stories. David Smith of "F" Force in Burma remembers, "Food seemed to be the centre of our thoughts, our lives, and our morale was affected by it more than by any other single factor. Food took priority over the inhumane treatment such as bashings, long hours of work, terrible living quarters, monsoons, you name it. The thought of food never left us and it must be recorded that stealing from our mates and fellow sufferers was rare. Stealing from the Japs whenever possible? Well, that was another matter."

Many had similar recollections:

"An hour before dawn the workers would rise and the mess orderlies would flounder through the mud to the kitchen and collect a bucket of rice pap which they would bring back to the hut. The men would then file past and by the light of a candle or a slush lamp each would be served a dixie of pap. This would have to satisfy them for

several hours. It would probably be raining but, no matter what the weather, they would be off to the tool shed to collect their picks and shovels, sledgehammers and dog spikes. While it was still dark, they would struggle through the mud to the railway line, where they would start to lay another two or three kilometres of rails. Perhaps by three or four in the afternoon a meal of rice and stew would have been sent out from the camp, and it was usually stone cold by the time it reached them. Squatting on a sleeper or a water-soaked log, the men would consume the unappetising mess, usually in the rain, for the wet season was not yet over."
Jim Jacobs, Singapore, 1942

"Several times I nearly had a riot on my hands, mainly because of the food which certainly was not very palatable; it consisted mainly of rice with a tasteless papaya stew or some very thin milk. Am afraid the men had my sympathy, but that could not be shown when they started getting fractious."
Gerard Harvey Veitch, Singapore, 1942

"Food was something you thought about all the time. You got a cup of 'pap' – stewed rice – for breakfast, watery slop, and that's what you went out and worked on, and if you went to the toilet soon after, well, that went. Lunch was rice again, which you took out with you in the morning in your dixie, and that usually soured by lunch. You might, if you were lucky, have a piece of dried seaweed or horsemeat in a mug of rice at night. If you were even luckier, there might be a weak stew, which was mostly pumpkin. It's surprising how a lot of blokes kept their weight up, especially with the work we all did."
Jim Kerr, Singapore, 1942

"On one occasion during the time at one of the Sonkurai camps, Bob Murray had to go and work in the Japanese cookhouse. He took the opportunity to bring a big piece of dried fish back with him. As the work party did not come in till 9 or 10pm, Bob boiled the fish and the maggots started coming to the top. After taking a few out, he decided that we would not see them so he left them. Then he left it outside so the smell would not attract attention. It put a good taste in the rice and was lovely and salty. A couple of days later he told me about the maggots!"
Walter "Wally" Holding, Singapore, 1942

"In the beginning we got boxed meat. The first lot we got was about the size of a butter box and very salty, but unfortunately

Altamura, Italy, 1942. Allied POWs at the internment camp Campo CPG 65

AWM Neg. P00866_001

German POW camp, kitchen area, Langensalza, 1917

PRG1300_15_5

it was full of maggots. We soon solved the problem, though, by pouring water into the kwalis and putting the meat in on top of that and a fire underneath. As it got hot, the maggots came to the top and crawled out and we scooped them off."
Neville Merrigan, Singapore, 1942

"On the Burma Line our rations were a pint (two cups) of rice a day. Not enough to keep body and soul together, let alone support bodies during long hours of back-breaking manual labour. As the result of the lack of nutrients in our diet we were very vulnerable to deficiency diseases such as beri-beri, scurvy and pellagra as well as succumbing easily to infections. The problem was compounded by the fact that the Japs penalised the sick by cutting their rations by half. Naturally, this was secretly supplemented from the rest of our rations. If the Japs had found out, they would have reasoned that if we were giving some of our food to the sick we must have been getting too much – and our rations would have been cut still further."
Jack Thorpe, Java, 1942

" I have eaten rat and snails. Rats are a delicacy and nearly everybody has a rat trap."

Knowing they would not be able to survive on the undersized rations the Japanese provided meant that soldiers often substituted their food with local fauna and flora. Japanese guards often kept chickens and ducks for eggs to supplement their own rations, so POWs would occasionally risk the chance of a bashing for a good meal and the odd one would go missing. If the opportunity arose they would kill more substantial creatures such as goats or pigs that were either feral or farmed by the natives. The Australians' bush skills were put to great use, skinning and preparing the animals for cooking. Extreme hunger meant that very unusual fare was used to supplement the pap: rodents, snails, all kinds of bug, leaves and Pacific jungle plants.

"Most men have lost weight. The average weight for the 204 men is 116lbs. I am not exaggerating when I say I can put my two hands around the waist of at least 10 men. I have eaten rat and snails. Rats are a delicacy and nearly everybody has a rat trap. We cook them with onions and tomatoes from our garden and they taste like beef stew. It is funny to see grown men down on hands and knees chasing snails, horrible slimy things but still protein."
Tom Pledger, Ambon, 1942

"We had little chance of supplementing our meagre diet in the remote jungle camps. Maggots added some nutrition, when available. I still remember Colonel Coates telling us in the early days of the Burma railway that if you could see the bottom of your dixie after you'd finished eating, you had a bloody good chance of making it back home. 'Don't worry what's in your dixie, just eat it', he'd say. He instilled in us the need to eat every morsel of food we got."
Jack Thorpe, Java, 1942

"We were working at Victoria Point at an aerodrome digging out landmines, and there were a few goats about. They used to take us down for a swim and my mate and I said let's 'dodge off and see if we can grab one of those goats'. I grabbed one by the leg and took him into the scrub. I had a potato knife that I had cut a point into, so was able to skin him. We cooked him in the scrub and it fed about 12 of us."
Robert Sproull, Singapore, 1942

" I left Germany weighing seven stone eight, and my weight from the age of 14 on has always been over 10 stone."

While Australian soldiers were generally better off when captured by the Germans or Italians, they often struggled to make do with the food provided by their captors. This changed during the course of World War Two, when the Germans in particular generally fed Australians so they were just better than starving. Logistical issues may have been partly to blame. That said, both Germany and Italy had signed the Geneva Convention. Ron Lister describes his rations as a "starvation diet". "Lukewarm mint tea and a three-quarter share of a large hard biscuit was breakfast. The big meal of the day was lunch which consisted of a breakfast cup-sized portion of soup, mainly water, laced with a small part of rice, barley or peas which gave the illusion of being fed. The evening meal was more tea with a piece of brown bread equal to a thick slice of a sandwich loaf."

"You had soup and sometimes you'd get a bit of meat in it. Fairly inadequate. I left Germany weighing seven stone eight, and my weight from the age of 14 on has always been over 10 stone. But the German ration was inadequate; there's no question of that."
Doug Crawford, Greece, 1941

"Food was mainly rice with sultanas and grapes. Very hot and dry in the compound so after a couple of days of mumbles of discontent a few groups made their plans and began sizing up their chances of escape."
Rick Hunter, Crete, 1941

"They would have cabbage and macaroni and rice. Very little of anything, but some of the cabbage used to be rotten and all slimy. Well, they'd chuck that out. Well, Jimmy and I would get that and we'd take all the slime off it and we'd cook it in some straw."
John Hawkes, El Alamein, 1942

"Rations were watery soup twice a day, plus a minute bun called bread, so Red Cross parcels became the prime goal – one between two men weekly. Some camps worked on one parcel daily per six men (and) they punctured all tins to prevent storage or sale. Talk was of meals and recipes, and we literally dreamed of food. Then, and each year thereafter, winter brought on Red Cross parcel shortages, just when our needs were greatest. British bombing was the usual excuse, but we felt it was a little of 'let them suffer too'."
Ray Middleton, El Alamein, 1942

"At our concentration camp in Salonika it was hell. They were starving us we could hardly walk about. We were living like dogs you could not move around the compound at night without fear of being shot. A few of the boys have been shot. If we are here much longer we will be mad or dead."
Reginald Lindley, Crete, 1941

"The last we ever saw of this lovely old lady was when she walked out the door of our hut holding the ring in front of her eyes with a big, toothless grin on her face."

POWs often supplemented their diet by buying or bartering for additional supplies. Wages, cigarettes and even other types of food were used to obtain additional supplies from locals, guards or other prisoners. Eric Donnelly, a POW in Korea, remembers how his mate tried to barter with a North Korean peasant woman. He had a brass ring and she had apples. His diet at the time consisted mainly of tasteless, boiled rice which "stuck to your mouth". "We used to wish that we had a little sugar, salt, curry or any bloody thing at all that would give a bit of taste."

His mate Jack Davis caught the eye of the woman as she passed the POW hospital. It had a cruel and unnecessary consequence. Donnelly recalls: "We started advising Jack that 15 was a reasonable price to pay for a brass ring and to accept her offer; this he did and the ring changed hands at 15 apples. The last we ever saw of this lovely old lady was when she walked out the door of our hut holding the ring in front of her eyes with a big, toothless grin on her face. Jack shared the apples around and we each got one and a half apples. I don't think I have ever tasted a nicer apple. It was the measure of the man that Jack Davis shared his apples equally so that we all got the same amount. Two days later Dr Whong came into our hut and asked us who had sold this ring, holding it up for us to see. Jack admitted that he was the culprit and asked the doctor if he had done anything wrong. Dr Whong said that the Korean peasants were not allowed to fraternise with the prisoners of war and the old woman had been shot as an example to others not to have contact with us. Dr Whong handed back the brass ring to Jack Davis and warned him not to do this again as he could not stop the army from carrying out these executions. Thus the People's Liberation Army put a value of 15 apples as the price for this poor old Korean lady's life. Whenever I eat an apple now, I think of her toothless smile and her face."

Others would pinch anything they could get their hands on, especially if it belonged to the enemy. It was one thing to steal food or contraband for bartering, but getting it past the guards was another matter. Those working for the Japanese often wore nothing but rags. When these disintegrated they were replaced with Japanese underwear, a piece of cloth about a 1.5 metres long and six inches wide. This was tied around the waist, brought up between the legs, tucked under the waistband and finished in a flap that hung down in front of the groin. Walter Holding recalls how fellow POWs quickly discovered other uses for the spare cloth on these "lap-laps".

"Anything pinched was put inside this and hung between your legs. They would drop us off up the road when we came in off work. We had to fall in to be searched – five ranks open order, in front of the guardhouse at the corner of the jail. One day, the search was over, and a guard who had nothing better to do smacked one of the boys

Pile driving on the Burma-Thai railway
Sketch by Fred Ransome Smith

on the backside and nearly broke his hand. He hit a bag of salt. After a full search there was a great heap of salt on the ground in front of the guardhouse. The Japanese in charge of the guard spoke some English. He told us it was very dirty to carry salt like that. Salt was always a problem. The boys pulled tankers of salt – seawater – to the jail to boil the rice. The 'G-string', as it was known, was used right through our POW days. I got a carton of cotton into Selarang area. We were on 10 cents a day (when we got it) and the carton of cotton was worth eight dollars through the fence. Walking with the carton of cotton reels in my G-string was a bit awkward."

" They never knew that the entire bottle was crammed full of whatever contraband we could lay our hands on during the day, especially tobacco."

Richard Armstrong remembers: "There was not a single way of stealing that we didn't adopt and promptly improve on and perfect in every way." In Singapore, Armstrong worked on the wharves where the men took anything they could get their hands on, especially medical supplies, to send back to the line. Whenever they got caught by the guards they would revise their methods and do it again. He recalls;

"When the guards found that some of our numbers were taking loot, such as sugar, out in our army water bottles, they promptly began checking these every day. The next move was to get some of our plumbers to open the bottom of the water bottle and solder a false bottom into it about an inch from the top. This top inch was filled with water and when the Japs checked it we splashed a little water out, thus satisfying the Jap. They never knew that the entire bottle was crammed full of whatever contraband we could lay our hands on during the day, especially tobacco.

"Another joke we enjoyed at the Japanese's expense was when loading tinned pineapple at the wharf. We would often open a case, take out the tins and puncture them then drink the juice and replace the tins in the case where they would ferment and rust, thereby spoiling other tins on the slow trip to Japan."

Armstrong also took great satisfaction from the time his crew stole 500 packs of sewing needles, netting them $12,500 on the local black market.

"He did not care how many men died, or if every sleeper meant a dead POW. If things got bad he would fill the gullies with dead POWs. And he was as good as his word."

Work for pay as a POW was meant to be determined by belligerents during a War. This rarely happened or was not enforced. Soldiers could be compelled to work, as long as the work was considered reasonable and was not directly related to the war effort. Whether they worked or not, the Conventions insist that prisoners are paid a wage by their captors. In German camps throughout Europe, better food was offered instead of money and prisoners accepted. They worked in glass factories in Munich, mines in Poland and on farms in Slovenia. In big Japanese camps like Changi, men were offered the chance to join a "force" to earn extra money for their labour. These forces were sent to different parts of the Pacific. 'F', 'H', 'K' and 'L' Forces went to Thailand and 'A' Force went to Burma. If enough men did not volunteer, soldiers were coerced into joining. At one point Changi's prison population slumped from tens of thousands to a few thousand as these work groups were dispatched.

Another aspect of the Geneva Convention is that a POW should not be forced to do excessive daily labour and be allowed at least one hour's rest a day and 24 consecutive hours' rest every week, preferably on Sunday – or on the day of rest in their country of origin. According to Jack Thorpe, the workload on the Burma-Thai Railway represented more than 400 kilometres of pain and death. Those who volunteered soon regretted it.

"Basically we lived the lives of slaves. The Japanese just wanted to get as much out of us as they could while we still lived. After our morning rice we marched off to work and worked all the hours there were then marched back home to another cup of rice and got what sleep we could until it was time to start again. When we moved camp it was always at night – never during working hours. In his 'welcome' address to us at Kunknitway, Colonel Nagatomo told us he had all Japanese POWs at his disposal. The Emperor had given him one year to build this railway from Burma into Thailand and he would do it. He did not care how many men died, or if every sleeper meant a dead POW. If things got bad he would fill the gullies with dead POWs. And he was as good as his word. During the 'speedo' (an intense period of construction that started in January 1943) we worked long into the night and the farce of sick parades was dropped altogether. Men died like flies. Nagatomo's second in command, Lieutenant Naito, was fond of saying, 'Your sick shall starve until they die or go back to work. Any sick prisoner, who can even just make it to work and dies, even if he has laid only one sleeper, will not have died in vain.' Inspirational words."

"Of the 7,000 odd who were in 'F' Force, over 3,000 died in the eight months in Thailand. That is 44 percent of the force."

Walter Holding discovered a way of reducing his workload for a while. The Japanese would usually specify a section of road or rail that had to be cleared each day. If the prisoners finished it easily and before knock-off time their workload would be doubled the following day. Holding's mates were a bit more fortunate.

"While we were working on the business of building up the formation of the track and getting the trucks running through again, I was lucky to be given a job with a little Japanese called Matsidor, who had been conscripted into the army. He had been going to technical school or college in Japan and because he had read quite a lot of books and had some knowledge of English. He was given the job, with 10 of us, to go out and cut the logs for the culverts at various places along the line.

"Of course, the usual thing was they would give us a quota of so much work to be done in a day. Matsidor had the lowest rank of all Japanese there and they all used him for a punching bag sort of thing all along the track. He was like a typical cartoon character – a tiny little bloke with his garter on his trousers wound right up to his knees, big thick horn-rimmed glasses and a great big pith helmet that just about covered him up. He looked like a mushroom. Matsidor was quite a reasonable little bloke. He was dead against the war and everything that was going on, but he had a job to do.

"He realised straight away that we could meet our quota in about three hours or so, so we would go out in the morning and get quite a bit of the work done then we would sit down and have a discussion. Matsidor wanted to know about Australia and we quizzed him about everything else for as long as we could to keep him from getting on and doing work but he did not get our quotas increased which was good."

Unfortunately, Matsidor was the exception when captured Diggers found themselves working for the Japanese Empire.

"Of the 7,000 odd who were in 'F' Force, over 3,000 died in the eight months in Thailand. That is 44 percent of the force. Of that, I think the British casualties were about double that of the Australians. It's hard to work out why, but I think a big thing was that they could not keep their hygiene up and a lot of them sort of packed it in the finish. They just did not have the will to carry on. Of course, so many Australians were people who, like me, had been on the farm and were used to swinging an axe. Any physical outdoor work gave us a lot better chance than those blokes who had been working in offices and had not had a chance to rough it. Probably the troops that had been in the Army for a couple of years were a lot better off too. They were quite hardened to that sort of business."
Walter "Wally" Holding, Singapore, 1942

"The railway to be constructed from Bang Pong to Thanbyuzayat was 415 kilometres long. At least 200,000 native labourers were dragooned or conscripted to build this railway, as well as British, Dutch and Australian prisoners of war. At least 13,000 Australians were involved. They were cared for during the construction of the railway by 37 medical officers and 458 medical orderlies from the Australian Army Medical Corps. There were 7,300 prisoners of war on 'F' Force, half British, half Australian, taken to Thailand in April 1943. By April 1944, 1,058 Australians and 2,029 British from F Force had died."
Gerard Harvey Veitch, Singapore, 1942

"Our job on the Burma Line was to excavate the earth and build the earthworks to a certain level under the supervision of Japanese engineers. One section did the picking and shovelling while the rest of the men carted the earth in bamboo baskets. Each group of men was given a quota. And if, say, one square metre of earth per person had to be removed, you weren't allowed to stop before you'd shifted it. Early in the piece the Japs had told us we could knock off when we'd done our quota so some idiots rushed to finish early. Of course, this was just what the Japanese wanted because then they pretty smartly increased our quota. When we started work in the mornings we'd have no idea what the quota would be until the engineers marked out the plots for us. The quotas continued to increase to around two square metres a day, and free time quickly became nonexistent. During the height of

the 'speedo' the quota could be four square metres a day and we had to work long into the night to complete it."
Jack Thorpe, Java, 1942

"My gang would be working all right and then would be suddenly told to stop. The men would then be stood with their arms outstretched horizontally, shoulder high, facing the sun without hats. The guards would be formed into two sections, one standing back with rifles and the others doing the actual beating. They would walk along the back of us and smack us underneath the arms, across the ribs and on the back. They would give each man a couple of bashes. If they whimpered or flinched they would get a bit more."
Hector "Bill" Sticpewich, Singapore, 1942

"We had it easy the first 12 months. I reckon only half a dozen died at the top. Sure we hud to work on the drome and we used to get flogged, but we had plenty of food and cigarettes."

The amount prisoners were paid to work was at the discretion of the detaining power, although the Geneva Conventions stipulated the daily rate must not be less than a quarter of one Swiss franc. Officers were generally paid more than their men. The extra pay helped POWs supplement their diets and purchase "luxury" items like soap and tobacco. Another requirement was that canteens be established wherever possible. In theory, prisoners were allowed to set up a canteen and buy groceries from local markets. In practice, however, most were operated by civilians or military personnel of the detaining power. All too often the canteen was an opportunity to take further advantage of the prisoners by selling goods at exorbitant prices and pocketing the profits.

"Well, you got paid if you worked. You got paid 10c, 15c a day, or 25c or 30c a day, something like that. The officers got much more than us; they got dollars. While we were in Singapore in the jail, they had a canteen. The people running it – the Chinese or the Indians or somebody – used to buy the food in and sell it to the troops. Tobacco, the tobacco weed, java weed, you could buy that. You could buy anything to supplement your food – if you had the money of course."
Cyril Gilbert, Singapore, 1942

"There was a problem in the camp over money. Our pay, when we worked, was 10 cents a day, which would have been less than one Australian penny at the time. The Japanese, however, paid our camp administration in large denomination notes of occupation currency. A means had to be found to break the notes down to 5c notes so the men could use it. Eventually an idea was hit upon, to make our own money for use in the camp. Old, now useless, chequebooks were collected and cut into small chits about half the size of a bus ticket. A stamp was carved that showed a figure '5' in the centre of a circle of small dots, each chit branded and signed by the colonel. He must have put his name to hundreds of them. There was a sequel one day, when the sergeant in charge of our hut called for silence and announced: 'Someone in this camp is forging the money chits. It had better stop. If caught he will go back to a work camp without the option.' We heard no more about it."
Gordon Nelson, Singapore, 1942

"We had it easy the first 12 months. I reckon only half a dozen died at the top. Sure we had to work on the drome and we used to get flogged, but we had plenty of food and cigarettes. We actually had a canteen in the prison camp. We were getting 10 cents a day. I think a coconut was about one cent, a turtle egg one cent and a fair sized banana went for a cent. It was a good camp."
Keith Botterill, Singapore, 1942

"We were in Thailand. Then they chose 2,500 of us to go to Japan and they took us up to Vietnam and we were in Saigon in a very beautiful, big, French legionnaires' camp. Admittedly, it was full of bugs and lice, but it was a roof over your head and you had electricity, running water and a canteen where you could buy toothbrushes, soaps, fruit and everything. Then all of a sudden it was 'pack your gear and off we go to Japan'."
Roydon Cornford, Java, 1942

Many prisoners in Europe were forced to work, but there were always volunteers desperate to escape the sheer boredom of camp life. Their German captors usually followed the safety guidelines outlined in the Conventions and for the most part supplied workers with additional rations. Doug Nix recalls how work was a way of escaping his mundane existence and getting his hands on better food. "Now a sergeant didn't have to go to work. According to the Germans, he was privileged so he did not

" The postcard provided by the Japanese so we could let our families know what a lovely time we were having while we were guests of the Emperor." Jack Thorpe

105.

IMPERIAL JAPANESE ARMY.

Our present place, quarters, and work is unchanged since last card sent to you The rains have finished, it is now beautiful weather. I am working healthily ( ). We receive newspapers printed in English which reveal world events.

We have joyfully received a present of some milk, tea, margarine, sugar and cigarettes from the Japanese Authorities.

We are very anxious to hear from home, but some prisoners have received letters or cables.

Everyone is hopeful of a speedy end to the war and with faith in the future we look forward to a happy reunion soon.

With best wishes for a cheerful Christmas.

RECEIVED SOME OF YOUR LETTERS OK. REMEMBER ME TO ALL AT HOME AND ELSEWHERE. TONS OF LOVE AND BEST OF LUCK

From _Jack. R. Thorpe_

Richard Leggo and winners of the
"Every Cup" at Campo PG 75, 1943

have to go out and work in camps. But if you went out to work, you got a little bit better tucker."

Nix also noted how the Germans were forced to comply with the requirement that POWs be protected in areas that were likely to be bombed or attacked. The doggedness shown by Nix and his fellow prisoners would have made any trade union delegate proud. "They made us work on the railway siding unloading coal and coke from railway stations. We proved to the International Red Cross that it was in a dangerous position. It was under air attack all the time, so they could not put you in a position where you either helped their war effort or put you in a position where you were going to be under attack. They had to move us."

"An old Digger said to me (he was taken prisoner in the 1914–18 war), 'Look, do as you're told in Germany and nothing will happen to you'."

Ernest Brough was an NCO in the same camp as Nix, near Graz. He believed the reason sergeants overseeing soldiers in the enlisted men's camps didn't have to work was because the Germans thought they were more likely to organise an escape. To alleviate their boredom, Brough and some fellow sergeants decided to hide their insignia and join a work party. They quickly found themselves confronting a German major over a breach in the Geneva Conventions because of the work the prisoners were doing. The Germans were making the POWs build an air-raid shelter to protect them from the bombing that Doug Nix and his work party had complained about.

"We had a pay book (that identified their rank), but we weren't going to show it. I just said I didn't have one. Well, they can't do much about it, can they, if you haven't got one? 'Where's your proof?' 'Haven't got it'. 'Righto, out you go'. So we were sent to Graz. We got to Graz and they were digging a big air-raid shelter in a bit of fascia rock, somewhere up in the town. We said to one another, 'We're not going to dig a bloody air-raid shelter for them to hide in, that's a bloody war effort. We're not helping them to live in there'. They said, 'Righto, you'll be going out to work tomorrow'. 'We don't have to go to work, we're not going'. 'Righto, we'll get someone down here to make you go'. So they got an officer down there. He lined us all up and said, 'You'll go out to work or we'll shoot you'.

"This big New Zealander, he could speak very good Germ
that major a tongue-lashing. He said he would report h
Geneva Conventions. Then they sort of compromised, be
pulled our pay books out then. 'Here you are. We're NCOs'. The
officers in the Graz camp said, 'Well, how the hell did they get here?
They were supposed to be kept in the camp'. They weren't game
to go back and say, 'Look, we've got NCOs here. They've got the
proof and we can't send them out to work because it's part of our
deal.' So, they said, 'What do you want to do?' We said, 'We're all
farmers. Australians and New Zealanders – we all love the land and
we like working on farms'. 'Right, out you go on the farms then'. So
they sent us four, the big New Zealander and Eric Vady and Alan
Berry and me to this camp at Spittal. Well, the big New Zealander,
I think he flunked out. He said he had a bad knee, but I don't think
he did. He was probably more educated and thought, 'The war is
going to come to an end soon and I'll stay where it's safe'."
Ernest Brough, El Alamein, 1942

Others enjoyed a more positive experience working for the German
civilian community in factories or on farms. Not all work as a POW
was abusive, degrading or arduous.

"An old Digger said to me (he was taken prisoner in the 1914—18
war), 'Look, do as you're told in Germany and nothing will happen
to you'. It wouldn't. Four of us were taken to a glass manufacturer
in Munich who supplied glass to the smaller firms around the
country. Of course, we got to know Munich. The old German
'civvy' didn't care where you went. He took me to his house one
day and his wife gave me a cup of coffee. They wanted English
cigarettes. They gave us a bottle of beer a day too. I'm not a beer
drinker but I did drink it."
Archie Whitehead, Crete, 1941

"Local farmers came to villages where we lined up like cattle and
they picked out prisoners to work for them. They asked us what
work we did in 'civvy' street. I was a baker at home. They weren't
very impressed with my efforts at the village bakery and I only
lasted one day before being sent to do odd jobs for a mangy Hun.
While shovelling snow one day, the house frau called out for me
to come to the door. She showed me inside and gave me a lovely
hot bath and new clothes to wear. She was a kind old lady married
to a Hun mongrel."
Les Manning, Crete, 1941

Some European prisoners were sent to work in coal mines. The conditions they worked under were better than POWs in Japan, but they where still dangerous. At least many of the German camps complied with the Geneva Conventions and provided extra rations for those doing hard labour. Archie Whitehead recalls the dangers of working down the pits in Poland: "They were grim days. And we spent two years there. There was a British soldier killed there. I don't know how I wasn't there then. They staged a strike, the fellas down in the mine, (but) they went back to work though. A German fired a shot down the mine."

In Europe the camp conditions varied considerably from country to country. It should also never be forgotten that while many Australians, Britons and Americans were generally well-treated, millions of Slavs, Soviets and Jews worked and died in the mines and factories during the Third Reich.

"We were trained as Field Ambulance Officers, our duty was to patch up a wounded soldier, put him on a stretcher and get him to a Casualty Clearing Station - now we were nursing orderlies, lives depended on us."

Sickness and disease were the main causes of concern for imprisoned Australians. Large groups of people in confined spaces and sharing primitive amenities over long periods of time meant a significant risk of contracting and spreading disease. Even camps with basic plumbing and running water failed to cope with the sheer volume of POWs. No camp was immune to the ravages of disease regardless of the era or location. On the scale of priorities, the health of POWs ranked lower than the war effort and occupation. Although the Conventions compelled nations to ensure a reasonable level of health care, the medical facilities and care provided by Turkish camps in WW1 and Japanese camps in WW2 were more than inhumane. In contrast some German camps, like Colditz, even offered dental care. The contrasting levels of medical care meant some prisoners were fairly well looked after while others were forced to use their own meagre resources and medical personnel to take care of their own.

Some of the medics were thrust into doing things they were not qualified for, they were not doctors and many not even trained nurses yet often they had the most medical knowledge in the group so found themselves having to step up to the plate. Joe Zeeno captured at Singapore in 1942 recalls: "We were trained as Field Ambulance Officers, our duty was to patch up a wounded soldier, put him on a stretcher and get him to a Casualty Clearing Station – now we were nursing orderlies, lives depended on us. The doctors needed sleep and during the night when we were working we would be needed to certify and remove the dead. I was also one of the Orderlies who used to hold the ulcer patients down – we had no anaesthetics, no other treatment, the dead flesh just had to be scraped out; it was just as hard on us as the patient – we were nerve cases."

Many soldiers were in awe of the brilliant work performed by their medics and doctors who were pushed to the limits with minimal resources and medical supplies. They would also never forget the times they helplessly watched a mate die a slow death simply because there was nothing more they could do. The doctors and medics shouldered a personal level of responsibility that is hard to imagine. The anguish surfaces in the words of Major Kevin Fagan, a prisoner and doctor on the Burma-Thai railway: "There were about 300 of us left out of about 600. From that group – none of whom were well, all of whom had malaria, were malnourished, and some of them were shivering on parade, dressed in a lap-lap or a pair of shorts, rarely any boots. I had to choose 100 men to march another 100 miles into the unknown, certainly to worse and definitely not to better. I never saw any of those men again. It was the most terrible thing I've had to do. If I hadn't done it then the Japanese would have taken the first 100 they found, and they would all have died. Some of these men had a chance of surviving. None of them should have been asked to do any more. Later on that day the Japanese medical officer came by. I said to him, 'Unless you change your treatment of these prisoners they will all die'. He said, 'That would be a very good thing; it would save the Japanese army much rice'."

Many other Australians had equally harrowing recollections of the impact disease, parasites and illness had on them and the treatments and awful facilities they witnessed.

"I arrived at Konquita at 11:45hrs and met Mr Woolfe, who seemed to be most despondent and almost in tears with weariness and his inability to make the Japanese realise the seriousness of his patients. The Japanese doctor just laughed at all requests for drugs and said,

'If men get sick and have no medicine I have no medicine, and if men die, they die and I can't be worried'."
Gerard Harvey Veitch, Singapore, 1942

"The Japs always put the sick on half rations. 'No work, no eat.' However, not content with that, they had some formula at the hospital whereby the weight of rice allocated to the camp was related to the weight of the camp's inhabitants. They re-weighed them regularly and as their weight went down so did their rations. Of course, the point was that the men were all so ill as a result of serious malnutrition and should have been fed more, not less."
Jack Thorpe, Java, 1942

"I developed beri-beri on July 25th, 1943. This time it was wet beri-beri and last time dry. I have been the third worst so far, but now we have about 70 odd in hospital and really everybody outside has it. This time my weight increased from about 10 stone 10lb to 12 stone 8lb in six days. This consists of fluid in the tissues. For anybody who hasn't seen it, it is hard to imagine what a chap looks like. I was the same thickness from the top of the head to the shoulders and everywhere you have a joint it just cracks open. My testicles were the size of a small football and every time you walked you carried them in your hand."
Tom Pledger, Ambon, 1942

"One man produced a 13-inch worm. I think a number of us must have them. When Frank Hern was starved for his appendicitis operation, one came out of his mouth."
Alexander Bourne, Singapore, 1942

"I had severe diarrhoea this day and I went off to the toilet. Standing astride a 'benjo' with everything pouring out, I heard a Pommie voice from behind me say, 'Hey, mate, yo' guts are hanging out'. I looked between my legs and there was a length of what looked like my intestines, but it was a tapeworm, a big fellow, about 12 to 15 inches long. I tugged it away; the poor thing was lifeless, starved to death, no doubt."
Gordon Jamieson, Singapore, 1942

"The thing I remember, is that during all that time I only laughed once. It was during the cholera epidemic and I was digging a couple of graves with a few blokes. By then we were mostly down to G-strings; I was lucky and still had the remnants of a pair of shorts. One of the Diggers, must have had a bit of dysentery, because when he bent over, in the trench mind you, a grave, he squirted straight across at

the other blokes, just like a squirt from a bloody hose. I just couldn't help but laugh; it was the way it happened and where as well. That was the only time I saw anything that made me laugh."
Bert Mettam, Singapore, 1942

"Medical supplies were practically nil. The only medicine I recall having seen was a small quantity of aspirin. Many prisoners were suffering from diarrhoea, dysentery, beri-beri and malnutrition diseases, but no medication was available for their treatment."
Geoffrey Underwood, Singapore, 1942

"After two nights without food we eventually arrived at Tanbaya. The camp was situated on both sides of the railway and we were greeted by a myriad of flies and the overwhelming stench of suppurating ulcers emanating out of the ulcer ward on the western side of the railway. My work commenced there and the most devastating experiences of my time on the Burma railway began. Stricken men were found with gaping ulcers on legs, arms and backsides. Almost every man in that ward of thirty had ulcers, malaria and dysentery – their only relief was a merciful death."
George Morgan, Singapore, 1942

"Then I got ulcers on my feet, a bad one on my right foot and a small one on my left, so I used the puttees to bind my feet to keep the mud off. I got rid of one lot of ulcers with maggots and the other with a sulphur powder, but the maggots did the best job. The docs couldn't scoop out the big one, because there wasn't enough flesh to scoop. It was right across my foot and for a while there I was worried I'd lose it. The maggots were a nuisance, though, as they'd keep you awake all night, wriggling."
Ted Whitmore, Singapore, 1942

"I remember one bloke on the other side of the aisle, he was dying. You could hear him all night with the death rattle and there was nothing anyone could do. Next morning his little mate took out two dixies to get the breakfast pap. He came back in and sat down next to his mate. He put one dixie on his dead mate's chest while he ate from the other, and then he ate from his mate's dixie. That's how callous it was."
Thomas Smith, Singapore, 1942

"The huts were divided up into different categories or wards for pellagra, beri-beri and dysentery. The job I got was probably in the worst ward in the camp: the ulcer and dysentery ward. It's hard to describe, but when you are leaning over a man's suppurating

Distributing Red Cross parcels to allied POWs at Kriegsgefstammlager
(camp) at Limburg am Lahn, Germany, 1917

AWM Neg. P03236_004

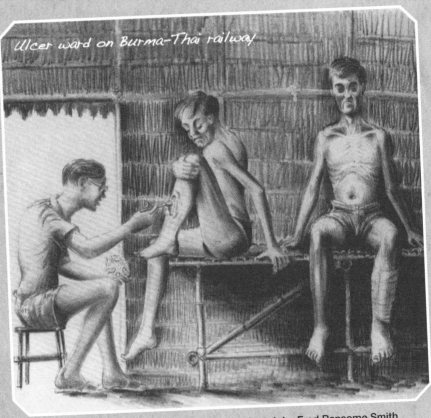

Ulcer ward on Burma-Thai railway

Sketch by Fred Ransome Smith

ulcer which has turned black and he has dysentery, you are pretty close to the centre of things. I've seen cases where the whole of a man's calf was eaten away by a tropical ulcer and others where shinbones were exposed and the skin was black and the bone was a dull yellow and perforated and the tendons exposed. Apart from very few medicines, all we had was boiled water, with which we bathed the ulcers."
Norman Anderton, Singapore, 1942

"It was a hellhole and we knew we were in for a bad time under the Italians' control. Water was scarce, so there was no opportunity to wash, shave or cut our hair. This did not help the never-ending plague of lice and fleas. To sleep, you had to dig out a hip hole and lie on the ground. Everyone had dysentery; there were no medical facilities at all."
William Hoffman, El Alamein, 1942

"To save our boots for the coming winter, most of us spent the summer barefoot. One day in October I stepped on a jagged, rusty half bully beef tin. I trailed blood to the camp infirmary where I was given an enormous anti-tetanus injection and put to bed in sheets but found next day that the beds were infested with crab lice (not to be confused with the body lice we'd largely beaten). I had to shave all my body hair and take a special ointment and disinfectant. Medical facilities were scarce as I found when two teeth decayed. When I couldn't stand it any longer I joined the dentist's queue, watching those before me faint or yell as teeth were pulled without anaesthetic. As the lesser evil I let them pull it."
Ray Middleton, El Alamein, 1942

"Despite some individual experiences to the contrary, there was no real medical attention available to POWs in most of the camps. The only inoculations were given just prior to the prisoners going south for repatriation. Although many POWs were sick and wounded, none of the doctor prisoners were permitted to practice. Captured airmen in particular were subjected to a pattern of intimidation, deprivation of basic physical needs, isolation, physical and mental torture – the pattern varied. Many prisoners became filthy, full of lice, with festering wounds full of maggots; they were unshaven and without haircuts for months on end and faced with squads of trained interrogators. They were bullied, deprived of sleep and browbeaten."
Phil Greville, Korea, 1952

"I was given a spinal injection and a Chinese doctor who spoke no English performed an operation on my leg. The operating room had an earthen floor, thatched roof and the illumination was supplied by a pressure lantern which was pumped every now and again to brighten the light output. As the Chinese doctor made the incision in my swollen thigh, he explained in Chinese what he was doing. Because the spinal injection only deadened the lower half of my body from the waist down, I was operated on in the sitting position which allowed me to observe the whole operation.

"After the first rush of rotten matter which had caused the swelling had dissipated, he started probing for shattered pieces of the femur bone which he proceeded to remove with tweezers. The operation lasted for about half hour. As he stitched the six-inch cut in my thigh to close the incision, the feeling started to return to my leg. However, as he continued to stitch I became more vocal about the pain in my leg. Four attendants physically restrained me as he completed his handiwork. Just as I was lifted off the 'operating table' the stitching came undone, and I thought I was in for another struggle when he again tried to close the wound. However, instead of trying to re-stitch me, he got an American pack of sulphanilamide powder and sprinkled it all over my wound before I was carted off to another room. In this room they had an ancient type of device for stretching limbs and applying a plaster cast. I was seated with one buttock on a small oval platform while my leg was stretched until I thought it would rip my hip apart. When they decided my leg wouldn't stretch any further, two female attendants or nurses started to apply a plaster cast to my right leg, hip and chest. This effectively made it impossible to even sit up and it meant I would spend the rest of the war on my back being dependent on others for my every need."
Eric Donnelly, Korea, 1953

" The lice made our days and nights miserable in the extreme and though we stripped every time a chance occurred it seemed impossible even to keep them down."

Prisoners of Germany and Turkey during WW1 endured a daily pattern of worry about health, food and sanitation. The Germans captured 3,850 Australians during the 1914—18 war of whom approximately, 330 died in captivity. Of the 217 captured by the Turks, 62 died. The death rate of approximately one in four is almost the same as that inflicted by the Japanese 25 years later.

"The filth was indescribable and we were packed so close together that it was impossible to sit down for rest. We just managed to crouch with our head between our knees. We were given a bag of hard biscuits for the journey and a few dates, which were promptly confiscated by our escort. My wound, which had not been attended to, was festering and causing me great pain. Most of us were suffering from dysentery and as there were no sanitary arrangements in the cattle truck we were soon in a filthy condition."
George Handsley, Romani, 1916

"As the weather got warmer and time went on, our bodily condition became awful. For eight weeks we never washed with soap and soon learned that of all scarce articles in Deutschland, soap was the scarcest. The lice made our days and nights miserable in the extreme and though we stripped every time a chance occurred it seemed impossible even to keep them down."
Justin Dawson, France, 1917

"The vermin in the house was beyond what I can describe and the majority of us got typhus. At one time 90 percent were in hospital, me amongst them, and I was unconscious for 15 days. They told me I had a temperature reaching 103.2 (39.4°C). An Englishman in this ward looked after me with medicine and food and I would certainly not have lived had he not done so, because the Turks stole the food and medicine as well as the few poor rags of clothing I possessed and sold them. When I was discharged from hospital I was almost without clothes. By the end of May 1917 I was declared fit for work, but malaria again attacked me and then I had rheumatic fever."
Leslie Richardson, Suez Canal, 1916

It is hardly surprising that the content of Australian newspaper reports about the Boer prison camps was to reappear 40 years later in reports about German camps. Separating officers from soldiers was not motivated by snobbery; the idea was to deprive the men of leadership. POWs at Waterval near Pretoria were freed six weeks after the following report on life as a prisoner of the Boers was published in *The Queenslander* on 5th May, 1900. It was published as the Boers retreated:

"The Boers fully understand the various uses of barbed wire. They have employed it to confuse a charging enemy and when sections of that enemy have fallen into their hands they have utilised this comparatively modern invention to keep their prisoners within bounds. The captured British officers who have been taken to Pretoria are housed in the State Model School from which it will be remembered Mr Winston Churchill made his escape. The school is a modern and well built building, having many large and lofty rooms and surrounded by a broad and cool veranda. The officers have their own cooks and servants. The bathrooms are commodious and books can be procured from the state library. The rations supplied to the prisoners are of much the same quantity and quality as those issued to the wives and families of burghers throughout the state.

"The great bulk of the captured men, however, are in camp at Waterval, the new military prison camp outside Pretoria. Their quarters consist of a series of long galvanised iron sheds. In them the soldiers make themselves comfortable and seem to have settled down to a regular garrison existence. The large enclosure is surrounded by a barbed wire entanglement. Each corner is protected by stockades, on which Maxim guns are mounted. Each stockade is in electric communication with the others and the whole camp seems to form an absolutely secure detention ground for the prisoners. The sentries appear to be men of middle age. They are in everyday mufti and look anything but military, the only evidence of soldierly duties being their rifles and bandoleers."

"The first man counted 'ichi', the second 'ni', and what did I get from the little man Peanuts,' Well scratch the bloody thing'."

Prisoners did everything they could to alleviate their boredom. In Germany, Les Manning recalls, they would lie on their bunks in the evening and "pass the time away talking of things we used to do before the war. All the stories would feature a beautiful girl along for the ride". A German guard showed Ray Middleton how to crochet. He collected as many old socks and cardigans as he could find, unstitched them and used the wool to crochet a blanket. In true Digger style, Australians would, wherever possible, make stills to create their own jungle juice.

Sadly, there were times when men would lie down and die; simply giving up the will to live in their new-found world of suffering and lost freedom. In such tough times it helped to have a larrikin in the group to lift spirits, as Richard Armstrong, a prisoner of the Japanese, recalls: "When lined up in three ranks we must number in Japanese as follows, *ichi, ni, san, shi* (or *yon*), *go, roku, shichi, hachi, kyuu, jyuu,* etc. On this occasion I was in charge of the party and 'Peanuts' was number three in the front rank. I should have guessed the bugger was up to mischief as this was his favourite pastime. The first man counted '*ichi*', the second '*ni*', and what did I get from the little man Peanuts, 'Well scratch the bloody thing'. At this the Jap guard jumped up and down in the one place and roared like all hell. I immediately pointed to Peanuts and said to the Jap, '*byoki*', as I turned my finger around my head. I was telling him Peanuts was sick in the head. After a few moments the Jap agreed with me that the bugger was *byoki*, because Peanuts couldn't stop laughing and without finishing the count the Jap took us back to camp."

Life for our POWs created a rollercoaster of emotions. At times life was frustrating, degrading, painful, boring, agonising but at others it was tolerable. Hardship can bring out the best in people; they might share meagre amounts of food with a mate who is sicker and needier. It can also bring out the worst, and find people taking a dying man's personal belongings. But judgments should not be made about those who had to endure a life of incarceration as a POW. Judgment should be reserved for those who were responsible for ignoring, or very loosely adhering to, the Geneva Convention and acting inhumanely.

A prisoner working on the Burma-Thai railway had a one in two chance of dying. For prisoners of the Third Reich, who numbered almost 9,000, the odds of surviving were one in 30. Many may have realised that they would have had a better chance of surviving on the battlefield. In battle a soldier sometimes needed luck on their side. Aussie soldiers could appreciate that. Unnecessary death and hardship at the hands of merciless captors was something else entirely.

Chapter 4
Punishment

"Prisoners of war shall be subject to the laws, regulations, and orders in force in the army of the State into whose hands they have fallen. Any act of insubordination warrants the adoption, as regards them, of such measures of severity as may be necessary."

Hague Convention, 1907

June, 1942, Bukit Timah, building a shrine. For fun, the Japs after belting a POW, would make them stand in the blazing sun in a post hole

Sketch by Fred Ransome Smith

Chapter 4 – Punishment

The Hague and Geneva Conventions stipulate how prisoners of war should be treated. They were first brought into being in 1863 and have been amended several times. Australia signed in 1900, initially as part of the British Empire, but after Federation signed in its own right. Germany, Japan, Italy and Turkey signed in 1907. Punishment for a crime committed by a prisoner is meant to be based on the laws of the country that has detained the prisoner. Theoretically, a POW in a country under Sharia or Islamic law could have a hand chopped off for committing theft. If a POW in Australian custody committed murder, he or she could be sentenced to life imprisonment, whereas in the United States they could be given the death sentence.

Australian POWs were at the mercy of the law of the land that held them and the sometimes arbitrary upholding of that law by their captors. The personal discipline of guards and commandants – and their state of mind – could determine whether a POW was given a warning, thrown in the cooler, beaten or executed. As the war progressed, and if their captors believed they were losing, punishments could increase in ferocity and frequency. Some Allied POWs in the European theatre during WW2 saw their captors loosen their control as the war turned against the Axis powers.

"He had been buried upright near the guardhouse for some days with just his head sticking out. Every bloody Jap who went anywhere near the guardhouse would walk over to where he was buried and kick him in the face."

It could be argued that the cruel punishments inflicted on Australian POWs stemmed from the brutal regimes their captors lived under, and their underlying lack of civil liberties. During WW2 the Nazi or Japanese parliament were renowned for ruthlessly suppressing their own people and they did not treat prisoners gently. An Australian POW speaking out against the treatment delivered to another prisoner in a Japanese camp received exactly the same punishment as a Japanese soldier who spoke out against a superior officer – a severe beating or even a court martial and execution. In fact, the Japanese would argue they were complying with the Conventions because they meted out the same military justice their own soldiers received. Nonetheless they conveniently forgot other articles of the Geneva Convention which contained words like "humane".

Prisoners, who committed crimes, were insubordinate or tried to escape, faced disciplinary action or even trial. Disciplinary measures might include confinement, fatigue duties, loss of pay and restriction of privileges. Conventions clearly state that punishment should not be inhumane, brutal or dangerous to the health of prisoners. This was not something the Japanese appeared able to grasp. Their prisoners were subject to measures that were frequently arbitrary and at best barbaric. Jack Thorpe recalls, "I don't know what poor Captain Drower had done to offend the Japs in our last days at Tamarkan, but when we finally left the camp he had been buried upright near the guardhouse for some days with just his head sticking out. Every bloody Jap who went anywhere near the guardhouse would walk over to where he was buried and kick him in the face. The only time we could get close was when we were marching out past the guardhouse. Anyhow, I saw him the day we marched out and he was a horrible sight. His whole head was swollen so much you couldn't see his eyes or mouth. His ears were barely poking through the swelling. We were all sure we'd never see him again."

Many years later, well after the war was over, Thorpe discovered that Bill Drower had survived and had gone on to enjoy a successful career in the British diplomatic corps. "The human body is a remarkable thing. As I found out for myself after I had done a further two and a half years as a guest of the Japanese military, the cruellest, most brutal army on earth."

The human body, mind and spirit are remarkable. It is hard to believe that people are able to survive such harsh treatment at the hands of sadistic captors. Stories like Bill Drower's are not unusual, as Don Doddy, another prisoner of the Japanese, recalls: "The man was then made to kneel with a section of bamboo behind his knees. His arms were outstretched and tied across another piece of bamboo. The final and perhaps fatal addition was a sharpened stake poised up under his chin. If the prisoner slackened down he would be dead. The man was later strung up by the neck for a slow death, which took 48 hours. Padre Thorpe pleaded hourly for the Japanese to release him, but they refused. After the slow hanging, he was taken inside a hut by his mates and laid out as dead. It was late and they were all exhausted, so it was agreed they would bury him tomorrow. Death wasn't unusual to these men. The dead could wait and so could their mate now. Then someone walked past and his toes wiggled."

Many Australian prisoners used black humour as a coping

mechanism. POW Richard Armstrong recalls the name Australians had for a punishment dished out by the Japanese for stealing from the Imperial Army; it was called a "Bukit Timah haircut". "This was the way we described the Japanese habit of chopping heads off people and placing them on long poles with warning notices attached, stating why the person had been beheaded. We first came across this delightful Japanese practice when we were shown heads on poles along the Bukit Timah Road in Singapore during the first three months of our captivity. Simply stated, a Bukit Timah haircut is a short back and sides with a Jap sword."

" They only had to 'think' you were going to do some wrong, either real or imagined, to punish you, even up to and including death."

The random nature and unpredictability of punishment, beatings and torture handed out by the Japanese are described by others as well.

"Lieutenant Bill Rowe of 2/29th Battalion got himself into a spot of bother, with the result that all officers were paraded and Bill was asked his rank and then called out to the front where he had his face slapped by a second class private and told to stand to one side. Unfortunately he did not stand to attention so the Japanese officer went over to him, kicked Bill on the shins and then hit him over the head several times with a stick, after which he was made to stand rigidly to attention while we received a lecture in very poor English which we could hardly understand. When the lecture finished, poor old Bill collapsed and cut his face as well as knocking out a tooth, but fortunately his glasses were not broken. As a result of the Bill Rowe incident that particular camp received the name of the 'Basher Camp' but later parties called it the 'Hitler Camp'."
Gerard Harvey Veitch, Singapore, 1942

"Most guards had nicknames. 'Holy Joe' claimed he was a Christian, though that didn't help us much. 'Baby Grand' had teeth that protruded straight out from his mouth like the keys on a piano. We had a couple of really hateful, mongrel Korean guards at the 105 Kilo, who were known as BB and the BBC – the 'Boy Bastard' and the 'Boy Bastard's Cobber' –they were absolute sadists who just delighted in bashing blokes around. They seemed to vie with each other as to who could be the most vicious. One of their favourite games was to get an Aussie and a Dutchman and make

the Dutchman slap the Aussie's face, or vice versa. Or they might vary things by using an American. If he didn't slap hard enough, the BB or the BBC would give him a hiding and they delighted in putting a rifle butt or a boot where it would hurt most – again and again. The trouble with these two bastards was that if you didn't slap hard enough and they gave you a bashing it would take you a couple of days to get over it and you'd still have to go to work. A good slap across the face was definitely the better of two evils! BB and BBC were hanged at the end of the war for their cruelty and use of torture."
Jack Thorpe, Java, 1942

"My gang would be working all right and then would be suddenly told to stop. The men would then be stood with their arms outstretched horizontally, shoulder high, facing the sun without hats. The guards would be formed into two sections, one standing back with rifles and the others doing the actual beating. They would walk along the back of us and smack us underneath the arms, across the ribs and on the back. They would give each man a couple of bashes. If they whimpered or flinched they would get a bit more."
Hector "Bill" Sticpewich, Singapore, 1942

"It was at Kami Songkurai Camp that we came across the *eisho* for the first time. This little Japanese play toy was one of their favourite forms of bastardry, torture and torment. It was a small box-like structure made of bamboo slats about four feet wide by four feet high and five feet long. Its purpose was the incarceration of prisoners who were considered to have sinned against Nippon. They only had to 'think' you were going to do some wrong, either real or imagined, to punish you, even up to and including death. As you can gather there was neither room in the *eisho* to lie down, sit up or in any way ease your terribly aching muscles and anatomy. The usual treatment was anything from a day up to a month cooped up in this prison. You were not allowed out except for your regular daily, or hourly, bashings. The food may have been as little as nothing for several days up to a generous one meal each day. Here you stayed for the duration of your tormentor's pleasure and there was absolutely no appeal to anyone. Like all Japanese treatments, the sole purpose of this inhuman punishment was firstly your complete and utter humiliation and degradation, and secondly to emphasise to you that Japan was all-powerful. I have seen four men all crammed into the *eisho* at the one time on one

97

occasion and there they stayed for about five days, all the while being forced to urinate and defecate on each other much to the amusement of their tormentors."
Richard Armstrong, Singapore, 1942

"He never stood by and did nothing if he saw a Jap belting one of the men. He always intervened, so then the Japs turned their attentions to him."

It is hard to come to grips with the rationale the Japanese used to select those articles of the Geneva Convention they would abide by. They seemed to pick and choose at random. Strangely, for the most part they abided by Article 49 which states soldiers could be used as labour while officers were not compelled to work. However, they certainly failed to stick to the articles about forced labour, such as ensuring workers were in a good state of physical and mental health, working conditions including the provision of food, clothes and quarters, the duration of daily labour, and not forcing the sick or injured to work.

For some POWs discretion was the better part of valour and they kept a low profile. Drawing attention to yourself increased the possibility of punishment. Lieutenant Colonel Jack Williams, Majors Wild and Hunt, and Captain Gwynne realised that by taking punishment for the "crimes" of their subordinates they achieved three things. First, they demonstrated to their men they were willing to suffer as they did. Secondly, it showed they possessed far greater moral fibre than the enemy. Finally, it proved they were still leading and protecting their men even in captivity. Many soldiers never forgot how some of their officers stood up to defend the rights of their men.

"Death rates and torture got steadily worse at the 75 Kilo camp where Colonel Jack Williams saved more lives than just mine. I believe he was the bravest man anybody could possibly meet. He never stood by and did nothing if he saw a Jap belting one of the men. He always intervened, so then the Japs turned their attentions to him. The bashings that this man took in the defence of his men were unbelievable. Every time you saw him he was sporting a piece of loose flesh or skin hanging off somewhere or had an arm in a sling. I saw him getting some of those bashings. They would lay into him with fists, rifle butts or bamboo rods but he would never flinch.

Blood could be streaming from his wounds but he wouldn't even wipe it off. He would just continue to stare the bastards straight in the eyes with a smile on his face – something the Japanese rightly interpreted as outright defiance. According to the Japanese code of behaviour you were not supposed to look at the person who was beating you. But Jack Williams absolutely despised the Japanese and would not let them get the better of him under any circumstance. It was a great morale booster for us to witness his courage. He stood up for his men and what was right and didn't give a damn about the consequences."
Jack Thorpe, Java, 1942

"The three men set about me with bamboos, causing extensive bruising of on my skull, hands and arms, and a fractured left five metacarpal bone."

"The first time we met Toyama was when we got off the train at Ban Pong. Toyama always carried a light wooden stick with him, which was nearly as tall as he was, and he would swing this stick around. Captain Gwynne and another major from the 29th or 30th Battalion, I think must have upset Toyama or something. Well, Toyama swung his stick at Captain Gwynne, who wore big horn-rimmed glasses, and knocked him over and his glasses off. Everyone was ready to sail in, but we could not do anything about it because if anyone had made a move we would all have been in trouble. We had the awful little bastard Toyama right through."
Walter "Wally" Holding, Singapore, 1942

"I was informed that all sick had to be sent for examination by an Imperial Japanese Army medical officer (MO), who was quartered about half a mile away. The total number of my sick on this occasion, derived from my own and previous parties, was 37 – 27 had infected feet and 10 had malaria or dysentery. The Japanese medical officer agreed that none of these men were fit to march. The corporal of the guard, however, only gave permission for 10 to remain. A further conference with the Japanese MO, Major Wild (interpreter) and myself resulted in a letter of instruction from the MO to the corporal. This was also ignored, as was a further visit from Major Wild to the MO later that afternoon. At the time scheduled for parade I fell in the 37 sick men in two batches – 27 and 10 – and Major Wild and I stood in front of them.

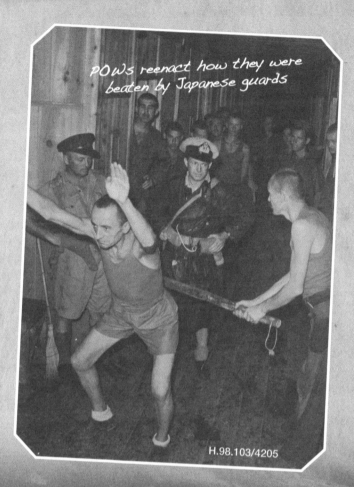

POWs reenact how they were beaten by Japanese guards

H.98.103/4205

Doug Nix and John Tasker at a German work camp

The corporal approached with a large bamboo in his hand and spoke menacingly to Major Wild, who answered in a placatory fashion. The corporal's only reply was to hit Major Wild in the face. Another guard followed suit and as Major Wild staggered back the corporal thrust at the major's genitalia with his bamboo. I was left standing before the patients and was immediately set upon by three guards. One tripped me while two others pushed me to the ground. The three men set about me with bamboos, causing extensive bruising on my skull, hands and arms, and a fractured left five metacarpal bone. After I was disposed of, the corporal then made the majority of the 27 foot-sufferers march with the rest of the troops. This episode took place in front of the whole parade of troops and caused much resentment amongst them. During this bashing the men were infuriated. There were some who wanted to get in and 'do' the Japanese. Major Hunt told them, 'Keep out of this you blokes – this is my fight!' The men were restrained. Soon after, I arrived in a truck and the men were still fuming at what they had witnessed. I saw Major Hunt standing alone amongst the tall bamboos. He was holding his left arm up in pain. There were groups of men scattered around talking about the bashing. I went up to Hunt and spoke to him. He deeply resented the suggestion he should go forward by transport. 'My duty is to protect the men,' he said."
Eric Stone, Singapore, 1942

"It's in their culture, they only knew one thing and that was strength. Black Jack Galleghan was the CO of the 2/30th Battalion. He was in charge of us at Thompson Road, and he walked along there one day and one of his men got smacked by one of the Japs. He went up to him with his walking stick, and swung it over the top of that cove's head. 'You will not touch a single one of my men.' And when he went back to the officer in charge, the Jap officer in charge of the camp, and said, 'You will not touch one of my men. If you want them punished, hand them over. I'll punish them, but don't you lay a finger on them.' Well, while Black Jack was there not one of us were hit. He used to inspect the Jap guards before they went on guard over us. He used to stand over them and they'd recognise one thing and that's strength. We got more out of them if we stood up to them. You just had to gauge how far to go, because if you went a bit further, you could get your head knocked off. While Black Jack was in charge of us there wasn't any one of us hit, but as soon as he went back to take over the AIS Malaya, Colonel McCracken took over. Of course the Japs

struck him straightaway and said, 'Our men will carry out their own punishment now.' Gilding, three others and myself were the first ones to get bashed."
Cyril Gilbert, Singapore, 1942

" *The cruelty began as soon as we became prisoners of war. Brutal treatment and torture became part of our daily lives from then on.*"

Jack Thorpe tells of his own punishment at the hand of the Japanese. At times the guards appeared to act out of personal resentment towards the POWs. At other times the punishments were a deliberate attempt to intimidate and subdue the Australians' will to resist. Jack's escape from a death sentence was due to the persistence of his commanding officer and his sense of duty and mateship.

"The cruelty began as soon as we became prisoners of war. Brutal treatment and torture became part of our daily lives from then on. I'd been to the sick parade in the morning with a bad dose of malaria, but the bloody Jap guard insisted that I had to go out to work. Anyway, I was put on a log-hauling gang where the other men told me to just put the rope on my shoulder but not do any pulling. Well, the Jap engineer saw that I wasn't doing my bit and hit me on the head with a shovel, laying me out on the ground. As I lay there he prepared to bring the shovel down on me edgeways, and I knew it would cut me in pieces, so I grabbed the shovel as it came down and took it from him. With that he blew his whistle to call the armed guards (Japanese engineers were not armed.) The guards responded quickly and I was surrounded. There was a lot of talking and they marched me back to camp. I had committed the unforgivable sin and resisted the Japanese Imperial Army – a capital offence.

"Back at the camp they tied me to a tree near one of the huts and just left me. I didn't know what was going to happen to me. I knew what the penalty was – death. In the afternoon the Japs from the guardhouse came around and looked at me and I told them that I was '*tuxan beoki*' (very sick), which they could see for themselves. That evening as the men were coming home from work, the Jap guards from the guardhouse came over and let me go. I thanked them and made for my hut. The ropes that had been around my upper arms and neck left burn scars which I carried for about thirty years, but which seem to have finally disappeared now. I later found out that my unexpected release was due to the efforts of Colonel Jack Williams."

Sometimes the Japanese used a court martial to determine guilt. This was seen as a means to dispense the Emperor's justice in line accordance the Hague Convention, especially when the verdict often resulted death. Usually the Australian officer or NCO in charge of a work detail was given the same or similar punishments for the actions of subordinates. While this cohered with elements of the Japanese military system, it was designed to hold POWs in line by fear and intimidation rather than to be just.

"One of our chaps had been caught at a village with a bag of clothes he was trying to sell. The Japs made out he was trying to escape. The trial came off at 11am on 1st March. What an ordeal! It lasted until 5pm. I thought I was to be a witness, but it turned out that I was being charged with neglect of duty. I should have had more control over the men in camp. I was an orderly sergeant. The orderly officer was also charged. We were told by Nagatoma that we were definitely to blame. Near the end of the trial another Jap officer, Lieutenant Naito, got up and gave what we thought was the verdict but which only turned out to be the prosecution. He sentenced one of the witnesses to death and fined the orderly officer 100 days' pay and me 50 days' pay. Brigadier Varley got up and wanted to know why the witness had been sentenced to death while the prisoner had not been given any punishment at all. They then found out they had made a mistake and sentenced the wrong man to death. They corrected that and we were then given half hour's break while Nagatoma came to his decision. The chap concerned was eventually sentenced to two months' imprisonment and two months' hard labour. The orderly officer was fined 20 days' pay and I was fined 10 days' pay. What a relief when it was all over. I certainly never want to go through it again."
Alfred Burkitt, Java, 1942

"We were taken inside the tent where the Japs were. They were trying a 2nd/30th Battalion sergeant, one of Black Jack's sergeants. He was marching his men home and they said, 'Why were you marching your men home?' He said, 'Nippon (we weren't allowed to call them Japanese of course, they were Nippon soldiers) soldier told us to march them when we'd finished.' So they asked the Jap and he claimed he hadn't said that. So they belted the hell out of the sergeant, knocked him to the ground and kicked him and

everything like that, not for marching his men home but for telling lies. 'No Nippon soldier tells lies,' the Jap officer said. We were the next ones to get tried and, of course, we didn't say anything because no matter what you said, they'd twist it round."
Cyril Gilbert, Singapore, 1942

" *Floggings were given daily on the slightest pretext and very often we received thrashings for offences of which we were ourselves totally ignorant.*"

The sheer number of Australian POWs captured by the Japanese far exceeded any other era or theatre of war in which Australia was involved. The scale of the abuse and brutality they endured was also far worse. In other conflicts, some captured soldiers faced equally brutal treatment while others were lucky to fall into the hands of captors who dealt with them in a far more measured way, and in accordance with the Geneva Convention.

Australians taken prisoner by the Turks in the First World War found their captors foreign in both culture and attitude. Turkish guards considered physical arbitrary punishment to be totally justifiable. George Handsley, a prisoner at Istanbul in 1917, recalls the ferocious nature of the Turks in one camp.

"This camp was described by the prisoners who had been there some time as the worst in Turkey, a hell on earth. Floggings were given daily on the slightest pretext and very often we received thrashings for offences of which we were ourselves totally ignorant. On one occasion a whole gang of 100 prisoners was flogged. The reason was that on the occasion of a Turk religious festival they were, according to their religion, forbidden to eat bread, so no ration was issued to the prisoners. As a consequence they refused to work without food. The commandant of the camp ordered the whole gang to be flogged."

Many of those captured at Gallipoli and in other battles suffered more from Turkish neglect and inefficiency than deliberate maltreatment. Food was poor, medical care primitive, and all experienced a casual brutality. Many POWs laboured to build the Taurus railway in southern Turkey in extremes of heat and cold. Of

Robert Parker as a motorcycle dispatcher in Korea prior to capture

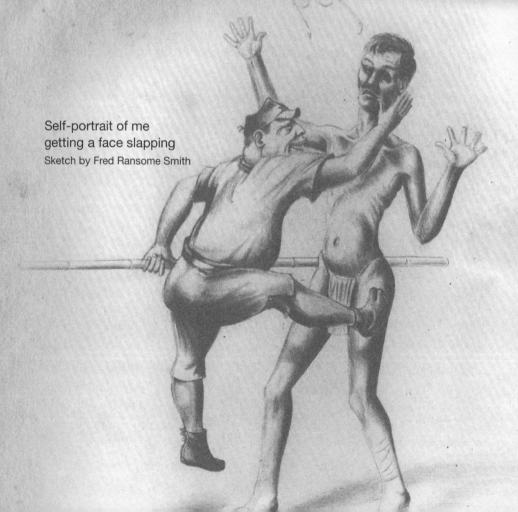

Self-portrait of me getting a face slapping
Sketch by Fred Ransome Smith

the 217 soldiers captured by the Turks, a total of 62 – nearly one in four – died in captivity.

By way of contrast, Doug Nix was a prisoner in Austria during WW2 and he found for the most part that his German guards were quite reasonable. "The guards were fine until the end of 1943 and on to 1945. That was when we started to get a bit of a bashing. I'm not talking about the older generation. I'm talking about the younger ones, who were between 19 and 24. They were made to go to the eastern front, the Russian front and they learnt a lesson, so when they came back they were very bitter. You had to be very careful how you approached them. They were Hitler years, and when they got back they found their parents had been killed in air raids and towns destroyed and what have you."

"One chap found himself outside his block during a bomber air raid alarm and was shot dead at the entrance to his block as he was attempting to get indoors. A mate went to him to pull him inside but he too was instantly shot dead."

Generally, however, the prisoners in Stalag 18A were treated with some respect. Nix could only remember one occasion when he was actually struck by a guard and in hindsight he could even see the humour in it. He did not understand that in German his name meant "nothing". This confused the guard who gave him an order.

"I got belted once for arguing back with one of the guards, but it wasn't anything. Well, the name Nix is spelt '*nichts*' in German and it's pronounced '*nicht*', which means 'nothing'. I had a German guard at a glass manufacturing company and I was a bit crook one time. He came in and demanded that I to go out to work. I just said to him in German, '*Ich bin kranke*' (I am sick). But he argued and argued and argued, and in the end said to me: 'What's your name?' So I said, 'Nix.' He asked again, 'What's your name?' And I said, 'Nix.' He raved and raved and welted me across the forehead. That's the only incident I ever had with him, and when he found out about my name later he thought it was a great joke."

Article 42 of the third Geneva Convention states that the use of weapons against prisoners of war, especially if they escaping or attempting to escape, is an extreme measure which should always be preceded by warnings appropriate to the circumstances.

In reality the situation would often find a nervous guard with a loaded weapon pointed at a potential escapee with little time to react. The results of such situations were varied. Sometimes compassion took hold. On other occasions the itch of a trigger finger resulted in quite different actions. John Crooks, a prisoner of the Germans, recalls two similar situations that ended in profoundly different ways.

"On one occasion a prisoner jumped the trip wire and attempted to climb the perimeter wire. Without an alert POW urgently calling out to the guard in the nearby tower not to shoot – as the poor chap was obviously in the middle of a mental breakdown – it would have been his last day. Not all guards would have been so humane. Not so two days after this. One chap found himself outside his block during a bomber air raid alarm and was shot dead at the entrance to his block as he was attempting to get indoors. A mate went to him to pull him inside but he too was instantly shot dead."

Doug Nix tried to escape several times and believed that the punishment he received related more to damage done to German property in the course of his attempt than actually trying to escape. "If you did any damage to a German establishment, that's why you've got 21days bread and water – not for the escape, but because you damaged the wire and stuff like that to get out."

"We had just exchanged one brutal regime for another and we assumed we would go back to the hunger, boredom and constant harassment with different lousy food, but we were in for a surprise."

Jack Calder was captured in North Africa in 1942 and experienced both Italian and German POW camps. The first was run by one of Mussolini's right-hand men, Colonel Vittorio Calcaterra. The camp was efficiently run but operated on brutal punishment and fear. Calcaterra offered his guards incentives – 1,000 lire and a fortnight's leave to anyone who shot a prisoner attempting to escape. He also posted a visual reminder in his office, a sign that hung above his door for all to see. Those who read it left with little doubt as to the lengths he would go to ensure his prisoners were kept in their place. The sign said, 'THE ENGLISH ARE CURSED – BUT MORE CURSED ARE THOSE ITALIANS WHO TREAT THEM WELL.'

When Italy capitulated, all the POWs became the responsibility of the German guards. "A German officer announced we were now prisoners of the German Army and any person who tried to escape would be shot," Calder recalls. "They gave us a graphic demonstration of how accurate they were with their Spandau machinegun by shooting from the windows of a nearby elevated sentry box. The message was quite clear. We had just exchanged one brutal regime for another and we assumed we would go back to the hunger, boredom and constant harassment with different lousy food, but we were in for a surprise. The next day, the Germans separated the various nationalities and we Australians were transported to Stalag 18A at Spittal in Austria as unwilling guests of the Third Reich."

" Hammelburg was famous because there were a lot of Russians there. The Russian prisoners had just started to arrive, and the Germans used to starve the poor buggers."

George Morley was at the same POW camp. He was working night shift in a brewery for extra rations when he met a Polish woman called Myra who offered him a home-cooked meal. Security for POWs working outside the camps was a little less strict so often only one guard would be with them. George decided to make the slip from his job with a mate, thinking it would be worth the punishment if he was caught. It was. "We had a good evening. Myra had a girlfriend with her. We had a good meal, drank wine and played records. The next thing was to get back to the camp. Being early morning, no trams were running. The only thing we saw was a police car. We heard it coming a long way back so we had plenty of time to hide. We had arranged with the work gang where we would meet them. They had spread out, giving us plenty of time between the guards to rejoin them. They told us that the guards knew there were two missing. When we got to the gates the Hun sergeant counted us and found that he had the right number. He was a lot smarter than most. He came along with his torch looking at everybody's boots. Danny and I were the only two without clay all over our boots. He put the torch on our faces and stood looking at us for some time. Then he decided to let us go as we were back."

The Germans considered the Australians, like the British, to be Aryans - a superior race Hitler described in his 1924 book *Mein*

Kampf as destined to rule the world. Aryan Australians formed part of this plan, once they had realised their true racial destiny. This may have been why Australian prisoners were not so rigorously punished by German guards. The Russians on the other hand were labelled *"untermenschen"*, or sub-human, by the Nazis. The treatment of the Russians shocked the Aussie POWs.

"Hammelburg was famous because there were a lot of Russians there. The Russian prisoners had just started to arrive, and the Germans used to starve the poor buggers. I'd made another escape attempt with Tom Bennett of the 3rd Battalion and we'd got caught. We were in a punishment company at Hammelburg and we used to throw bread and whatever we had over the wire. It was an interesting punishment company. We had Frenchmen there who wouldn't buckle down to the Germans, we had Serbs, we had Scots but Tom Bennett and I were the only Australians. We used to throw food over the wire and you'd see these Russians carrying a dead mate, stark naked, down to the communal graves at the back of the camp. But when they saw the food they'd just drop him and go for the food, cigarettes or whatever.

"There would have been at least 30 Jewish boys in our camp. I've always thought it really interesting that the Jews were never persecuted if they were in British uniform. I don't know about American uniform. Americans are different again. Having read some of the books written by my friend Charles Whiting, (I know) the American Jews who got captured got a bit of a rough deal."
Keith Hooper, Crete, 1941

"The Nazis, having the well-known German inclination toward good order and discipline, came upon a macabre method of enforcing these on us. One day spent burying the corpses of dead Soviet prisoners became the standard penalty for minor breaches of discipline; the number of days served in this way increased with the seriousness of the breach."
Ralph Churches, Greece, 1941

"Our camp commander, known only as John the Bastard, had reportedly shot an Englishman in bed when the five percent 'kranke' or sick quota was exceeded and he'd refused to budge. I also watched him make a Russian POW dance with bullets at his feet. He had dared to scrounge at our rubbish tip for food."
Ray Middleton, El Alamein, 1942

"The result of this was broken teeth and torn mouths. Another trick would be to ram the stick straight into the prisoner's throat, a dangerous and painful act of cruelty."

Prisoners of the Chinese and North Koreans during the Korean War discovered that the Geneva Convention meant very little to their captors. Although the People's Republic of China (along with the US) had not signed the revision in 1949, it agreed in 1950 to abide by it. Article 87 of the third Geneva Convention states that collective punishment for individual acts, corporal punishment, imprisonment without daylight, and all forms of torture and cruelty are forbidden. Not only were United Nations' prisoners subjected to brainwashing by their guards, but other punishments were given out that resembled those given by the Japanese six years earlier.

"On 25th June, 1952, four Australians were involved in a breakout of 24 UN POWs. It was organised by Corporal Buck. The group escaped in small parties, intending to converge on a selected rendezvous. Keith Gwyther, using civilian skills, magnetised some wire for compasses. Unfortunately one UN POW withdrew at the last moment and informed the Chinese of the intended breakout. The Chinese were waiting at the rendezvous and captured all the escapees. The foiled escapees were punished by being gaoled in the 'sweat box', a small cell four metres square and 2.5 metres high, with small windows set high on three sides and a heavy door with a grille on the fourth side. Guards, following the example of the provost marshal of Pyongyang, would push a pencil through the grille and force one of the POWs to hold it between his teeth. Occasionally the sentry would suddenly knock the outer end sideways, causing a split mouth and loss of teeth. Alternatively, the stick was driven sharply inwards to damage the mouth or throat. Because of his part in organising the escape, Corporal Buck was taken into the guardhouse and beaten frequently over a period of two weeks."
Phil Greville, Korea, 1952

"The head guard at Pyoktong by the name of Tong visited the prisoners often. He amused himself by battering the captives with a club, rifle butt or pistol. Often his treatment left the victim unconscious. On one occasion when Gwyther and Parker were caught talking, they were forced to squat and balance on their toes. This they had to

do on round saplings that made up the floor. When they lost their balance and fell they were beaten with rifle butts and clubs. Tong hated Americans as he had been forced to leave that country. They suffered most under him. Tong had yet another pastime involving the prisoners. This was to force one to hold a pencil like a piece of wood between his teeth. Then a guard would unexpectedly knock the wood in a sideways swipe. The result of this was broken teeth and torn mouths. Another trick would be to ram the stick straight into the prisoner's throat, a dangerous and painful act of cruelty."
Tom Hollis, Korea, 1951

Without a doubt war can bring out the worst in people. It would be foolish to deny that Australians have breached The Hague and Geneva Conventions with respect to the treatment of prisoners. Sadly, it only takes a rogue or two to undo the good work many others have done. The Aussie psyche generally believes in a "fair go" for all and this also applies to how we treat captured prisoners. Interestingly, the handling of captured terrorists since 9/11 and in conflicts such as Iraq has led the world powers to push for a re-examination of terms such as "non-combatant" and "torture". The Geneva Convention has always strictly banned torture as a means to obtaining information, but Australia's coalition partners in Iraq have admitted to doing this. Those individuals who humiliated prisoners under the guise of extracting information may have been atypical, however, the administration is ultimately responsible for controlling the behaviour.

The Geneva Convention strictly bans torture for information and yet many Australian POWs endured conditions and treatment that contravened these Conventions. Prisoners during WW2 were arbitrarily executed, starved and tortured by Japanese guards using cruel and violent methods. One out of every three Australian prisoners would die in captivity; you can only wonder how many wished they had died on the battlefield. The tragic end for some of our POWs shows that a country with every intention of acting with justice can be waylaid by the actions of the individual. Individuals who follow their own misaligned moral compass and set out in the wrong direction. While there are "rules" and Conventions designed to protect a POW, he or she remains at the mercy of the regime and the individual who happens upon them.

Work party on the
Burma-Thai railway

Sketch by Fred Ransome Smith

Chapter 5
Glimpses of Comfort

" Prisoners of war shall be allowed to send and receive letters and cards. If the detaining power deems it necessary to limit the number of letters and cards sent by each prisoner of war, the said number shall not be less than two letters and four cards monthly."

Article 71, third Geneva Convention

The Red Cross and the Red Crescent emblems at the Red Cross museum in Geneva

Prisoners of war experienced periods of terror, violence and deprivation during their incarceration. Ironically, these traumatic experiences were often the only breaks in what was otherwise a boring and mundane existence. POW camp life meant the same faces, the same routine and often the same food, or lack of it, for months on end. Winston Churchill memorably described the long and drawn out day of being incarcerated stating "the hours crawl by like paralytic centipedes".

Maintaining both physical and mental health was incredibly challenging for POWs. For many, their meagre diet and gruelling conditions meant the fight to survive ate up the little energy they had. They also had to invent ways of occupying the long hours, weeks, months and years in captivity and simultaneously keeping their sanity. Whenever prisoners worked – voluntarily or otherwise – the jobs were generally mind-numbing and repetitive. Even so, POWs would often volunteer to work so they could escape the tedium of the prison compound. Creating distractions was the means of dealing with the boredom and lifting the spirits. ANZAC Day, the Melbourne Cup, Mothers Day, birthdays and Christmas each reminded soldiers of home and forged a sense of unity that set them apart from their captors. Cricket matches against English POWs or holding mock Empire games emphasised the strength of the bond between Allied nations, particularly for the enemy.

"The German sentries sniffed the smell of frying bacon and saw all kinds of dainties coming out of tins and sighed in vain."

Until the middle of the 19th century no organisations existed that treated the wounded on the battlefield. In June 1859, a Swiss businessman, Henry Dunant, witnessed the battle of Solferino during the Austro-Sardinian war. He was shocked by the appalling aftermath of the battle, where around 40,000 soldiers lay dead and wounded without medical attention or basic care. On his return to Geneva he set about establishing a voluntary relief organisation to assist the wounded in battle. His vision resulted in the creation of the Red Cross. Dunant's recommendations were also the catalyst for the international treaties protecting volunteers, medics and the wounded on the battlefield. This would later form the basis of the Hague and Geneva Conventions.

With the outbreak of World War One, Red Cross nurses from around the world supported the medical services of the European armed forces. Immediately after the start of the war, the Red Cross set up the International Prisoners of War Agency, run entirely by volunteers. By the end of the war the Red Cross agency had sent out about 20 million letters, two million parcels and 18 million Swiss francs in donations to the POWs of all affected countries. The agency also became a pseudo police force for POWs as it monitored compliance with the Geneva Conventions through camp inspections. By the end of World War One over 500 camps throughout Europe had been visited.

During World War Two, the Red Cross increased its activities significantly, but the number of people it was to care for increased too. With advances in aviation, bombing raids became a major part of war so a significant number of civilians were affected too. The Red Cross assisted in much the same way as it had in World War One. By 1945, they had performed over 12,000 visits to POW camps in 41 countries, checking the conditions of the camps and the people inside them. They had also delivered almost 30 million Red Cross (and later Red Crescent) parcels.

A Red Cross comfort parcel helped the POWs supplement their diet, but it also broke the monotony with a small, but welcome, relief. These comfort parcels were sent through neutral nations such as Switzerland, Argentina and Sweden.

Red Cross and Crescent parcels were a godsend to all POWs, especially when their captors themselves were short on food. The Conventions protecting these parcels meant that most made it through to European prison camps. But POWs in Asia were not so fortunate. Their parcels were often damaged, stolen or withheld. Sometimes the Japanese would keep the parcels to supplement their own meagre rations instead of passing them on to their prisoners. Hungry guards would also occasionally deny prisoners their usual rations if Red Cross parcels had been handed out.

A typical Red Cross parcel contained cereal, dairy and meat products. Tinned fruit, jam and tobacco were also common. The British parcels received by Australians in European camps during the Second World War could sustain one POW for a week, but they were designed to supplement the prison diet, not replace it. They were meant to be shipped weekly but that often did not happen. In 1918, German prison guards who had lived on 1,000 calories a day since the blockade of 1916 would have found it torturous to watch prisoners eating more than them. Justin Dawson, who was captured by the Germans in 1918, recalls one such incident.

"The accumulation of months of parcels came in avalanches and we had quantities of everything, and Fritz – having a great liking for English tobacco not to mention grub – roared like a sucking dove and smiled sweetly on the Englander. But there was nothing doing. The German sentries sniffed the smell of frying bacon and saw all kinds of dainties coming out of tins and sighed in vain. The tables were turned with a vengeance and we did not forget to rub it in. From that time on, no one did any serious work, and curiously enough though we were soon strong and fit and able to do it, Fritz never tried his old games again."

"We feel that we all owe a debt of gratitude to the Red Cross that can never be repaid. Most assuredly the Red Cross food parcels enabled us to live to tell the tale."

Between 1916 and 1918 almost 400,000 parcels were sent from Australia to POWs. During WW2, the Italians were denied many simple pleasures. Doug LeFevre, a prisoner of the Italians in 1942, recalls their reaction: "When we got the Red Cross parcel, the Italians saw such things as chocolate that they hadn't seen for a number of years because Mussolini forbade it. There was powdered milk and all these different foods."

Captured by the Germans, Ralph Churches reflected on the "miraculous ability of the Red Cross to take its mission of mercy across the bloodiest battlefronts and bombed-out war zones". For others, the Red Cross parcels were the difference between life and death because their inadequate prison rations had dried up. At times, the arrival of the parcels gave POWs an unexpected advantage. They were then in the uncommon position to barter treats like chocolate and cigarettes with locals and guards in exchange for more nutritious food or even female company. Others recall how their parcels were received or used:

"We were supposed to get an American Red Cross parcel each. Well, we got one between seven men and the Japs kept the other six."
Cyril Gilbert, Singapore, 1942

"I never received a Red Cross parcel in my three and a half years as a POW of the Japanese and never even saw any distributed.

When I was working on the wharves in Saigon, after work on the Burma railway had finished, there was a go-down, or warehouse, about half full of Red Cross parcels on my section of wharf. However they were being transhipped to Japan and any POW 'stealing' from a Red Cross parcel took his life in his hands."
Jack Thorpe, Java, 1942

"We feel that we all owe a debt of gratitude to the Red Cross that can never be repaid. Most assuredly the Red Cross food parcels enabled us to live to tell the tale."
Unnamed officer, Germany, 1918

"We had a small issue of Red Cross supplies which were followed about one month later with a good issue which was planned to span out for about three months. It was a great addition to our diet and with its advent deficiency diseases died almost to nil."
Gerard Harvey Veitch, Singapore, 1942

"Thanks to the Red Cross, parcels came in regularly in Germany. Germany's a signatory to the Red Cross so they had to stand up to it. We were never allowed to talk to Red Cross men but they come into the camp with the Polish. We traded items in Red Cross parcels for what the civilians had. Especially in Poland, it was chocolates for their family. They'd give us about 18 eggs for it. The guards used to search us and take everything that was not a Red Cross parcel off us. This one time they lined us up and the German searched the front line and he give an open order march and I went from the back row into the front row, so he missed me. I was the only one who got in with about 20 eggs. What luck."
Archie Whitehead, Crete, 1941

"Without the Red Cross supplies of food, and not forgetting the medical stocks, we would have had the hope of a snowball in hell of surviving the war without serious illnesses."
Ron Lister, Crete, 1941

"I had 400 fags in my box, a pound of tobacco and a good bed. That's all we wanted. Cigarette and food parcels are a prisoner's dream in Deutschland."
Reginald Lindley, Crete, 1941

Food wasn't the only thing on a prisoner's mind. Prisoners were desperate to get their hands on basic toiletries, such as soap, warm clothing and books. John Crooks, who was captured in Greece in 1941, was one of many POWs to remember the delight he felt when he received a few very simple luxuries. "Shortly after our arrival at Corinth, Greek representatives of the International Red Cross visited the camp. They brought a supply of 'goodies' of which I scored a toothbrush, a box of matches and a neck-to-knee nightshirt. I was grateful for the first two, but I was glad a little later that I disposed of my camera because I thought that Fred might coerce me into letting him take a photograph of me wearing it."

"Some fellas were always planning escapes. But mostly we read books. People would send us books through the Red Cross and you'd pass them round."
Archie Whitehead, Crete, 1941

"A fair quantity of medical equipment arrived together with some comforts in the form of one toothbrush between two, shaving cream and toothpaste between two, five razor blades, one pencil, a few towels, some civvie suits, a few woollen socks, some woollen underclothing and a few handkerchiefs."
Alexander Bourne, Singapore, 1942

"We received an issue of soap and three packets of cigarettes from the Red Cross and there was some tinned food which was sent to the hospital."
Alfred Burkitt, Java, 1942

"Oh Mum, I would give all my money to get a line home to you, to show you I am still alive, but the Japs don't seem to think it necessary."

Letters from loved ones were prized above all else. A letter from a captured soldier brought relief to families that were waiting to learn the fate of their loved ones. And a letter from home reassured a soldier that all was well and reminded him of one of the reasons he was fighting – to defend his family and way of life. The importance of written communication was not lost on those who drew up the Geneva Conventions. Several articles specify the conditions surrounding letters and correspondence to and from prisoners. The rules state that within one week of being taken prisoner, every POW is to be allowed to write directly to his family and to send a card to the central Prisoners of War Agency that will notify them of his capture, address and state of health. The POW agency then catalogued the cards, which proved vital in terms of identifying who had been captured and informing loved ones. The agency had indexed around seven million by the conclusion of WW1, and by the end of WW2 it had indexed collectively 45 million cards, relating to both military and civilians amongst the Allies and the Axis powers as well.

After their initial card and letter, prisoners were to be allowed to send and receive letters and cards on a regular basis. If the detaining power deemed it necessary to limit the mail sent by each POW, then the minimum was to be two letters and four cards each month. As it turned out, the detaining powers simply did not have sufficient linguists to censor the mail so the number of letters sent was reduced. For many prisoners, the restriction of mail was used as punishment, so that a prisoner's right to correspond with home was frequently ignored. Tom Pledger, who was captured at Ambon, expressed his frustration in his diary. "Oh Mum, I would give all my money to get a line home to you, to show you I am still alive, but the Japs don't seem to think it necessary."

Other soldiers recall the frustration and joy of corresponding:

"It was nearly two years before I got a chance to write anything, for the Japs did not let us have any paper or writing materials."
Jim Parker, Singapore, 1942

"When we were first given the opportunity to write a card home by the Japanese it was a little card like a postcard (but) smaller. We were able to write 30 words including the address. And we were told that we each had one card and one card only, and if we made a mess of it we didn't get a replacement."
David Griffin, Singapore, 1942

"I was thinking quite a lot about home when instructions came through that we could write a letter and would be able to do so once a month. We did it, but didn't expect it to get far."
Alfred Burkitt, Java, 1942

"The communists permitted mail to some POWs and not to others – some never got a letter despite relatives keeping up a flow of mail throughout their captivity. Similarly, if POWs wrote in glowing terms of their captors and the treatment they were receiving, those letters would be delivered into the international postal system. In no way did the Chinese conform to the spirit of the Geneva Conventions."
Phil Greville, Korea, 1952

POWs at a camp in Austria, Frantschach, St Gertraud, 1944

Living conditions at
Langensalza, 1917

PRG1300_15_4

"We have at last been allowed to write home, but only a postcard of 24 words so could not say very much. And whether they will ever get home is very doubtful. There have been several repatriation ships for civilians from Japan and whenever we hear of one we always hope for some mail, but to date no luck although we have heard that there is mail on the last ship to go through."
Gerard Harvey Veitch, Singapore, 1942

"I remembered with sadness, a letter given to me by one of the English soldiers with whom I had become friendly. It was to his wife in case he didn't make it. I later found he had died several months before the war ended. One of the saddest things I had to do when I reached home was send the letter off to his widow. She wrote an appreciative reply and we corresponded for a little while. I sent her some food parcels, as England was short of food for a long time after the war."
Gordon Nelson, Singapore, 1942

" At last to see the old familiar handwriting, to be brought into touch with the outer world. At the sight of those letters I broke down completely."

The despair POWs felt due to the lack of direct contact with loved ones was felt by those back in Australia as well. Often the first correspondence received by a family was a telegram from the Australian government advising that their loved one had been captured, or more likely the telegram would simply state they were MIA – missing in action. It often took a long time for POW identification cards to filter back through the POW agency to the military chain of command. During the long periods without news, many families feared the worst, so to find out that they are alive and a prisoner was always welcome news. Jean Griffin tells us how she felt when she received the first card from her husband in 1942, after he was captured during the fall of Singapore: "I was sitting having lunch with my father and I could hear the postie blowing his whistle. And he was blowing it so hard that I felt that there must have been a reason. I went down to the gate and he was sitting on a horse holding up a card. And, as I maintain, even the horse was smiling, everybody was happy, and he handed me my first 25-word card (stating that David was alive, well and a POW)."

Most prisoners doubted their letters would make it home, so when mail from loved ones was distributed, morale soared. Men who received letters shared them with mates who had none, so that each could experience the hope and optimism. In 1917, Tommy Taylor was a prisoner in Germany. He explains how the emotion and significance of letters created that much needed connection with the outside world. "Letters from home! Who can imagine what it meant to us? For 15 weary months we had been forced by starvation and hardship to submit to humiliation and indignities, allowed barely sufficient food to keep body and soul together, and forced to gather weeds and herbs for sustenance. Gaunt, unwashed, unshaven and devoured by vermin; knowing practically nothing of what was going on beyond our barbed-wire enclosures; seemingly dead to the world, and, for all we knew, mourned as dead. Would we ever see our loved ones again? And at last to see the old familiar handwriting, to be brought into touch with the outer world. At the sight of those letters I broke down completely."

The importance of letters and their impact on POWs' spirits can be found in the following diary entry again from Tom Pledger in 1942. His passionate description about sharing letters with his mates highlights how meaningful news of events at home can be a world away in a POW camp. One of the most amazing pieces of news for Tom was discovering who had won the Melbourne Cup.

"It has been a gala day for us lonely boys. Three days ago we heard there were some letters at Kokorie for us and we have been out to meet the ration truck each day since with a beaming smile and an ache of hope in our heart, only to turn away downhearted because there were none. But today the lorry pulled in with our mail, about 400 letters, and the camp was one big noise. Everyone held their breath as it was being issued. You could see eyes hungrily watching the sergeant as he read the names out and the look of joy as your name was read out. Anxiously I held on, oh how those moments seemed like years, but at last my name, then everything stopped still and I could picture you sitting down to write just as excited as I am. One, two, three, four. Fancy four whole letters from my dear ones, they had held the pen in their actual hands and written their thoughts on that single sheet of paper.

"How far away it seems. You have no idea how hard it is to conjure up your image in one's mind after three years. I couldn't open it. I just ran round like a kid with a new toy telling everybody that I had got four. If this is how I am going to feel when I receive a letter it will kill me when I am to arrive home again. At last I plucked up courage and going away by myself with the letters tucked away against my heart I opened them one at a time. The first was Mum's and it was written two years ago, but it didn't matter, I was so pleased to hear of you all, but it seemed so short, only one page, then one from that big brave true blue girl, Jessie. Gee, my heart went out to her to think I have a girl like her waiting for my return. God look after you, dear.

"One from Marie and one from Ray, it was as though you were all sitting around me urging me to read your letter first. Since then, I have read and re-read them a dozen times and Neil has read mine and I have read his. Some of the boys have not been so lucky, some have had bad news and others did not get any mail at all, but I think they have got over it as we have read them part of ours. We even know that Colonus won the cup at 25/1 and beer is 9d a pot and the pubs are closed from 2.00 p.m. 'till 5.00 p.m. We have not been allowed to write, but if we could only get word to you that would be the greatest joy of the lot as it would relieve your minds. Well, dears I will have to read them again so will sign off."

Letters could also be a way to say goodbye and a chance to share your last words with a loved one. James McCracken was one of more than 30 POWs who escaped from an Italian camp in 1943 after Italy capitulated. He fought with the partisans until he was recaptured. He was wearing civilian clothing which was a clear breach of the conventions of war. He was put on trial, found guilty of being a spy and was shot in 1943. Before his execution McCracken was allowed to write to his family in Bendigo. Sadly, the simplicity of his note, which leaves much unsaid, would give little comfort to his family. "Just a line to tell you that I will not see you again as I am going to be shot."

Special occasions and holidays are often hard when we are separated from family or friends, but for a captured POW there is very little hope of having a real celebration. A Digger was sometimes surprised to receive an unexpected meal or a gift usually made by his mates to lift his spirits. Even the Japanese demonstrated some thoughtfulness at Christmas, according to an entry in Gerard Harvey Veitch's diary. He woke on Christmas morning feeling miserable and lonely and his thoughts were consumed by what his family would be doing at home that day. "This is my first Christmas as a POW and the second away from home. Went to church parade at 10:00 hrs. Had Christmas dinner with the boys and had to sleep it off afterwards. In the evening we had our mess dinner, quite a repast with the menu of: tomato soup, roast pork and bully beef, green peas, potatoes, parsnips, boiled pudding with white sauce, fruit in season, rice wine and coffee, cigars and cigarettes and bonbons. Once again, a very large meal sufficient for everyone's needs. After mess, went to a carol concert at the camp theatre. During the evening received instructions to move back to Changi on 28th Dec so we would have to march 11 miles. Am feeling brighter than in the morning, but have an uncomfortable, full feeling that is not pleasant."

"On Christmas morning we had a POW 'first' for breakfast. Instead of the tasteless rice pap we had endured for years, we had sugar to go with it!"

Others recall some of these special occasions;

"They have a system here that on your birthday you receive an extra of some sort. I was extremely lucky and I got a meat pastie. Tommy Betts, an old cobber, gave me a tomato he grew. We sat down to meal fit for a king, but lacking in quantity. Food is getting very scarce. All we hope is that the Japs are feeling it too."
Tom Pledger, Ambon, 1942

"We had to send out a work party on Christmas Day and the boys weren't allowed to come back early. We built a table in one of the empty huts and had quite an enjoyable Christmas dinner. The best since Syria. We had pap and a small pork pie for breakfast, hash for lunch and nasi goreng, pork stew and peanut sambal with a piece of cake for dinner, plus a rissole with coffee for supper. New Year's Day again and still everything was very quiet. There was no work, so our boys put on a boxing tournament and a concert in the evening."
Alfred Burkitt, Java, 1942

"Christmas Day 1942 found us still at Hlepauk (18 kilometre camp), and to celebrate the festive season the cooks had contrived to accumulate a few extra rations in order to provide a better than average meal. In addition to the inevitable rice and stew, we had a little extra meat, plus some rather tasty sweet potatoes and baked pumpkin."
Jim Jacobs, Singapore, 1942

Les Manning's POW barracks,
Germany, 1942/43

Volunteers packing Red Cross parcels, 1944
SRG770_40_179

"On Christmas morning we had a POW 'first' for breakfast. Instead of the tasteless rice pap we had endured for years, we had sugar to go with it! Also, there were scrambled eggs, rice cakes and coffee. We toasted the downfall of the Japanese army with the coffee. I went back to my bed space on Christmas Day after visiting someone. I found a banana waiting for me – a present from Bill, one of my friends. A year earlier, Arthur had given me tripe, now I had been given a banana. I was able to reciprocate by giving Bill a packet of cigarette papers. Of all the Christmas presents I have received over the last 50 years, none have represented more sacrifice than that shown by those two gifts."
Gordon Nelson, Singapore, 1942

" Our cruel workload, combined with starvation and the ravages of disease, meant that our entire focus was on survival at the most basic level."

When tedium and boredom set in, the POWs set to work conjuring up imaginative ways to pass the time and remain sane. Even prisoners of the Japanese, with little energy or free time, came up with something, although it often depended on where they were being held. Some camps in Thailand were reasonable while others had a mortality rate greater than 50 percent and were focused more on work duties than providing any downtime for their POWs. At a weekly sports day arranged by Weary Dunlop to maintain community spirit he demonstrated his "secret weapon".

"Next we moved to Bandoeng (in Java) which was a really big area, and with Weary Dunlop in charge of the whole camp it was soon organised and running as smooth as silk. We had a sports day every Saturday, all nations participating. The Ambonese (South Moluccans) were beaut little chaps and good athletes. The Manadenese from the Celebes were real Jap crawlers and most of them did turn over to the Japs early in the show. I remember the hop, step and jump. Weary was two foot taller than the Ambonese and he took off... big hop, huge step in mid-air and only had his jockey undies on and out pops Percy and balls before he lands for the jump. He was yards and yards in front of everyone else's mark."
Milton "Snow" Fairclough, Java, 1942

"The crude jungle camps of Burma didn't offer the kind of resources available at Changi and our cruel workload, combined with starvation and the ravages of disease, meant that our entire

focus was on survival at the most basic level. However in our early weeks on the Burma railway, while we still had some free time and a bit of energy left, Lieutenant Rivett organised evening discussions to keep the blokes' brains busy and alleviate boredom."
Jack Thorpe, Java, 1942

" To read, say, Elizabethan poems to a group of 250 starved prisoners living in the most appalling sort of conditions, it was something I did very timidly to begin with."

"Although we were all supposed to perform some task each day, we had a lot of time on our hands. There were many ways of filling in these idle hours. Firstly, a camp library was established under the supervision of Major E.W. Swanton, well known English cricket writer of the *Evening Standard*. Joining fee was one book and there was no further charge. The number and variety of books which had been brought up from Changi was amazing, so something could be found to suit every literary taste. By far the most popular indoor games were bridge and chess, and many tournaments were arranged. For outdoor games we played basketball, volleyball and circles, or deck tennis. Our physical condition at this time was better than it had been since early 1942. Siam was a land of plenty, and although our diet was monotonous and still consisted mainly of rice and stew, there was more of it. In addition, canteen supplies were fairly regular. It was possible to supplement the standard ration with an average canteen purchase of one egg, two bananas and an ounce or two of peanut butter per day."
Jim Jacobs, Singapore, 1942

"They hit upon the idea of having some sort of a library which they could get started by asking the troops who had books in their kit bag to deliver them. Also, that we should be enrolled as teachers and two of us even as lecturers. To read, say, Elizabethan poems to a group of 250 starved prisoners living in the most appalling sort of conditions, it was something I did very timidly to begin with. I thought there would be raspberries and all sorts of things coming back from the audience. But not a bit. They realised, those that were there, that there was something in this. You know, that poetry wasn't just a lot of muck. And we had some real converts. And then I thought of the idea of having a literary competition. So we got a group of writers, identifiable group of writers, British and Australian mixed, and that was the nucleus. From that was born the 'Literary Society'."
David Griffin, Singapore, 1942

"This was the newspaper printed in English for all the European people living in Sannomiya rather than all the different languages, because they could all speak and read English evidently. In it was the fair dinkum news of the war and they knew every blow that was being struck. They even got news of the Battle of Stalingrad in Russia and the different island conquests as the Americans and Australians fought their way through the islands. Every time the Japs lost a battle we lost one too, but it was good that we were getting a bit of news. Ken got onto this fellow somehow or other. He had made a deal with him: he used to get the newspaper about once a week and he would put it under his crotch the Japs were reluctant to feel around that area when they were searching you. I think they had an inferiority complex. The paper was taken back to camp and read by a person in each hut and the news would be relayed so that everyone in the camp knew what was going on except the Japs."
Mick Kidley, Singapore, 1942

Melbourne Cup ranks high on the Australian Army social calendar. Today in non-operational messes around the country, like the rest of the nation, people gather around to watch the race. Even on operations, soldiers tune in their radios wherever they can. Interest among Australian soldiers was just as high on the first Tuesday in November during World War Two. There were no radios at Jack Thorpe's work camp in 1942, but the Aussies convinced the Japanese to let them have the day off.

"The Japanese told them that they knew all about the Melbourne Cup in Japan and after a discussion it was agreed that we should have the day off," recalls Jack Thorpe. "But we were not allowed to rest. We must clear an area in the camp so that we could hold a mock Melbourne Cup. We must cut long pieces of bamboo to use as horses between our legs; we must have mock bookmakers, and a mock bar, etc. Their little joke. Well, we'd get what laughs we could out of the situation, as well.

"Morning arrived and there were bloody Japs all over the camp, eager to supervise the preparations for the Cup in the afternoon. Apparently we were to recreate Flemington in the Burmese jungle. Some of the blokes built a bar about elbow height, complete with a price list sitting up on the bar. I can only remember a few of the items and only two of those are publishable. The cheapest was a 'Yellow Nip', at one cent, while a glass of 'Maiden's Water' was £100. The drinks were coloured water with burnt rice.

"We had a lot of fun with the horses' names as well. One I can recall was 'Scanties – Out of Place, by Foul Play'. Another was 'Rice Bubbles – Out of Erection, by Wet Dream'. During this supposed day off the armed guards were constantly going through our huts and anybody caught inside was touched up by the back end of a rifle and sent out to spend time on the parade ground. Sheer bastardry. We'd come to expect nothing less and we were never disappointed.

"What we hadn't expected was for one of the Jap engineers to tell us the name of the winner the next day. According to him the winner of the 1942 Melbourne Cup was Colonus. I checked on this after I got back home and blow me down but the bastard was right. But how on earth did he know?"

"The only one I stayed with was soccer, rationing myself to one game per week, which seemed to be about my physical limit."

In comparison those POWs held in Europe, generally had more food and spare time than their counterparts held by the Japanese and found more ways of filling in their days. POWs at Stalag 383 at Hohenfels held an ANZAC Day and sports carnival in 1944, as well as an Empire Games in 1943 and 1944. This featured posters, medals and, in true Aussie soldier style, betting on the outcome. In 1918 Germany, officers in POW camps such as Gustrow and Karlsruhe boasted a batman for every eight officers. It is hardly surprising the officers had this extra time as they were exempt from labour under the Geneva and Hague Conventions.

"We actually had an Australian Rules football competition; we competed for a cup, which was won by the Western Australians incidentally."
Keith Hooper, Crete, 1941

"We used to hear the BBC news every night. They had a little wireless there. How the hell they got it there I don't know."
Ernest Brough, El Alamein, 1942

"We used to gamble, cigarettes and what have you. We made a Crown and Anchor set. It was made on a bit of hessian, and the covering of it was made from a Red Cross parcel. The dye out of the Red Cross parcel, the red and the black, was soaked in water and then impregnated into the cloth."
Doug Nix, Greece, 1941

"There were many and varied summer activities to kill time apart from study programs. Musicians combined to form an orchestra and sporting and theatrical groups soon became popular. There was a library and those who favoured card games or board games such as chess soon found each other's mutual interests. There were some strange by-products of these efforts to kill time. One of these, during a dry spell, consisted of a number of officers engaged in a race of pushing table-tennis balls along the road with their noses. It was also observed, after rain, that there was a race of paper boats down the water-filled drains. This was strange as the Warburg camp was notorious for its mud and unmade roads. This then became part of life of a POW, together with some time allotted to sport within each man's physical capability. This capability was limited by the low calorie intake from the available food as well as an individual's genetic makeup. Added interest was sometimes given by some contests such as a cricket test. One such cricket match, Britain vs the Dominions, saw the Dominions 139 runs, Britain 110. At one time or another, I attempted to play tennis, baseball and hockey, as well as soccer. The only one I stayed with was soccer, rationing myself to one game per week, which seemed to be about my physical limit. I am still a fan of the English soccer competition."
John Crooks, Greece, 1941

Cigarettes were of great significance to all POWs whether they smoked or not. They were a valuable commodity in a war-torn country and were used for bartering in Europe as well as Asia. Non-smokers would sell theirs when they arrived, others would store up the cigarette parcels until they had sufficient to exchange for something they needed. POWs would barter with other soldiers, locals, and even the guards who seemed to love British tobacco. It did not take some soldiers long to work out there could be a profitable business in the cigarette trade regardless of the origin of the tobacco. Gordon Nelson, a prisoner of the Japanese, found it even more profitable to make his own: "I heard about a chap who for 50 cents would make a small machine for rolling cigarettes. It appeared to be a rough imitation of something available commercially in Australia. I had enough money to buy some tobacco and cigarette papers, and both were available in Thailand. With some trepidation I spent almost all my remaining cash on those items and went into the business of rolling cigarettes. As glue for the paper I used some sloppy breakfast rice, and the nail scissors from my little sewing kit were ideal for trimming the ends. I was able to make a couple of hundred a day with the machine. The tobacco was a light brown, stringy stuff of doubtful quality but there was nothing else available.

"I charged five cents for a neat bundle of five held together with a strip of paper stuck with rice glue and had no trouble selling the cigarettes. Eventually I was able to pay another chap to go round the huts selling my wares. They were a boon to chaps on work parties who, instead of having to lose precious smoking-time rolling their own, could light up a 'tailor-made' with hardly a slow down in work or when there was a 'breather'. A smoke was about the only pleasure available in our deprived circumstances. I gave a few smokes to sick chaps from time to time."

" We would smoke almost anything, leaves, grass, you would dry it out and crumble it up and roll it in paper."

Others recall how valuable cigarettes were during their time in captivity:

"The boys were working on the docks unloading ships so they managed to steal a lot of stuff such as sugar, peas and tobacco. The Japs used to search the work parties each night but the boys used to put it over them pretty easily. Sugar was worth 9 dollars (about 1 pound 4 shillings) a pound, while cigarettes were 100 dollars a carton. Some of the boys made thousands of dollars. One of the punishments used by the Japs if they caught anyone was to make them eat whatever they had stolen. Some chaps had to eat tobacco leaves, some dried peas and even dry rice. That was in addition to the usual beating."
Alfred Burkitt, Java, 1942

"Cigarettes and chocolate being an essential part of the Red Cross ration. They provided a basis for price fixing – 1 point = 1 cigarette, and 40 cigarettes or 40 points equalled quarter pound of chocolate. These basic values fluctuated in times of scarcity or plenty but remained as a firm foundation for pricing other goods. Good old bully beef became a standard for food, being usually equal to 80 points. Food and clothing were two separate departments with food and chocolate as the common currency, i.e. food for food and clothing for clothing."
Ron Lister, Crete, 1941

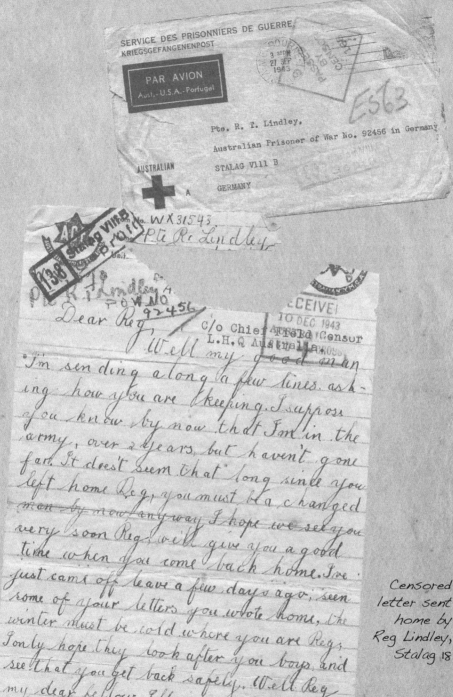

No. WX 31543.

Pte R Lindley

Pte R T Lindley
POW NO
92456

Dear Reg.

C/o Chief Field Censor
L.H.Q Australia

RECEIVED
10 DEC 1943

Well my good man
"I'm sending along a few lines asking how you are keeping. I suppose
you know by now that I'm in the
army, over 2 years, but haven't gone
far. It does't seem that long since you
left home Reg, you must be a changed
man by now anyway I hope we see you
very soon Reg, will give you a good
time when you come back home. I've
just came off leave a few days ago, seen
some of your letters you wrote home, the
winter must be cold where you are Reg,
I only hope they look after you boys and
see that you get back safely. Well Reg
my dear fellow I'll see you soon, look
after yourself, with very best wishes
from your loving brother Ross.

WRITE HOME FIRST!

Censored
letter sent
home by
Reg Lindley,
Stalag 18

"We would smoke almost anything, leaves, grass, you would dry it out and crumble it up and roll it in paper. Paper was hard to find but the *Bible* was the best, if you had a Bible, oh god that was beautiful. You could sell those sheets for anything at all because it was beautiful rice paper."
Cyril Gilbert, Singapore, 1942

When Archie Whitehead was shipped to Munich to work, the POWs were in an unusual situation. They had a large female workforce in their vicinity. Once again the universal appeal of the cigarette came into play and was used to buy a little private time and a very rare glimpse of comfort as Archie recalls. "You would be up on top pushing the coal trucks away with the girls. Women did all the work on top, but they had to have some men as the work was heavy. Some of the prisoners had girlfriends but they couldn't get out (of the coalmine complex). They might have bribed a German who wanted English cigarettes, because English cigarettes spoke all languages. You could offer them to the guards and he might let you out to see your girlfriend."

Soldiers found comfort in many of the physical and spiritual things we take for granted today. A simple toothbrush or a change of clothes could make a prisoner feel like a new man. A kiss from a stranger with a warm heart could sustain a soldier for some time as Justin Dawson, who was captured in Belgium in 1918, recalls. "While there I made friends with a Belgian barrister in Tournai who supplied me with a toothbrush and hairbrush, articles to which I had long been a stranger, and many other necessities, including that article more precious than gold in Germany – soap. He introduced me to a dear old Madame, and her daughters, who kissed me for my mother and gave me a warm scarf and quite a nice parcel of food. The daughters did not participate in the kissing, much to my disappointment. I will not forget these people in a hurry, for I can assure you I was pretty unkempt and none too clean. At this time I weighed eight stone and my clothes were in rags. The next time they visited us, Madame brought me a fine pair of warm riding trousers from M. Frison (the barrister) and from that time out I was easily the dandy of the party and an object of envy."

When prisoners found a creature comfort they often went to great lengths to hang on to it, as Les Manning found out in Germany: "We left Geroldhausen for Wittighausen and worked to keep the rail tracks in good condition. Our living conditions got worse as we moved up the line. One day six of our men were spotted carrying a bath, a big beautiful concrete bath. How great for us, at last we could wash this war off us, at least for a while. That bath went wherever we did."

> *"Morale suffered under such terrible conditions; with men dying so rapidly that each man would wonder if his turn would be next."*

The smallest comfort can be so important, it may take only the simplest gesture to bring a man back from total hopelessness as Peter Hendry, a medical officer at Changi recalls of a soldier in his ward: "He was at the point of despair. He was hungry, sick and exhausted. He had lost all his mates and was so depressed that he lay down in the mud to die. He said and I quote, 'The medical officer (MO) who ran the hospital came to pick me up. I refused to move, all I wanted to do was die. He had me carried to the hospital ward against my will. Soon after my arrival the MO and his staff began a concert. It was so stupid that I started to laugh. I never looked back'."

Medical officers and orderlies on the Burma-Thai railway have been hailed as heroes for a long time and rightly so given the accounts of how they saved so many lives with limited medical supplies. Padre Paddy Walsh reminds us that even without medicine you can still help your mate in some small way to lift spirits and raise morale:

"There was no way we could ease the sick men, the best we could do was to supply smokes to some when tobacco was available, or an occasional tin of milk. We arranged different lectures and concerts and for one period it was possible to have lecture in each hospital ward almost every night, but the supply of lectures soon ran out and we had spread them over a greater time. Earlier the Japanese had objected to the men singing but later we were able to arrange concerts about once a week.

"Morale suffered under such terrible conditions; with men dying so rapidly that each man would wonder if his turn would be next. Some of them even took to stealing from their mates; no article was safe if it had a saleable value among the natives. Strict measures were taken by our own authorities but a certain amount of stealing still took place.

"But these actions were outweighed by the many cases of noble work and selflessness shown; I have seen many cases where men who themselves were sick and had to go to work each day would spend half the night looking after sick comrades, carrying them on their backs to the latrines, washing them and caring for them as best they could."

Soldiers can be away from home for years at a time during a war. For many the small tokens of home that they carry link them to their families and the comforts that await them on their return. A photo, letter, a special gift from a wife, the ribbon once worn in your daughter's hair or even just a memory. Such treasures were kept close to the heart. A captor could strip a prisoner of his material belongings but if the spirit is strong a memory or a small token could be kept alive forever. Gordon Gafney, a prisoner of the Japanese, recalls how they preserved the special occasions: "As dawn came we had not reached our camp and word came down the column of very tired men – it was Mother's Day – so the men picked a tiny white jungle flower and draped it over their packs as they marched to their next stop. Mother's Day was never forgotten."

The experiences of these soldiers should remind us how we take many things in our lives for granted. Taking a bath, reading a book, having a beer or a piece of fruit was an enormous luxury for most of these men. Simple items such as Red Cross parcels or letters from home made an enormous impact on their lives and boosted their morale. What these so-called "privileges" gave prisoners bore no resemblance to the size of the package. For a POW to have a taste of some of the liberties he had been denied, such as playing sport or following the Melbourne Cup, reinvigorated his spirit and kept his dream of freedom alive. An extra ration or a piece of fruit pinched from a captor could be just the nutritional supplement a man needed to be able to push on for a few more weeks, giving them the energy to fight whatever setbacks they might unexpectedly face. The simple and potent belief that they were remembered beyond the walls that trapped them was significant for many. For countless prisoners these little things kept them going and charged up their will to continue their fight, so they could one day return to a normal life.

Stripped of luxuries, entertainment and freedom, POWs had to examine their own values, appreciate what they had and what they were fighting for. Soldiers who became prisoners were forced to accept the reality of their situation and to learn to treasure whatever they had, large or small. They were intent on survival and the hope that one day they would be free.

POWs at Campo PG 57
during a delousing session

Chapter 6
Escape

" Offences committed by prisoners of war with the sole intention of facilitating their escape and which do not entail any violence against life or limb, such as offences against public property, theft without intention of self-enrichment, the drawing up or use of false papers, the wearing of civilian clothing, shall occasion disciplinary punishment only. Prisoners of war who aid or abet an escape or an attempt to escape shall be liable on this count to disciplinary punishment only."

Article 93, third Geneva Convention

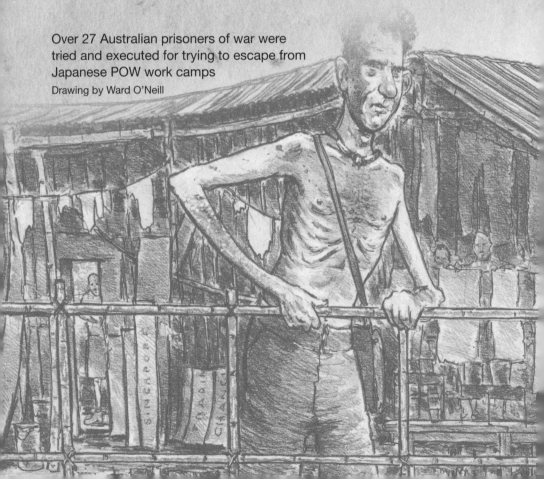

Over 27 Australian prisoners of war were tried and executed for trying to escape from Japanese POW work camps

Drawing by Ward O'Neill

For almost a century the exploits of prisoners who escaped from POW camps have inspired books and hundreds of hours of movie and television entertainment. These exciting stories about outwitting the enemy, forging papers, creating ingenious disguises and the hazardous crossing of enemy lines have gripped our imaginations for decades. Whether they were famous people, such as Winston Churchill during the Boer War, or famous Allied prisoners in WW2 Germany, like those in "The Great Escape", most POWs throughout history have felt it their duty to do more than just sit out the war. An escape attempt would tie up a captor's resources. They would be obliged to muster search parties, conduct camp searches and establish disciplinary tribunals for those that were caught. Prevented from fighting, many POWs hoped they could at least aggravate the enemy by placing a burden on their resources. Some POWs found that involvement in escape plans cultivated hope, kept bodies busy and fostered a spirit of mateship that would help pass the long days. Escape plans were the only way they could continue to contribute to the war effort. Some escapes were meticulously planned, while others came about by a fleeting moment of opportunity. Nevertheless, all escapes involved ingenuity, resourcefulness, cunning and courage.

> "Though we were lightly guarded, we were 150 miles from anywhere in the desert, with no food or water, only enemy posts en route, so we had little scope or inclination to try to escape. Later we regretted losing even that slender chance, but it remains a might-have-been."

There is nothing in the Geneva Convention that states a soldier has a duty to escape. But countries on both sides of conflicts encouraged, or even ordered, their men to resist their captors and attempt to escape if possible. Between 1906 and 1949, the Conventions did state that escapes were a disciplinary matter, not a criminal offence. During WW2 this part of the Conventions was followed by some but not by others. Doug Nix recalled how some WW2 escapees from German Stalags were put in solitary confinement in the "bunker". "You got 21 days bread and water, not for the escape but because you damaged the wire and stuff like that to get out." Less fortunate were the prisoners involved in "The Great Escape", who were shot as an example to others.

Prisoners of the Japanese had next to no chance of escaping. Negotiating the difficult terrain throughout much of Asia was virtually impossible and as "Europeans" they would have needed more than a clever disguise to blend into the local populations. However, that didn't stop some from trying and invariably they paid with their lives for their bravery. "I thought about escaping, but never tried," said Willoby "Bill" Wharton. "Changi is on the south-east coast of Singapore Island and there was nowhere to escape to, other than the waters which were shark-infested and patrolled by the Japanese air force. It was impossible to blend in with the Asians, unlike in Europe where they could disguise themselves easily. The few prisoners that did try to escape were mostly caught and beheaded or tortured, or both."

Those held captive in the deserts of North Africa faced a similar problem. Ray Middleton was captured at El Alamein and believes he could have escaped his guards while being moved across the Libyan Desert, but there was nowhere to go. "Though we were lightly guarded, we were 150 miles from anywhere in the desert, with no food or water, only enemy posts en route, so we had little scope or inclination to try to escape. Later we regretted losing even that slender chance, but it remains a might-have-been."

Most of the Australians captured by the Germans or Italians during WW2 found themselves in countries where they could blend in if they escaped. Many tried almost the moment they were taken prisoner. Some attempted to escape from trains and others from the makeshift compounds in which they were initially incarcerated.

"Only two got away from our camp. They got under the train. That was early in the war. All the Germans were awake to that sort of thing afterwards. But they got away, an Australian and a Brit in Munich. Another mate of mine escaped too, him and his mate. Swung along on the train and dropped off. They were trying to get into Yugoslavia. The Russians had entered the war, but they jumped off in Bulgaria! When they knocked on the door of a house, the fella came out with a gun. They were in the German part. Bulgarians were fighting with the Germans. Anyway, they put them up, they billeted them with the Bulgarian soldiers and, gee, they were great blokes, the fella told me. They were all interested in you and would do anything for you."
Archie Whitehead, Crete, 1941

"They took us up to Solingen. I tried for a second time to escape there, and this was a funny one. We had to get out of one train and walk over a makeshift bridge to get on the train on the other side. I ducked under the train and then went for my life for a stone wall. I jumped over the stone wall and here's a German soldier up the end having a pee. I saw him and smiled, laughed. He smiled at me and we walked back to the train. Then we got on the train. I don't think I shook his hand, but it would have been quite appropriate. You were dealing with the front-line soldiers, as we were until we got to Solingen. They were pretty easy on us, because they could have the same experience. It was when we got to Solingen that we started to fall into the hands of these other fellows…other units that didn't go to the front. They started to kick us around."
Keith Hooper, Crete, 1941

"One bloke that I heard a lot of stories about he escaped. He made a hammock out of the cord we tied around our Red Cross parcels strung it under a train and got away."
Lansell West, Crete, 1941

German camps were usually well-constructed and had a perimeter of barbed wire fencing and a warning wire about one metre off the ground that ran parallel to the perimeter wire. POWs were informed that if they crossed the warning wire they could be shot. The Geneva Conventions permit shooting as "an extreme measure" during an escape attempt, but they also insist that guards give warnings. That wire was their warning. This "implied warning" applied to western prisoners only. In stark comparision captured soldiers from the Soviet Union were very rarely given any warnings and frequently shot unmercifully by the Germans for the most trivial of reasons.

In Allied POW camps, escape committees were quickly formed to improve the control and planning of escape plans. It was the responsibility of the committee to approve and prioritise escape attempts. Once a plan was approved, the committee was responsible for planning and the gathering of resources. Prisoners demonstrated amazing ingenuity as they put their minds to producing escape equipment.

"They (the committees) were usually controlled by senior NCOs. We had an RSM, his name was Shanker; he was a British warrant officer. You had a multitude of fellows who didn't want to go out to work from main camps. That way they could stay in the main camps

and get together and form a body like a musical entertainment squad or a physical instructor squad and escape committees. But the escape committees were kept very quiet from the Germans. Their job was to bribe guards with cigarettes to get certain things into the camp, such as parts to make crystal sets, parts to make wirelesses, and even to buy a bullet off them."
Doug Nix, Greece, 1941

"There were many attempts to escape, usually involving a small number of would-be escapees. But the most brilliant and the most successful from this camp was on one night in August 1942, when a bold attack on the perimeter fences was made using teams of prisoners and systems of ladders to scale the perimeter. Being a later inmate, it was not until close to the end of the war, in fact, the end of 1944 while in Oflag VIIB, that I and four others became involved in planning and rehearsing a similar 'over-the-wire' attempt which did not come to fruition, probably fortunately. The cancellation was due to unsuitable weather conditions on the day. Also, news had come through of the massacre, on direct orders from Hitler, of 50 recaptured escapees from Stalag Luft 3 in Northern Germany. This would have also influenced the escape committee's decision to cancel the attempt anyway."
John Crooks, Greece, 1941

" I could analyse you - if you were guarding me - down to every step you took, whether you stopped and lit a cigarette, whether you patted your dog or whether you looked up at the sky."

Elaborate escape attempts could take months to plan. Papers and passes had to be stolen or forged. Food had to be hidden and prepared for a journey that could take weeks. The Germans knew that food was vital for an attempt, so they restricted the way tinned food from Red Cross parcels could be used – they punctured the tins so they could not be stored. Individuals would volunteer some of the contents of their Red Cross parcel to the escape committee. Uniforms needed to be altered too so they were not recognised. According to the Geneva Convention, civilian clothing could be worn, but soldiers had to carry identification that proved they were POWs. Maps, compasses and survival equipment were also important, as were photographs for identification papers, stamps, seals, German money and railway timetables.

"Often an escape required a bit of bluff to get out through the main gate, and to do this a German uniform and equipment had to be made. Rifles, hand-carved, took some months of work, with details being checked against the genuine article by studying guards' rifles while they were in position around the parade ground before and after parade. Badges of rank could also be carved or embroidered. Some of the chaps did fine needlework. Another method for badges was to make clay moulds, bake them, and then heat the thick 78-rpm gramophone records and press them into the mould; we also used this method to make badges for our own uniforms."
Ron Lister, Crete, 1941

"One of the men was busy making a compass when a guard came into the room. He stopped right in front of him demanding to know what he was doing, but Jack said he was only mucking around. The guard turned to us and made a circle with his finger around his head, meaning Jack was a bit silly. They never found out where the food was hidden, ready for our escape. I hid mine on a ledge above the door of an old pigpen where the guards never thought to look."
Les Manning, Crete, 1941

"POWs have got an immense amount of time. I could analyse you – if you were guarding me – down to every step you took, whether you stopped and lit a cigarette, whether you patted your dog or whether you looked up at the sky. I knew exactly how long it took you to walk 100 yards, and in that 100 yards I've seen 15, 20 fellows go out through the wire. Mass escape numbers weren't a good idea. That was proved, in the 'Great Escape' where they annihilated 50 percent of them, but that was in the later part of the war. You could sit for days and days, and you could work out exactly what you were going to do because you had so much time on your hands. And when you were ready to move, you moved at that exact moment. You didn't hesitate. You just took the opportunity, but you still put yourself in a bit of danger."
Doug Nix, Greece, 1941

"We decided we would get things going. Because on Sunday you could intermingle with the other camps that were about, we used to walk up the road to Dobl. We got a map of Austria there. We got a compass off this Polish soldier. Allan Berry gave him an

overcoat for that. We got the map from these British fellows at Dobl. We tried to trace it on paper, but you couldn't get any real good paper, so we thought we'd make it out of what paper we did get in the camp. But the Germans pinched it. We thought: 'Well, they've (the British fellows) had the map for two or three years and not used it so we will just keep it and, we'll use it'."
Ernest Brough, El Alamein, 1942

"Within a month I planned an escape together with a 2/43rd chap, but my diarrhoea put paid to any attempts to walk the length of Italy. So I gave him my stored rations, helped him over an eight-foot wall (not very tightly guarded) and we used a dummy for two days to get him free. The panic which followed the discovery of 'man missing' can only be called comic opera, as a detachment of troops – with fixed bayonets – lined our path between beds and cookhouse. The whole party was returned to Campo and the only complaints were from those who'd bought the weekly issue of rough red wine and now missed it."
Ray Middleton, El Alamein, 1942

"We had compasses, we had maps. You could get German money if you wanted to try with transactions and bribes. But we didn't need German money. We had supplied warrant cards the forgers used to do it. You'd get a party that might have to be sent down to clean their German quarters out. You'd get a slice of potato and soon as they would turn their backs you'd pick up one of their stamps and you'd stamp it on the back of the potato slab. Then you'd take it back to the camp and the fellow in there would be a forger or an engraver, and he'd engrave the stamp out, and you'd get little bits of rubber or whatever you found and make a stamp and there it was on the outside.

"The escape equipment was in the roofs of places, under the floor, in the back of your shirts and in the cuffs of your trousers, everywhere. We got impounded into a camp near a dynamite factory and (the Germans) knew we were getting in and out for food. They come pounding in and they banged the walls with their rifles and all this and that. We had a carpenter in our section and you couldn't tell where he'd cut the wall. You could have a cache in the middle of the hut and they would walk past and say: 'We're not looking for that, we're looking for the hole in the wall.' So one-track minded."
Doug Nix, Greece, 1941

Secret radio hiding place
German camp Stalag Luft

Prisoner's intricate hand
made escape map showing
area in Germany 1944

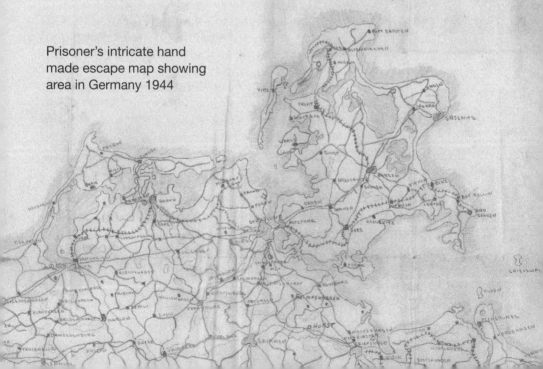

"To make a compass, a magnetised needle or pointer is the first essential and you can imagine that a POW camp would not be a likely place to find one lying around. Again, ingenuity came to the fore. One brand of British safety razors advertised a good gimmick: 'Why cut your fingers when picking up dropped razor blades? Use our razor with a magnet in the handle!' So every POW who wanted a compass requested one of these specials in his next clothing parcel from home. And there it was: an innocent razor, not a suspicious item but something that every soldier possessed. Later on, the escape committee would organise metal to be magnetised on the transformer of our 'canary' – the secret wireless set. We made quite reliable compasses out of razor blades and sewing needles. Every person had a Hussif (sewing kit), complete with needles and thread. The simplest compass was made with a razor blade magnetised by stroking the blade with a magnet and then cutting it to an arrow shape with a pair of scissors under water. An aluminium bridge was shaped to balance the blade on a needle point, and the compass was ready to be assembled in a case with a final fancy touch of a dab of luminous paint, which came from a watch, on the needle point."
Ron Lister, Crete, 1941

Some escape attempts were well planned and orchestrated. But occasionally it was a spur of the moment decision, taken when an opportunity presented itself, that could create the push for freedom.

"Me and some others were planning to escape (from Stalag VIIIB) but our actual escape was not planned, it happened on impulse. Some of us were standing at the gate one night, just looking. The guard was walking up and down and a German came in, leaving the gate open. It was dark, so I said: 'I'm going out the gate. Is anybody coming?' And two chaps said: 'Yeah.' So that made three of us. And I said: 'Righto. Once we're out, don't look around. Just keep walking. If we get shot in the back, bad luck.'"
"Blue" Heron, Germany, 1941

"I said to him I wanted to go to the toilet and he was lax, so I just walked along and moved the door of the train and I opened the door and jumped out into the snow. The snow cushioned me and I got up and walked away. I hid, but a kid gave me away. This is what you had to be careful of, some people were lenient towards you and some people got scared of you and the next minute I've got the police on me."
Doug Nix, Greece, 1941

Chapter 6 – Escape

"I made six attempts to escape, and the first time was from the hospital. They moved the least wounded of us into a block of flats and I tried to get away. I got over the wall, but I almost fell on top of the German guard. So that was that."
Keith Hooper, Crete, 1941

"I became friends with a Welsh guard, Warrant Officer 2 by the name of Taffy Davis (Taffy is the nickname given to all Welshmen). Taffy and I decided that this place, Graz, would be perfect to escape from. If not, perhaps to the Yugoslav partisans. We didn't have a preference as long as we got away from the Germans. One night early in March 1945, while the Allied Air Force was carrying out extensive air raids, we decide to make our escape bid and without any hassles, we got away from camp. The guards were too occupied with the air raids in progress. Fortunately for me, Taffy had worked on some of the farms around Graz and knew the layout of the average Austrian farm. He seemed to know where the cows were stalled, where the farmer stored the vegetables and fruit and anything of value to someone on the run. We obtained sufficient food by raiding a farm during the night and hiding by day. We hid in the hills using whatever cover was available or something we had pinched from a farm."
Jack Calder, El Alamein, 1942

"All hell broke loose! All the prisoners were paraded and counted several times. The two escapees had their thumbs tied together behind their backs with a thin rope attached."

Under Article 93 of the third Geneva Convention, POWs who committed non-violent offences in the process of escaping should only be subject to disciplinary punishment. In Europe and North Africa during WW2, this stipulation was largely ignored by their jailers. Some punishments were excessive and even members of escape committees who did not participate in the escape were punished for aiding or abetting the attempt.

Jack Calder, a senior officer in an Italian-run prison camp at Benghazi – the Palm Tree Camp – had endorsed the following quick escape attempt. The punishment that followed was meted out to more than just the escapees. He recalled: "The plan was to escape under the ration truck and when they were out in the open and all was clear, they were to go inland hopefully to meet a friendly tribe of natives. They wangled themselves on the detail for unloading the ration truck which came into the area each afternoon. While they were on the unloading party, the pair got under the truck and spread themselves on the chassis under the floor. When the truck was nearly ready to go some idiot in the compound looked under the truck. The driver must have noticed this and as soon as the truck was outside the compound, he stopped and looked underneath the vehicle and naturally found the two men. All hell broke loose! All the prisoners were paraded and counted several times. The two escapees had their thumbs tied together behind their backs with a thin rope attached. The rope was then thrown over a tree and pulled tight until the men were literally standing on their toes. They were left there all night and released the following morning. The Italians had a spy in the camp who reported I was the one responsible for allowing the men to attempt an escape. I was subjected to four hours of the same treatment."

In late 1942 Keith Dodd was at Campo 57 in Italy. Some men had been preparing an escape for months but within a week they had all been recaptured. The Italians tried to charge them with theft so they could punish them outside the Geneva Convention. "It was in the last days of October that the one and only large scale attempt to escape was made from the camp," Dodd said. "Nineteen fellows went out through a tunnel, 118 feet long, dug at a depth of about 12 to 15 feet, from No.5 hut in our compound behind the sentry box in the field. While they were digging they had to use football bladders to make up for the lack of oxygen once they got about 30 feet along the tunnels. It was a futile attempt though because inside a week they had all 19 back, but they certainly fooled the old colonel who had claimed that it was impossible to escape from the camp. These fellows found out how hard it could be in that camp, because they chained them and whipped some of them, attempting to get information which would enable them to charge the escapees with larceny, which meant 12 months in a civilian gaol."

The standard punishment administered by the Germans to escapees was 21 days' solitary confinement. It was worse for multiple escape attempts. Stan McDonald was captured by the Germans in Kalamata. Four failed escape attempts meant he spent a great deal of time in the lock-up. Not one to give in, McDonald tried a fifth time and was successful. "'Disciplinaries', as we were called, were subject to rough handling and sent to Landeck, a tough prison not far from the Swiss Alps. Here we were given solitary confinement for 21 days then returned to Wolfsberg. A group of us was sent to a village in a remote valley north of Stainach in Steiermark. We were told that because of our previous escape attempts it would be all work, no recreation and any escape attempts would result in us being shot. We were later taken to another camp and treated more civilised. It was here I considered another escape attempt and became friendly with a Latvian conscripted worker. He was becoming nervous about the Russian advance, as he was from the Baltic States, so wanted to escape to Villach where he had friends from his hometown, Riga. This escape was easy as the guards were not as concerned about us as they were with air raids. We boarded a train carrying wounded troops back from the Russian front. We stayed on the train until Klagenfurt, where we met up with people who took us to Villach. We spent some time there. Then one morning in May we noticed tanks in the streets. We hesitated, because we didn't know whether they were retreating Germans, but then we heard English voices so we ran from the building towards them shouting: 'You bloody beauty.' They thought I was an Austrian gone mad but I told them I was Australian and had been a prisoner for four years and that really impressed them."

" It didn't occur to the Italians to look in the pit as they all had the same sort of smell which everyone disliked."

Despite meticulous planning and hard work over a long time, escape attempts often failed at the final stages. Jack Calder approved an elaborate plan which used the latrine system to disguise a mass escape from his Italian camp, "Sidi Hussein" near Benghazi. The latrines were called "12-holers". "I got quite friendly with another Australian, Jack Wright, and over a period of time we discussed an escape plan," Calder recollected. "Our idea was to dig a tunnel under the wire, out far enough for the end to be out of sight of the perimeter guards who always seemed to be half asleep. We would select a site near the barbed wire, in line with the latrine 12-holers. These boxed pine latrines had six holes on either side and if anyone wished to relieve themselves they sat on them and the residue went into a deep hole under them. We figured we could set one of these up and have 12 men in shifts

Two German guards inspect a section of an escape tunnel from the Holzminden POW camp. Dug by Allied escapees, the tunnel was used by some POWs to make a successful escape from the camp in July 1918

AWM Neg. P03473.006

GILLETTE BLADE

TRADE MARK

King C. Gillette

Small escape compass used during escape from Holzminden POW camp

AWM Neg. RELAWM16875

HOLZMINDEN TUNNEL. JULY 1918

sitting on them 24 hours a day. They would take away the dirt at night in small bags made from Italian groundsheets and empty them into any of the approximately 100 other 12-holers situated all round the camp.

"Jack and I estimated it would be necessary to make the tunnel about 150 feet long and at least six feet deep. The prisoners who dug the latrine pits told us the ground was very stable 6—10 feet down but rock might be a problem. We would simply have to go around any rock in the way. Another problem was light and air for the tunnellers. This was overcome by stealing some water pipe from the camp water system. The pipe was broken into manageable lengths and forced up from the tunnel to the ground above, allowing air to come down into the tunnel. Jack somehow managed to get some army torches and batteries which solved the lighting problem.

"We recruited 25 others who could be relied on to keep their mouths shut and were prepared to get stuck into the project. The idea was to work our way south and join a friendly native tribe who might assist us to eventually get back to Egypt and rejoin our own forces. Implements were made or obtained by trading with other prisoners, especially the South Africans in the camp (who for some reason were allowed to keep a lot of their equipment when they surrendered Tobruk).

"We got our 12-holer and placed it in position with twelve men sitting on the box at all times. To fool the Italians, a pit was dug under the box and like all the other latrines the dirt from the pit was placed in a heap at the rear. It didn't occur to the Italians to look in the pit as they all had the same sort of smell which everyone disliked. The tunnel proceeded without a great deal of problems and the day came when we were ready to break out. The men had enough rations for one week and were briefed on where to find water on their way south. It was estimated to be at least 75 miles before contact could be made with any friendly natives.

"After about two hours of darkness, 30 men of the group were in the tunnel waiting for the final breakthrough when all of a sudden the guards started yelling. They moved the 12-holer from the entrance to the tunnel and blocked some of the air holes. We had no choice but to emerge from the tunnel and be placed under heavy guard and then marched off to the guard compound. The next day all the men except me and three others were taken into

Benghazi and placed aboard an old cargo boat and sent to Italy. Us four were interrogated for some time, and then tortured by holding our thumbs in a steel vice and tightening it. I passed out and I believe the others did too. They wanted to know where we got the equipment to dig the tunnel and who disposed of the dirt for us. We told them nothing and we were placed in solitary confinement for some time. The longer we stayed there the more we lost touch with reality. We became weaker, unable to comprehend time and our thumbs had become infected as we received no medical treatment. We were a complete mess."

George Morley remembers the dangers and discomfort of tunnelling at Stalag 18a in Germany, and the heartbreak of getting so close before being discovered. "Every evening we would work on the tunnel. It was very hard going, lying on your stomach digging. We would try and do about three feet and then some of the others would take over and timber the roof. We went extra good until one of the men started complaining about their bed boards being used for the tunnel as it made their beds very uncomfortable. We had a meeting about this and it was agreed that we could have the boards. After many weeks we estimated that we were about 55 feet outside the wire in the paddock. I wanted to come up and go. The others thought we should go further. We had a night of very heavy rain. In the morning before we went to work we could see a depression where the earth had sunk but the timber had held. When we returned from work the boys yelled out that the tunnel had been found. What happened was that the guards saw the depression and checked under the building. It was like a mine with electric light, small trollies and piles of dirt. They were happy that they had found it before we had a chance to use it."

" It was half-light when they stood up, still under the overhang, and adjusted their gear and strolled away across the open hillside."

Ron Lister's description of an escape from his German camp reveals how complex the process could be and how coordinated a successful escape plan needed to be. Almost everyone in the camp was involved in larger escapes. Lister's account is an example of how a group of men would work together just so a few could escape. This intricate plan included stooges, a command structure and diversions to help the four men escape. Sadly, they did not taste freedom for long.

"Although I had not escaped myself, I was one of the back-up group who assisted with stooging, map-making and the numerous behind-the-scenes activities that went into getting bodies outside the wire. As the system evolved it became evident that the first essential was coordination, which meant that an escape committee with authority to control all escape methods be empowered, under the authority of the senior British officer, to approve or veto plans for escape.

"The camp was at Dössel-über-Warburg and was a couple of miles from Warburg which lay over the other side of a hill from the camp. Warburg had a railway station and we could hear the trains and make an accurate guess as to the direction they were running. So for a period of about a month, a 24-hour listening watch was kept with a room at a time covering the day and night.

"This became room 6's effort, led by Jimmy McDonnell and two mates, all blondish and posing as Swedish workmen on their way home to Sweden after working in Germany. This escape required a diagram to explain how it went in detail and to demonstrate the clever use of blind spots and synchronised stooging. The cast involved four active participants with only three making the escape. Number 1 went over the tripwire and lay alongside the inner wall of barbed wire, under cover of the top wire overhang but over the toughest part. He then set about cutting and clearing a way through the tangle of loose coils between the two fences and opening up the outer wire. Wriggling backwards he then gave the all clear for No.2 to come across the tripwire and crawl out and lay out of sight along the outside wire. No.2 and No.3 then followed in due course. All this sounds easy, but remember, any person crossing that tripwire could be shot without warning, not just shot with a rifle, but the whole area could be sprayed with machinegun fire.

"When the outside three had signalled that they were all set to go, the inside man crawled through the tangle of wire again and crawled backwards, closing the tell-tale gap behind him. Then he waited for the signal so he could dash back over the tripwire into safety.

"I watched all this going on and it reached a tense moment, which had to be timed perfectly and had been checked over many days. It was half-light when they stood up, still under the overhang, and adjusted their gear and strolled away across the open hillside. A dangerous moment – the guard in A tower shouted a challenge and one of the three yelled back something in German and kept walking. The guard hesitated and then turned to check the inside of the camp again and to make certain that the baseball players were not up to any mischief so now for the stooges and 'actors'.

"Diversions had been put in place to keep the guards in A and B towers occupied so they were looking away from the area of action. To this end a softball game had been arranged to take place on the open ground under tower A, the star performer being the man with the tin legs – Douglas Bader – and a very noisy crowd of supporters. Bader became the key man in the distraction of the tower guard A. He performed clumsy antics in swiping at the ball, falling over or attempting to hit and run. He was cued by the control point at C outside Hut 38, and by the coordinating signals from all the stooges. The word 'go' would send a man to jump the tripwire and lie under the fence overhang. You can realise that dozens of people would have to be coached in their parts and rehearsals were carried out over a couple of weeks so that seemingly un-related activities could be coordinated together as a whole. Jimmy's team had supplied the idea, which then received the full support of the escaping committee.

"The stooges and diversions were run by the committee, so the escapees could concentrate on getting their own act perfect. The fellow who cut the wire and returned into the camp was one of the committee's experts and deserved a medal for his part. Alas for this splendid evasion – which was not discovered till the next morning – Jim and his mates ran into one of those snags that could be anticipated but could not be covered completely – the necessity to have up-to-date travel papers that enabled movement from one zone to another. These were often changed and dated so that papers could soon became obsolete. Still they travelled some hundreds of miles by train before being challenged and returned to us, after a period in the camp cooler."

Persistent "offenders" were often sent to supposed escape-proof prisons. Doug Nix's fourth attempt was from one such facility. He decided to escape simply because he was told it was impossible. For Nix, the look on the commandant's face when 20 men did the "impossible" was well worth his punishment in the bunker.

"They sent me out to that place called Waldenstein which they reckoned you couldn't escape from. Now Waldenstein is like an old castle, but it has one approach to it. You come across a bridge leading into the courtyard, similar to Colditz. It was three stories high. There was the underground section where the Germans lived, and then where we had our cookhouse, and above it was where we used to live. Now the sewerage system was all connected by one tunnel that went from the top to the bottom. We got permission to go down to the creek to wash. When we got down there, there were four grilles where the sewer came out. You just sat on the seat and everything dropped from the top to bottom and out into the creek. We found the bars in the creek were rotted away. We bound together hessian bags and used these to lower ourselves down behind the toilet, straight down to the creek – 21 of us. We formed a group and marched back to the main camp, Stalag 18A, which was about 10 kilometres away. We pulled up at the main gate and the guard that was on wanted to know where our guard was. 'We haven't got one'. And he said: 'What do you mean, you haven't got one?' He said: 'Where did youse come from? What party? Waldenstein! No, you couldn't have.' Then the panic started. The camp commandant came out waving a pistol around, wanting to know how we got out of Waldenstein. We eventually told him."

" The picture's still in my mind of these old Austrian guards with their hands up and their rifles still hanging from their shoulders."

One of the most remarkable European WW2 breakouts was Ralph Churches mass escape in 1944. Ralph Churches made contact with Yugoslavian partisans while they working on a railway line and formulated a plan to break out more than 100 allies who were being held prisoner by Austrian guards. At first his goal was to escape with six men, but he soon extended this considerably. Unlike the "Great Escape" from Stalag Luft III, where 50 men were murdered after being recaptured, these men got away.

"I knew I was going to escape," Churches said. "I didn't know how or where, but I always knew I was going to escape." He convinced the partisans that they could free the other POWs, but he demanded that the Austrian guards, mostly older WW1 veterans, must be released after the escape. The partisans agreed and 14 days later 99 POWs reached freedom after marching 250 kilometres. "You're not going to like yourself if you are given an opportunity to do the right thing as a leader but you don't do it," Churches said. "I said to the partisans that I would not consider taking part in this action unless they could guarantee that in due course they would let the Austrians free. 'You let them free when we are safely away,' I said. So up we jumped, yelling and screaming. They were strung out over perhaps 100 metres or so. There was no hesitation. The picture's still in my mind of these old Austrian guards with their hands up and their rifles still hanging from their shoulders. It looked a bit comical. I said: 'Come on, chaps, we're on our way! Get yourselves together, you won't be coming back!' One man said: 'Good on you, Crow! I thought you'd be back!'."

Attempting to escape from a Japanese POW camp was a very different story. Soldiers captured by the Italians and Germans and transferred to camps in Europe could go through the wire and have a chance of blending in with the local population, or "natives" as they called them. Most Australian POWs in Asia were not Asian. They stood out because of their height, clothing, hair colour and facial features. Escaping into the jungle without rations or equipment was close to impossible. Friendly nations were hundreds of kilometres away, sometimes an ocean away, and the local population was more likely to report an escapee to the Japanese than to assist him.

The Japanese had another way of deterring prisoners from escaping which blatantly disregarded the Geneva Conventions. They announced that for every prisoner who escaped they would execute one of his comrades back at camp as a warning to the others. If they were recaptured they would almost certainly be summarily executed or beaten and tortured to death. Jack Thorpe maintained the situation was: "Dig your own grave and be executed."

"To try to escape as a POW of the Japanese was suicide. Our white skin made us too easy to identify in a population of brown skins, and we were also extremely susceptible to local diseases such as malaria. So we knew we had to stick it out somehow. There was no other way. However early in the building of the railway three men did decide to make a break for it, perhaps because two of them could speak Burmese. At that time the British and the Japanese were fighting a couple of hundred miles on the Rangoon side of the Salween River. Apparently the men said they could make it and the camp POW commanding officer agreed. He gave his consent and away they went.

Torture and bashings in
front of all the troops at
Kanburi for those members
found with a wireless and
planning an escape

Sketch by Fred Ransome Smith

"They'd been gone several months and the scrapping between the Japs and our officers about who was responsible for their escape had just settled down when one morning who should be walking around the camp but one of these escapees. Apparently they'd made it to the front line but were there for days waiting for a lull in the fighting so they could make a break towards the British lines. They didn't have any food and were getting weaker by the day so in the end they decided to just make a dash for it. The other two had been killed and this bloke had been caught by the Japanese and brought back to camp.

"Well, he wandered around the camp for weeks, telling everybody of his exploits. He had got a bullet in his knee and that leg was so stiff he could hardly walk. One day two guards walked up to him, grabbed an arm each, and took him into the jungle where there were more guards and a Jap officer. They handed him a shovel and told him to dig his own grave. However, he wasn't able to because of his injuries. So one of the guards came back into the camp to where a group of us were sitting, and grabbed the two blokes sitting right next to me. He took them back to dig the grave.

"Altogether there were few attempted escapes from the Japanese and then only at the beginning. This was partly because the odds were stacked so heavily against us that such attempts were futile. But the main reason was if you attempted to escape it wasn't only your own death warrant you were signing. After this escape attempt the Japs segregated us into blocks of eight. We were told if anyone from that eight escaped or committed any kind of misdemeanour, all eight would receive punishment – including the death penalty. It was very effective because they soon showed us they meant it. On our way home from work one night we saw eight POWs tied to trees with buckets of rock hanging around their necks. The bucket handle was just a bit of wire, cutting off the blood supply to their heads. Their crime? One of them not doing as he was told."
Jack Thorpe, Java, 1942

"No one escaped from our group, but (they did) from one of the camps where the British were. Five or six of them escaped, but they all got captured. The natives handed them over and they were all executed. So there was no place to go. You were a white man in a black man's country, and if you were in the jungle and you scratched your leg by going through bamboo and that, you'd

have an ulcer, and before long half your leg would be gone. So there was nowhere to go."
Cyril Gilbert, Singapore, 1942

"The Japanese regard the recent escaping of prisoners very seriously, and told us last night that for every man who escapes now a man in camp will be shot."
Jim Ling, Singapore, 1942

After the fall of Singapore, Australians were asked to sign a document stating they would not attempt to escape. This document was designed to do two things. The Japanese believed it legitimised an execution if a soldier did try to escape. It was also designed to lower the morale of the soldier by removing his obligation to escape.

"The Japanese caught two young chaps who tried to escape – one was a corporal and one was a private. They made Lieutenant Colonel Galleghan, 'Black Jack', go out there to watch and they used these Indian troops to shoot them. When the Lieutenant Colonel came back he gave us a bit of a talk. The Indians could not shoot properly. One bloke was down and the other was still trying to stand up with bullet wounds in him. In the end they killed him. He came back and he said: 'Righto, you have just got to sign this form. You are signing under duress so it does not mean much.' He stood up with tears running down his face as he told us the story. So then we all had to line up to go through and sign these forms to state that we would not attempt to escape. I would have loved to have seen the forms when they finished because all the blokes were going through and signing them, but not necessarily with their real names. They used any name they could think of. There were bloody film stars, Ned Kelly and Adolf Hitler, the whole lot and they all signed these bloody forms."
Walter "Wally" Holding, Singapore, 1942

"We were ordered to sign. But that didn't matter at all because I signed somebody else's and he signed mine. Some of the others signed Mickey Mouse and Pluto the Pup and everything like that. So long as they had a signature, that's all they were worried about."
Cyril Gilbert, Singapore, 1942

"On 1st July, the Japs tried to get us to sign a paper saying that we wouldn't escape and we would obey the Japanese army. The brigadier had a clause put in at the end saying that we would

obey all orders unless they ran contrary to our oath to the King of England which made the whole thing useless. We thought we had got away with it, but the next day the guards started a terrible blitz. We couldn't move without getting bashed up. The work parties were a welcome relief. The camp was wired off into compounds and they confined us to a separate compound. They also cut down the food ration to an absolute minimum. On the 4th, the whole matter came to a head. They sent the original forms around to be signed again but no one would. They sent guards around to the officers' compound to round them all up and march them out of the camp. They then tackled the Yanks and told them that they would not guarantee their lives if they didn't sign. They all signed, and as it wasn't much good half the camp holding out, we followed suit. The officers were ordered to do so by the brigadier. We had been told by the Japs that the Brig had ordered to sign but we thought they were just putting it on. About 60 of our boys held out but they were ordered to sign by the Brig himself."
Alfred Burkitt, Java, 1942

Japanese reprisals against escaped prisoners were brutal. Little, if any, mercy was shown. The Japanese considered escaping to be "desertion from duty" and execution was the punishment given to a Japanese soldier who committed the same act.

"Then one morning a group of men were selected by the guard sergeant and marched off to be shot."

"Two of my men, Stan Raft and Bert Barrett, went out one night and were not missed until roll call next morning. One night nearly a week later they returned to camp and told me their story. They had intended to search for a boat so they could get away to Java or Sumatra, but before going very far they had been apprehended by a Jap soldier and taken into custody. Both were locked in an enclosed tennis court with several other British and Australian troops who had been caught under similar circumstances, and here they were kept for two days and nights without food or water.

"When Raft was questioned by a Jap officer, he told the Jap that he and Barrett were only out looking for food. The Jap believed this story and told Raft that he and Barrett would not be shot but that they would be returned to Changi after being suitably punished. For the next day or two the two lads were stood up at the guardhouse and subjected to severe beatings by the guards. Then one morning a group of men were selected by the guard sergeant and marched off to be shot. Raft was included in this group. He was marching out with the firing party when the officer to whom he had spoken previously spotted him. Halting the party, the officer ordered Raft back to the guardhouse and next day returned the two of them to Changi. They reported to me soon after arrival and told me of their experience.

"'Well,' I asked Raft, 'do you still think it worth making another attempt at escaping?' 'Not for me, Sir,' he replied. 'I've had enough.' His pal Barrett was of the same opinion. They still bore the marks of their beatings, and their experience had taught them a severe lesson. Neither they nor any other members of signals attempted to escape while I was at Changi, although a year or two later an unsuccessful attempt was made by one or two others."
Jim Jacobs, Singapore, 1942

"Major Bell and two others took off in an attempt to escape and they got well up the 'Line'. I'm not sure now how many weeks it was before they were caught, although one of them was caught pretty much straightaway. Anyway, they were all brought back and shot at Thanbyuzayat. Word had filtered down to us that they had been captured and there were no illusions as to what was going to happen to them, especially after eight of our anti-tankers were executed at Tavoy. It was either a bullet or the sword."
Ken Dumbrell, Burma, 1942

"One afternoon 'Pinhead' (a guard), ordered Sergeant O'Donnell of Queensland to go with him, as he intended to shoot an ox which was straying in the jungle. O'Donnell had no choice, and the two of them disappeared into the tangle of trees which grew right up to the track. When our day's work was finished and we were ready to return to camp, O'Donnell and Pinhead were still absent, so we went back to camp without them. As we were walking back we heard three shots in the distance, but did not pay much attention at the time as we knew that Pinhead was still out on his shooting spree.

"We had been back about half an hour or so when the guards came rushing over to our huts and ordered the whole camp to go on tenko (parade) at once. Lieutenant Colonel Anderson was informed that one of the prisoners had escaped. The guards were in a terrific flap, and rushed about all over the place demanding that the rolls

Adventurous black marketers would take the risk of escaping for a day in a rubbish bin to trade. Burma-Thai railway

Sketch by Fred Ransome Smith

be checked at once and the missing man's name reported.

"We all knew that O'Donnell was the missing man, but when Anderson tried to explain to Tanaka what had happened, Tanaka denied that Pinhead had taken one of the prisoners into the jungle with him and insisted that one of our men had tried to escape. He maintained that it was up to us to find out who the man was. The whole camp was furious at being kept standing on tenko for nearly two hours while this farce proceeded, because we knew full well that Tanaka was bluffing, but could not work out why. Finally we were allowed to break off and have our evening meal.

"Anderson was then sent for and told to accompany Tanaka and some of the guards. They went into the jungle, where Anderson was shown O'Donnell's dead body, lying on the bank of a creek. Tanaka said that O'Donnell had been shot attempting to escape, but an examination of the bullet wounds clearly showed that he had been shot in the chest, and that two more shots had then been fired at close range while he was lying on the sloping bank.

"Anderson pointed this out to Tanaka, who would not listen to any explanation other than that O'Donnell had been shot while he was attempting to escape. When Anderson pointed out that a man wearing only a pair of shorts, boots and a hat, and carrying no food or water, would not be so foolish as to try and escape, he was told not to argue. The beastly incident was the talk of the camp for days. Thereafter Pinhead lost his initial nickname and became known to one and all as 'Dillinger' after the notorious American gangster."
Jim Jacobs, Singapore, 1942

According to Cyril Gilbert, prisoners had plans to escape, but were often thwarted by frequent Japanese searches for equipment while those on work parties were regularly moved from camp to camp and had limited opportunities to hide equipment. The only cache of escape equipment near Gilbert's camp was hidden in a well that no one used.

"Well, we had these great ideas of escape when we left Singapore to go up by train. We thought we'd escape to Burma and then on to India, but when we got to Bam Pong to go into the huts, those that were in there before said: 'As soon as you get in there, they move all the people out and they go through your gear.' There was a well inside Bam Pong. What was in that well was nobody's business.

There were revolvers (and) everything underneath the sun in there, so they couldn't take them from your gear. If they found anything there, they'd confiscate it, and then you'd get a hell of a hiding. So it was nobody's business what was in that well."
Cyril Gilbert, Singapore, 1942

" We have roughly six or seven hundred miles to go. If we are caught we shall be shot, as that has been the policy of our hosts to date."

Max Benoit left this letter behind and requested that it be given to his mother if his escape attempt failed. Max and his mates were never heard of again.

"Dear Mum. If you receive this letter before hearing from me I shall not be coming home. At the time of writing I am somewhere in northern Thailand, very close to the Burma border. We have recently been shifted from Singapore, where until about two months ago I have been held prisoner. Our food up to date has not been good, the main item of our diet being rice, very little else. Myself and two mates have decided to attempt an escape. We consider we have at least a 50/50 chance of getting through, and reckon on making the trip inside three months before the monsoons set in. We have roughly six or seven hundred miles to go. If we are caught we shall be shot, as that has been the policy of our hosts to date. The three of us are in fairly good physical condition and have decided to go whilst we still have our health. About eight men in 10 are suffering from vitamin diseases and beriberi etc."
Max Benoit, Singapore, 1942

In 1944, John Prosser tasted freedom for 14 hours. On the way to a labour camp in Japan, his ship was sunk by Allied submarines. He and his mates had to continue their war against Japanese survivors who seemed hell-bent on killing them.

"It was pitch-black dark and the next thing I heard an (American) voice. 'Anyone around swim this way, swim this way and I'll keep calling so you can get a line on where I'm calling from.' He didn't seem very far away and he kept calling, 'Swim this way, swim this way.' So I kept swimming and I found a raft. They are not very big. I reckon six men could get on the raft. There was a looped rope right around the raft and there was four men each side. 'Grab a rope', he said to me. 'Are you English?' 'No,' I said, 'Aussie'. 'Right, grab that rope we'll work something out.' He said there were two or three fellas on the raft. 'They are knocked about a bit so just hang on if you're not knocked about.' I said no, I had got hit on the leg. He said we would wait till daylight and see what happens.

"Just on daylight some Japs came along and tried to knock some of our chaps in off the raft. They grabbed hold of it and were screaming and hollering. They nearly tipped the raft over and they did it twice. So this American he told me he was a commander and he'd been sunk twice. He'd been on a destroyer. He said: 'Any floating bits of wood around? You're not too bad. We'll pick up a length of wood and if those bastards (Americans say ba-stards, we say bar-stards) grab hold of this raft and try to tip it over again, smack them on the fingers. We're still at war, Aussie. It's got to be done'. They tried it again. We gave the Japs a few taps around the fingers. Eventually they let go."
John Prosser, Timor, 1942

Some prisoners who attempted to escape from Korean and Chinese POW camps during the Korean War were brutally bashed and deprived of necessities but others avoided severe reprisals. The following two incidents occurred during the march north of the battlefields.

"Corporal Buck, captured earlier was now at the 'Bean Camp' and together with the other Australians, Private R. ('Bob') Parker and Private K.W. ('Mo') Gwyther were marched off to Camp 5. As they moved northwards their minds turned to escape. Don Buck and Bob Parker and a Frenchman made their plans while Keith Gwyther and an American made theirs. The latter dropped out of the column somewhere to the east of Pyongyang on the seventh day of the march. They moved north towards the Taedong River, the course of which they followed for some distance until they found a small boat. They set off for the far shore, but unknowingly struck an island and after they were cast off the boat, they were forced to swim to the far shore.

"They headed westward for the coast, moving along the flats by night and aiming to reach a high feature where they could lie up during the day and observe the route for the following night's march. They were detected by an alert Chinese sentry, recaptured and gaoled along with delinquents from the Chinese People's

Volunteers. After a month in that gaol they were transferred to Camp 5, where they met Buck and Parker, as well as Tom Hollis. In the meantime Don Buck and Bob Parker had dropped out of the march on the second night and set off for the coast. They had scrounged a few vegetables and some bran, and with this managed to keep going for 11 days until they took refuge in a hut occupied by an aged Korean. He professed to dislike the Chinese and gave them every assistance, but they decided to move off. Not long afterwards they were intercepted by a North Korean patrol and after a brief but energetic pursuit were overtaken and forced to surrender. The POWs were bound tightly with wire and subjected to many indignities. Chinese troops 'rescued' them, untying them and taking them to Camp 12 via Camp 9. Surprisingly, they were not punished but eventually were moved to their original destination, Camp 5."

Phil Greville, Korea, 1952

"The foiled escapees were punished by being gaoled in the 'sweat box', a small cell four metres square and 2.5 metres high, with small windows set high on three sides and a heavy door with a grille on the fourth side."

Australian POWs in Korea found themselves in a situation similar to that experienced by their comrades in Japanese camps a decade earlier. Most Australians were of European descent which meant they had to move quickly to reach the front lines in South Korea. The risk with larger breakouts was keeping it quiet and trusting members in the escape party that they would not give the game away. This was not always successful, as Phil Greville recalls. "On 25th June, 1952, all four Australians were involved in a breakout of 24 UN POWs. It was organised by Corporal Buck. The parties escaped in small groups, intending to converge on a selected rendezvous. Keith Gwyther, using civilian skills, magnetised some wire for compasses. Unfortunately one UN POW withdrew at the last moment and informed the Chinese of the intended breakout. The Chinese were waiting at the rendezvous and captured all the escapees. The foiled escapees were punished by being gaoled in the 'sweat box', a small cell four metres square and 2.5 metres high, with small windows set high on three sides and a heavy door with a grille on the fourth side. Because of his part in organising the escape Corporal Buck was taken into the guard house and beaten frequently over a period of two weeks."

During the Boer War and WW1, escapees faced their own challenges. Many soldiers captured in Turkey were interned near Istanbul. Others were sent further east to Anatolia. Anyone who escaped was presented with the same problem later faced by Australians in Singapore in 1942 and afterwards in the Korean War. They were simply too conspicuous, which made it easy for the Turks to find them. One exception was one of Australia's first pilots Thomas White, who managed to board a cargo vessel heading to Odessa in 1918.

"Vladimir Vilkovsky was a Ukrainian aviator of Polish descent captured in a seaplane when operating with the Russian Black Sea fleet near Trebizond," White later recalled. "We had been close friends at Afion and, as he spoke seven languages and had a determined effort to escape in 1916, I had a profound respect for his ability and courage. Having heard that a Ukrainian ambassador from the newly-founded republic had arrived at Constantinople, he was endeavouring on the strength of his linguistic abilities to obtain the post of secretary. To this end he frequently contrived to interview the ambassador and on my behalf called on Theodore for news.

"We were to escape during the week commencing August 24th. We would make our way to a German beer garden "Zur Neuen Welt" in the Grand Rue de Galata. There we should meet a Russian civilian who would take us to a hiding place. We should know him because of a cigarette behind his left ear. When the Batoum was ready to sail we were to go abroad as stowaways. And for substantial bribes our fares to Odessa would be concealed by the ship's engineer."

Having received permission to visit a dentist, White fled to his rendezvous in the beer garden.

"Here was the man for whom I had waited so long! Almost hidden by his hair and the turned-down rim of his hat, I saw a ragged cigarette. As soon as I could catch his eye I placed a cigarette behind my ear, but he ignored the signal and did not look in my direction for some time. I ordered two drinks and sat down beside him before he could protest and asked him in Russian if he spoke that language. He curtly replied in the affirmative. 'Are you waiting

for somebody?' I suggested, at the same time placing the cigarette I was smoking in the assigned position. He seemed horribly frightened, his hands rapping nervously on the table's edge. 'I am one of the British officers you seek,' I assured him. 'But there were to be two', he muttered. 'The other was caught, or you would already have met him,' I replied. (His 'British' comrade, Bott, managed to also make the rendezvous later). I told him I would wait outside till he came out. He agreed, so we shook hands with many farewells as if our ways lay in different directions. Outside, I manoeuvred around shop windows until my new-found friend appeared, whereupon with no sign of recognition I followed him about twenty yards in rear. When darkness fell, the ship's officer we had seen at the waterfront took us to his cabin, where we drank glasses of sweet tea and smoked his excellent cigarettes."
Thomas White, Mesopotamia, 1915

"If this were done at many different points along the fence, some men would undoubtedly get away, and the others would undoubtedly be shot."

Further west in Germany, Australian prisoners were as keen to escape as their fellow prisoners would be 25 years later. The great breakout at Holzminden involved several Australian POWs. They tunnelled for nine months until escaping in the spring of 1918. Sixty Allied officers were supposed to break out but only 29 managed to get through before the tunnel collapsed. Of the 29, ten made it to neutral Holland. Australians played a key role. Stanley Purves, who later worked on the Sydney harbour bridge, made compasses and was one of the ten who made it to freedom. Dick Cash found photographic paper for identification papers.

Several Australians escaped successfully during the Boer War, making good use of the fact that they shared similar dress, appearance and language with the enemy. However, the main POW camp in Pretoria was well guarded, as American journalist Richard Davis noted later. "The chances of escape from the camp are almost impossible. It might be done, however, by tunnelling under the fence, or by cutting the wires of the tell-tale electric lights, and, after throwing mattresses over the barbed wire entanglements, scrambling over them into the darkness. If this were done at many different points along the fence, some men would undoubtedly get away, and the others would undoubtedly be shot." It is evident that a number of prisoners had not read Mr Davis's report as they did escape. Hugh Vernon identifies the members who made the successful escape in 1900: "M. Ford and G. Whittington were taken to Pretoria as prisoners. They escaped from the prisoners' lager at Waterval and, after gruelling experiences and hairbreadth escapes, reported to the British Consul at Lourenco Marques in neutral Portuguese territory three months later."

Any escape attempt is inherently risky. Australian prisoners of war knew they were risking punishment, torture or death. Yet many considered it their duty to at least make an attempt wherever possible. For some boredom or patriotism was the motivation. Others were simply desperate or frustrated by being held captive. Others needed to escape the violence and torture administered by their captors. Regardless of cause or reason, they craved freedom and came up with ingenious escape plans that ranged from the simple to the elaborate. Determined prisoners frequently pooled their knowledge and time to devise innovative ways of breaking out. Many succeeded but, sadly, many others paid the ultimate sacrifice for seeking to rejoin the battle or to see their country and loved ones again.

Chapter 7
War Crimes

"Prisoners of war must at all times be humanely treated. Any unlawful act or omission by the Detaining Power causing death or seriously endangering the health of a prisoner of war in its custody is prohibited, and will be regarded as a serious breach of the present Convention. In particular, no prisoner of war may be subjected to physical mutilation or to medical or scientific experiments of any kind which are not justified by the medical, dental or hospital treatment of the prisoner concerned and carried out in his interest. Likewise, prisoners of war must at all times be protected, particularly against acts of violence or intimidation and against insults and public curiosity. Measures of reprisal against prisoners of war are prohibited."

Article 13, third Geneva Convention

Found guilty of war crimes
German General Anton Dostler
is tied to a stake before his
execution by a firing squad

Julius Caesar murdered hundreds and thousands of men, women and children during his conquest of Gaul in 58—50 BC. He wasn't the first General responsible for mass murder of this kind, and he certainly wasn't the last. For a long time such acts were not considered war crimes as such, they were accepted as part of warfare. Whether murder of this kind was prompted by a thirst for revenge, ideology or simple logistics, genocide was an acceptable way of instilling fear in the hearts of surviving enemy and bringing them to heel. Prisoners captured by Mongols were used as target practice. Aztecs offered their prisoners as blood sacrifices. And at the battle of Agincourt, bound French prisoners had their throats cut when the English thought they were losing the battle.

From a modern European perspective – and where Australia has created its Army ethos – the concept of chivalry and mercy, along with the increasing size of the 19th and 20th century battlefields, ultimately led to the Hague and Geneva Conventions.

"The Japanese also forced many women into sexual slavery. While civilians bore the brunt of these crimes against humanity, torture and unlawful killing were also carried out against military personnel and POWs."

The suffering of hundreds of thousands of prisoners prompted the creation of Conventions that outlined universal and humane methods of detaining POWs. The term "war crime" was introduced in the fourth Geneva Convention after World War 2 as a direct result of the brutality of the Nazis and Japanese towards civilians and POWs. Article 147 defined war crimes as: "Wilful killing, torture or inhuman treatment, including wilfully causing great suffering or serious injury to body or health, unlawful deportation or transfer or unlawful confinement of a protected person, compelling a protected person to serve in the forces of a hostile power, or wilfully depriving a protected person of the rights of fair and regular trial, taking of hostages and extensive destruction and appropriation of property, not justified by military necessity and carried out unlawfully and wantonly". Under the fourth Convention the term "protected persons" was applied to civilians, but it is widely accepted that POWs are also included in this category as they were under the third Convention.

The war crimes committed by Japan and Germany before and during World War 2 are comparable in scale. It is estimated that Nazis killed more than six million Jews and this number rises to over 10 million when Soviet POWs and civilians are included in the count. It should be noted that when Stalin was in power, the Soviets inflicted similar atrocities against the Germans. The Japanese are believed to have massacred as many as 30 million people, including Filipinos, Malays, Vietnamese, Cambodians, Indonesians, Burmese and Chinese. Both regimes were responsible for mass looting in the countries they conquered. Both Japan and Germany enslaved millions of people and exploited them for forced labour. The Japanese also forced many women into sexual slavery. While civilians bore the brunt of these crimes against humanity, torture and unlawful killing were also carried out against military personnel and POWs.

The Geneva Convention is a treaty signed by nations that provide guidance for the conduct of war. It is not international law and not enforceable. However the "victor" in a conflict can use the articles contained in it as the basis for charges of war crimes. During World War 1 war crimes also occurred, for example the slaughter of more than 6,000 civilians during the invasion of Belgium by Germany in 1914. No war crime trials were held after that conflict ended, although there were international reviews which delivered punishment in the form of financial reparations for the losers. The scale and brutality of the World War 2 atrocities forced the occupying powers, including Australia, to act decisively on the conquered Axis powers.

At both the Nuremburg and Tokyo war crimes trials, high-ranking leaders such Hermann Goering and Hideki Tojo were charged with crimes against humanity. POWs pushed for individual guards to be tried for brutality, torture and murder. The Nazis committed relatively few war crimes against Australian POWs during WW2, with one of the worst incidents being the Gestapo's murder of five Australian prisoners from the "Great Escape" from Stalag Luft III in 1944. From an Australian perspective, the trials of Japanese perpetrators were paramount, in particular the ones relating to the Bangka Island massacre, the Sandakan death march and the consistent inhumane treatment of POWs throughout the war.

The Bangka Island massacre occurred on 16th February, 1942. Japanese soldiers machine gunned 22 Australian military nurses in cold blood, leaving only one survivor. The nurses had left

Singapore four days earlier on board the merchant ship *Vyner Brooke*, just before the city fell to the Japanese. The ship, carrying many injured soldiers and 65 Australian nurses, was bombed and sunk. Twenty-two nurses reached the shores of Bangka Island where they were joined by another group of soldiers and civilian men and women. The island was held by the Japanese and some of the survivors went off to surrender, leaving the nurses to care for the wounded on the beach. They were found a short time later by ten Japanese soldiers led by an officer. The soldiers forced those amongst the wounded who were capable of walking to move around a headland where they were murdered. Then the Japanese soldiers returned to the beach and ordered the nurses into the surf where all but one were shot in the back and killed.

Sister Vivian Bullwinkel was shot, but not killed. She feigned death until the Japanese soldiers left. She evaded capture for 10 days and only surrendered because a wounded soldier she found faced certain death without medical attention. She was reunited with other *Vyner Brooke* survivors and survived the war. In 1947 she gave evidence about the massacre at a war crimes trial in Tokyo.

" It is the aim not to allow the escape of a single one, to annihilate them all, and not to leave any traces."

The Japanese War Ministry was adamant that the Imperial Army should dispose of its prisoners when they could no longer function as slave labour. During the Tokyo trials a damning government directive was put forward as evidence. Issued in 1944, it read: "When the battle situation becomes urgent the POWs will be concentrated and confined in their location and kept under heavy guard until preparations for the final disposition will be made. Although the basic aim is to act under superior orders, individual disposition may be made in certain circumstances. Whether they are destroyed individually or in groups, and whether it is accomplished by means of mass bombing, poisonous smoke, poisons, drowning, or decapitation, dispose of them as the situation dictates. It is the aim not to allow the escape of a single one, to annihilate them all, and not to leave any traces."

The Sandakan death march in 1945 was based on this directive. Almost 2,500 Allied soldiers were forced to march from Sandakan to Ranau. Only six survived. The prisoners had been shipped to the Sandakan camp in North Borneo to build an airstrip. In January

1945 the advancing Allies bombed the airfield which prompted the Japanese commander, Captain Susumi Hoshijima, to move the remaining prisoners west to the town of Ranau – almost 260 kilometres away. The first to leave were the fittest prisoners who carried the Japanese equipment for their relocation to the western coast. Over the next few months the remainder of the prisoners began their march. Those too weak to leave Sandakan were shot. Those who fell during the march and were incapable of continuing were shot. By the time they reached Ranau, only 38 were still alive. They were too weak to work so the order was given to kill them all. The only survivors were six Australians who escaped the march. Just three survived the ordeal and gave evidence at the war tribunal.

"I've seen men shot and bayoneted to death because they could not keep up with the party. We climbed this mountain about 30 miles out from Ranau, and we lost five men on that mountain in half a day. They shot five of them because they couldn't continue. But I just kept plodding along. It was dense jungle, I was heartbroken; but I thought there was safety in numbers. I just kept going."
Keith Botterill, Singapore, 1942

"Men from my own party could not go on. Bauto was the first place we actually had to leave anyone. They remained there, at this Jap dump. At the next place, at the bottom of a big hill, we left two more men. Later, we heard shots, and we thought the two men must have been shot. In all of my dealings with the Japanese, I have never seen any one of our chaps after they had been left with the Japs. Once you stopped, you stopped for good."
William "Dick" Moxham, Singapore, 1942

"If blokes just couldn't go on, we shook hands with them, and said, 'Hope everything's all right'. But they knew what was going to happen. There was nothing you could do. You just had to keep yourself going. More or less survival of the fittest."
Nelson Short, Singapore, 1942

Not all war crimes were committed on such a mass scale. Many crimes were inflicted on POWs on a daily basis. Guards carried out killings, torture, brutal bashings and even systematic cannibalism. Many written reports and testimonies collected by the Australian War Crimes Section of the Tokyo tribunal found the Japanese were involved in acts of cannibalism on a significant scale. An Indian POW testified: "The Japanese started selecting prisoners and every day one prisoner was taken out and killed and eaten by the soldiers. I personally saw this happen and about 100 prisoners were eaten at this place by the Japanese."

"From the amount of blood around it was clear that this savagery had been perpetrated while he was still alive."

Jack Thorpe had an inkling of what to expect after the murder of a POW was reported during fighting in Java. "We loaded our trucks with men and headed for the inland city of Bandung. When everyone had got clear, a group went back to retrieve any surviving members of the rear guard that had been covering our retreat. They were appalled to discover the disembowelled body of Captain Haines tied to a tree. From the amount of blood around it was clear that this savagery had been perpetrated while he was still alive. This was grim news for everyone. One of our own had died a horrible death and our enemy seemed intent on letting us know that similar barbarism awaited us if we fell into their hands – which seemed almost inevitable."

Following his capture, Jack Thorpe worked on the Burma-Thai Railway and recalls two occasions when Japanese guards murdered Australian prisoners. "One of the worst guards was nicknamed 'Dillinger' for a very appropriate reason; the man was a cold-blooded killer who had shot a man as he was relieving himself on a working party out from the 18 Kilo camp. The man had been given permission for a toilet break but didn't return. A search party went looking for him and he was found dead, shot in the head and chest. Dillinger admitted to killing him but claimed the man, who was carrying nothing and was next to naked, had been attempting to escape. The man had been shot at close range and from the front but Dillinger's explanation seemed to satisfy his Japanese officers. They moved him to a different camp for a while, reinforcing our belief that as far as the Japs were concerned it was open season on POWs. Simply put, the Japs saw us as dead men walking."

In the second instance, an Australian was murdered by firing squad after a failed escape attempt. Jack's description of this man's defiance inspired his mates. "The Japs then stood the man on the edge of the grave and the Japanese officer went up to him to put a blindfold over his eyes. He gave that Jap officer an almighty whack across the face and said to him, 'I don't want a blindfold, you bloody bastard. My mates will get you all and kill the bloody lot of you. You can fire away now!' I knew the two men who dug the grave and witnessed the execution very well and they told me about the man's courageous and defiant death."

"you simply couldn't work them out. I know hate is a terrible word, but I'll never forgive and I'll never forget."

Others Australian POWs recalled similar crimes at the hands of the Japanese:

"I was good friends with Mickie, a lovely bloke, a larrikin. He mixed with anybody. He was put in charge of a working party, but he got very sick and was sent to hospital. Apparently, some of the blokes from his group went into the bush and hid and didn't go out on the job. The Japs did a count and found out, so they got Mickie out of the hospital and, because he was in charge of those men, gave him a brutal bashing. I didn't see it. I remember one of the blokes in our tent was on the line up, so I asked him what had happened and he said, 'I don't want to talk about it.' They carried Mickie into hospital, but he was terribly battered. After Mickie died the next day, I was coming back from work and I remember talking to a bloke from the 11th Platoon, Mickie's platoon. 'They killed our cobber' (he said). That's the saddest memory I have got. To be bashed to death. I mean, it's one thing if you get a few slaps across the face, it's another thing to be bashed to death."
Arch Flanagan, Singapore, 1942

"A working party for the aerodrome was needed to replace the men who had gone there after we had landed at Mergui and were now moving on. Arthur and I were included in the party; we hiked out there and met up with our company commander and others. They told a graphic story of their experiences. It appeared that after they arrived at the Tavoy River three months earlier they had been forced to march something 60 kilometres to the aerodrome with no food. Exhausted on arrival, they were quartered in a hangar where the floor was entirely covered with a great quantity of large and small stones. They were given several bashings and little food, and with conditions so dreadful, a group of eight men decided

In effect by the Australian Militia

New Guinea. 1943.
A photograph
found on the body
of a dead Japanese
soldier showing Sgt
Leonard Siffleet
of "M" Special
Unit, wearing a
blindfold and with
his arms tied, about
to be beheaded
with a sword by
Yasuno Chikao

AWM Neg. 101099

Japanese
facing war
crimes
tribunals
H98.103/4690

that they would die if they stayed there and tried to escape. The Japanese however had offered a bounty to local sympathisers for the return of any escapees. They were all captured, tried and shot in spite of the vigorous protests of Brigadier Varley, the senior Australian officer."
Gordon Nelson, Singapore, 1942

"I do remember a terrible incident this one night. It can get cold of a night up there and so a few blokes were sitting around a fire. They heard some Australians marching past our camp, so two of our blokes went to the front of the camp to see if there were any anti-tank boys with them. For no reason that made any sense, the Japs grabbed these two blokes and shoved them back towards the fire. Then, with bayonets in their backs, they would not allow them to move from the fires edge. Jack had his shirt on and that saved him really, but the other fellow was that badly burnt; he died soon after. That's the sort of sadistic thing they did and you never knew which way they would go; you simply couldn't work them out. I know hate is a terrible word, but I'll never forgive and I'll never forget."
Jim Kerr, Singapore, 1942

"The Japanese rounded up quite a lot of people. Les McCann did not know too much about it, but he said there were about 15 of them and they were taken out to a big ditch, lined up facing the ditch and then they were shot in the back. That was on Thursday 19th February, 1942 at Pasir Panjang. When Les came to, everyone else was dead so he went off. He had a bit of a pinhole in his back but there was a hell of a mess in the front of his chest where the bullet came out and ripped him apart. He wandered around and a Japanese picked him up. When Les came through to us he told the officers his story, but they would not believe him. They said: 'Who was there that you know?'

"He said, 'The only bloke I know was Fred Airey, our Regimental Sergeant Major.' Our officers were never too sure about Les's tale, but a few months later the Java party came up, these were the people taken prisoner on Java. Word came through that Airey was with the Java party. So, of course, the officers raced over there and said, 'Righto, what's this tale we had heard about you being lined up and shot by a firing squad?' Fred Airey said: 'I have never ever mentioned that since it happened – they would knock me off quick and lively if they knew. How do you know?' And they told him about McCann, and he said: 'That's right'."

"Fred said the Japanese lined them up then with the first volley the Japanese fired into them. They were all falling over so he took a dive. He went down in the ditch and lay still, he did not move at all. He said after they were all down some of the blokes were moving about a bit. Then the Japanese came through and shot them again. Luckily McCann was out to it so he did not move. Fred said he waited until after the Japanese had gone, then had a look around and said everyone was dead so he took off. He made it down as far as Java. If he had not turned up no one would have believed McCann's tale."
Walter "Wally" Holding, Singapore, 1942

"Naito (a Japanese soldier) was a complete drunkard and in the whole time we were there I never once saw him sober. He used to drink Burmese whisky made by the coolies, who, I was told, made it out of anything they could find. Anyhow, this incident first occurred during our time at the 75 Kilo camp and it was repeated many times after, at both the 75 and 105 Kilo camps. Naito arrived back at the camp late one night, drunk as usual and riding his big black horse. He spotted a POW on his way to a piss-a-phone – a urinal made out of a piece of bamboo sunk into the ground. Naito pointed his revolver at the man and told him to run. By this time everyone in the hut was awake. The POW turned to run towards the hut, but Naito told him to run towards the jungle. As soon as he did Naito shot him for trying to escape. The man was a murdering mongrel."
Jack Thorpe, Java, 1942

"Meals were poor and light on and when two chaps went looking for food outside the school, they were caught. They were treated as escapees and ended up being shot in spite of strenuous efforts by our colonel to intercede for their lives. That was the first occasion we had faced brutality of this kind and it greatly shocked and upset us. It particularly hit the colonel and his officers, as they found themselves unable to make any impression on the Japanese commander."
Gordon Nelson, Singapore, 1942

Crimes were also committed against non-combatants regardless of whether they were men, women or children. Jack Thorpe recalls four heart-wrenching accounts of brutality dished out by the Japanese.

"She'd been stripped of clothing and tied down on this freshly-cut bamboo. Over there, when bamboo is cut it will grow about twenty centimetres overnight."

"I also witnessed many brutal crimes carried out by the Japanese against civilians. An awful event occurred during my time at the 105 Kilo camp. The Japs used to let four men go into the jungle every day to get firewood for our cookhouse. No Japs went with them, because there was nowhere the POWs could escape to. It was a permanent job for these men and they'd been at it for many months. Anyhow, this day while they were getting wood a little Burmese girl appeared from out of the jungle. She gave these men a letter with the latest news written in English, and then just disappeared. Rather than reading the letter and then destroying it, one of the men kept the letter on his person somewhere. They headed back to camp just before dark but were stopped and searched when they came in. The Japs found the note and the men received a terrible bashing. You could hear it going on all night.

"Morning arrived and we saw the men going off into the jungle as usual. We thought it was a bit odd, the Japs letting them continue with their jobs. Anyway, the men kept going out to work as usual for about four days. On the fifth day we came home from work and there was a little Burmese girl tied up outside the guardhouse. She only looked about nine or ten years old. That night, and for a couple of nights after that, the guards took her into their quarters. Then one day, instead of being tied up outside the guardhouse we saw her in a clump of bamboos. She'd been stripped of clothing and tied down on this freshly-cut bamboo. Over there, when bamboo is cut it will grow about twenty centimetres overnight. One of these bamboo shoots grew up inside her and that is how she died."
Jack Thorpe, Java, 1942

"When we were working on the wharf in Saigon we began encountering a young French girl on our way to work. She was between 16-18 years old, blonde, and the most beautiful girl you could ever wish to see. She usually rode a pushbike and I can vividly remember the first time she spoke to us. She had ridden past several times before so she was just another person until one day as she was passing she spoke in English and asked who we were. We told her we were Australian; she gave a big smile before pushing on past us. Several days passed and she was back again, this time giving us a bit of news about the war. We told her it was too risky to verbally relay news. She had to ride so close to us the Japs would soon realise that there was something going on.

"Several days passed before we saw her again. This time she just rode past us fairly fast and flicked a message wrapped around a small stone. It was how the war was progressing. This went on for a few weeks, then one day we were lined up in the road outside our camp waiting to be searched and counted when we noticed that there were more Japs than usual hanging around. Some were standing behind trucks and cars and they all had rifles. We thought that they might have been waiting for this girl but we hadn't seen her for a few days. Anyhow, we saw her in the distance and the Japs started moving around which indicated that it was her they'd been waiting for. Most of the Japs were in front of us, so some of our men could give her the signal to get going. When she saw it she started pedalling fast in the opposite direction but by then it was too late. They did not shoot her, but one of the Japs threw his rifle at her and knocked her off her bike.

"The Japs were proper mongrels in the way they handled her that evening. They took her into the guardhouse and she was crying out in English. 'Help me! Somebody help me!' And we couldn't do a thing about it with 30 armed Japs just looking for a reason to do a bit of target practice. We'd been held outside the compound while all this was going on. Suddenly the Japs said we could come in. Our Australian officer said to us before we entered the compound, 'They have tied this girl up under the tree near the guardhouse and the Japs will probably want us to look at her. You know what to do, fellas.' I have never felt prouder to be an Australian than that day when those Japanese bastards tried to make us look at this girl stripped naked and bleeding around the body. There was not one man who lifted his head and we were there for hours. Finally we were dismissed and no man spoke a word. They just walked to where their bed was on the floor and sat there in silence. She may have been dead when she was tied to the tree, I don't know, and we never saw her again. I'll guarantee that no man who was there will ever forget her and what happened to her."
Jack Thorpe, Java, 1942

"We were back in Singapore and had been cleaning up the area around the Ford motor factory for a couple of weeks when a terrible massacre occurred one afternoon. We'd been loaded onto

NLA vn4227531

Vivian Bullwinkel at Puckapunyal Army Camp, Victoria, before she left for Singapore, 1941

Vivian Bullwinkel giving evidence at a war crimes trial relating to the Bangka Island Massacre
NLA vna4227532

trucks to go back to camp, and all the workers in the factory had knocked off, so the road was full of workers walking shoulder to shoulder down the hill. Previously, they'd all gone home by the time we left but this day we'd finished early. We were in the first truck and there were others behind us, but when the driver of our truck saw all the workers, instead of blowing his horn, he pushed the accelerator down and deliberately ran the workers down. To make matters worse, he changed gear to get over the bodies piled up underneath the truck.

"He eventually stopped and you never saw such a mess of mangled, smashed and bloody human beings. They nearly all spoke English and were asking for us to help them. However, there was nothing we could do but pull them to the side of the road. What clothes we had on were only rags, so we couldn't attend to their wounds. Apart from this, the Japs wouldn't let us help them at all. Even when we were only moving them the Japs were bashing us with their rifle butts. After clearing a path through the dead and dying we headed back to camp. Most of those workers had been Chinese."
Jack Thorpe, Java, 1942

"We were back working on the wharves again and one morning before they loaded us on the trucks the Japanese officer in charge gave us a talking to. We were not working hard enough and not doing as we were told. This morning he was going to show us what would happen to us if we didn't work harder. They drove us through the Chinese part of Singapore and there on the side of the road, on stakes about a metre high, were all these heads of Chinese men. We were told that they had been punished for disobeying the Japanese.

"The night before, we had heard a few very large explosions down towards the harbour, but hadn't taken any notice because we were hearing them all the time. But apparently these explosions were from Japanese war ships being blown up in the harbour. The ones that were blown up were ships that had a hard time in battle and were being repaired by Chinese shipwrights. The Japanese blamed the shipwrights, but they were too cunning to lop the lollies off the shipwrights because they needed them. So they went into Chinatown and grabbed thirty or forty innocent Chinese men and chopped their heads off – naturally showing them to the shipwrights. The dreadful irony about this incident is that it wasn't the shipwrights who had blown up the ships but

those bloody Australian commandos, Z Force, on their boat *The Krait*. Of course we didn't learn this until we came home."
Jack Thorpe, Java, 1942

"Toyama never got as far as any court martial for war crimes or anything else. They told them the whole story about him so they took him out and shot him."

The Japanese inflicted slow starvation and appalling treatment on a daily basis to POWs throughout all its camps in the Asia Pacific theatre. The brutal and cold-blooded disregard for human life brought bout the greatest surge of outrage from survivors. Those fortunate enough to survive as a Japanese POW testified in war crimes trials. Many Japanese soldiers did not make it to trial. They either committed ritual suicide or were the recipients of "justice" outside the courtroom from survivors who had been incarcerated. Walter Holding recalls one such revenge attack on a brutal guard nicknamed the 'Little Bastard', who for years had murdered and beat POWs.

"After the war finished everyone volunteered to go and pick Toyama out of the camp, but the authorities gave Captain Gwynne the job. Toyama never got as far as any court martial for war crimes or anything else. They told them the whole story about him so they took him out and shot him."

An Australian Army doctor, Harry Windsor, was on the team set up to treat POWs when the war ended. He experienced intense disgust and loathing for the condition in which he found many Australian POWs. This man of healing officially recommended that the guards, the Kempeitai (military police) and all of the Japanese involved in their treatment, "be forthwith slowly and painfully butchered".

Some of the Japanese responsible had their crimes recorded at trial, and the frank accounts of their actions show not only their callousness but also how orders had come to them from high up in the Imperial Army.

"We were ordered by the admiral to kill them on the following day, for he had received a report informing him that the POWs

at Soeakodo were restive. In compliance with this order, I took about 30 other ranks to Soeakodo. I cannot recall now from which platoons these men were selected. We dug holes in a coconut plantation about 200 metres from Soeakodo in the direction of the airfield and killed the POWs with swords and bayonets. It began at 10am and took about two hours. I divided my men into three groups, the first for moving them out of the house in which they were confined, the second for preventing disorder on their way to the plantation, the third for beheading or bayoneting them. The POWs were sent to the spot one by one and made to kneel, with their eyes bandaged. Our men of the third group came out in turn, one at a time, to behead the POW with a sword or to bayonet him through the chest."
Company Commander Nakagawa, Laha, 1942

" One of the most significant trials and convictions involved the Japanese Prime Minister Hideki Tojo. Following Japan's unconditional surrender in 1945."

On occasion, some Japanese were found not guilty of war crimes. During the investigation of Major Katsumura's execution of Australian POWs, it was found that the POWs where not carrying military identification, so they could in fact be identified as spies as specified by the Hague Convention. An extract of a research paper, *The Australian War Crimes Trials and Investigations (1942-51)* by D.C.S. Sissons outlines the reason behind this.

"The Commander of the Bogor Detachment of the Military Police (Major Katsumura) and five of his NCOs were charged with the unlawful execution of a group of three escaped POWs (two Australian, one Dutch) in hiding and a woman member of the Dutch underground who had been harbouring them. The POWs had escaped from a camp at Batavia in May 1942 and had remained at large for more than a year. The Bogor Detachment on 12 August 1943 captured the three hiding in a concealed cellar in the house of a Dutch resident and on September 5th executed them and the woman by decapitation. Katsumura, the NCO in charge of the execution party, and the four executioners were tried by an Australian court at Singapore in September 1946 on a charge of 'committing a war crime in that they at or near Bogor on 5/9/43 in violation of the laws and usages of war were concerned in the unlawful killing of the four victims.'

"The Prosecution contended that the victims had been executed without trial in contravention of Article 30 of the Hague Rules 30 which provides that 'a spy taken in the act shall not be punished without previous trial'. Katsumura testified that following the arrest of the prisoners he had despatched the completed proforma and the attached testimony to Military Police HQ at Batavia which on September 3rd notified him that the C-in-C's (Commander in Chief) sanction had been obtained and instructed him to perform the executions.

"The Defence argued that in these circumstances the accused was entitled to believe that 'a trial by documents' had been performed which satisfied the requirements of Hague Convention Article 30. The Australian court made the following finding: 'The Court finds you not guilty. The court in its finding is guided by the amendment to Para 443 (as amended), Manual of Military Law, Page 288, Australian Edition'."

One of the most significant trials and convictions involved the Japanese Prime Minister Hideki Tojo. Following Japan's unconditional surrender in 1945, US General Douglas MacArthur ordered the arrest of the first 40 alleged war criminals, including Tojo. He was arrested after a failed suicide attempt and charged with numerous crimes including the ordering, authorising, and permitting of inhumane treatment of POWs and others. He was found guilty and sentenced to death. Before being hanged on 23rd December, 1948 he apologised for Japanese military atrocities and asked that the Americans be lenient towards the Japanese people whose lives had been devastated by the Allied bombing campaign and two atomic explosions. Two former Prime Ministers, Koki Hirota and Kuniaki Koiso, were also convicted. Many high-ranking officials were tried and convicted but the US administration and senior officers such as MacArthur have been widely criticised for exonerating Emperor Hirohito and members of the Imperial family from criminal prosecution.

For Australian POWs there was some consolation in knowing that many war criminals were brought to justice. Twenty-five people were tried as Class-A war criminals by the International Military Tribunal for the Far East. These became known as the "Tokyo Trials". Another 5,700 were indicted as Class-B or Class-C war criminals. A total of 920 were executed and 475 were sentenced to life in prison. The Allies imprisoned another 2,944, while 1,018 were acquitted. The remaining 279 escaped sentence or were not tried. Other trials were held around the Asia Pacific region, including Australia, who charged 924 Japanese personnel. Of those, 144 were executed and 280 were acquitted. The remainder were given prison terms.

Many perpetrators of war crimes were acquitted due to technicalities in the legal system. This apparent "failure of justice" did little to mend the mental and physical wounds of those who had been subjected to such barbaric behaviour. Cyril Gilbert lived as a POW and experienced the same suffering. He was not alone when he expressed his feelings: "I always maintained the only good Jap's a dead bastard."

"The harsh discipline at PG57 by the Italians kept us on our toes. A soldier nicknamed 'Old Socks' was shot because he stood up too fast to salute a guard."

During World War 2, POWs in Italian camps were treated roughly and some claim inhumanely. However, any breaches of the Geneva Conventions in this instance were generally isolated cases. This, along with Italy's capitulation and swift change of sides, is probably why there were no war crimes prosecutions in that country. Although more than a thousand Italians were indicted, they were not prosecuted. Having your freedom taken away by being held captive as a POW is traumatic enough. Enduring the excessive punishment and deprivation of liberty that the Geneva Conventions are supposed to protect against is inconceivable. For those who experienced or witnessed such incidents in Italian camps, the fact that no justice was served was like rubbing salt into an open wound.

"As the Italian capitulation began to take place, history shows that part of the agreement was that Allied POWs were to be returned. Remember we were in a compound farthermost to the south of Italy. Three days before the capitulation was announced everyone at Campo 65 was loaded onto a train, then battle trucks, and taken to Germany. The main reason we were not handed over to the Allies was that if the Allies had seen us, the Italians would have been charged with war crimes, as we were in a very bad way."
William Hoffman, El Alamein, 1942

"The harsh discipline at PG57 by the Italians kept us on our toes. A soldier nicknamed 'Old Socks' was shot because he stood up too fast to salute a guard. He was one of the older men sitting down when a guard came along and gave him a prod with a bayonet as he said: '*Attenzione*' (stand to attention). He stood up quickly and was shot. The guard's excuse was that he thought he was being attacked. There was another incident. During the cold winters our huts were only lit either when the Red Cross would come to inspect the camp or when you could steal some wood. Jack Richardson returned with a couple of sticks of wood from the cookhouse. He was bailed up by one of the guards, with their dog (they only used dogs at night), who demanded to know what he was doing. 'Just stealing a piece of wood,' he replied, thinking at worst he would get a week's solitary confinement. Without warning the guard shot Jack in the chest. They then allowed the men in a nearby hut to come out on the porch. The guards said, 'That's what's going to happen if we find anyone out at night. We will shoot you dead.' In the morning, when they came for Jack's body, he was still alive."
John McWilliams, El Alamein, 1942

"You could be punished for anything, and I mean literally anything. You could be punished for failing to salute a corporal. You could be punished for smiling or laughing. The Italians didn't like to be laughed at and they would dream up all sorts of punishments such as making you stand still out in the cold or sending you to the 'boob' or cutting all of your hair off – any little thing they think would annoy you.

"The Italians were like every other nationality: the good, bad and the indifferent. The Italian civilians up in the working camps were wonderful people, most generous, and they were very sorry for us because we were POWs and we were away from our family. But then their sympathies were not with Mussolini because basically they were communist and the communists were opposed to the fascists. In the camps it depended on your guards. We had one lot of guards who had fought in Russia for the Germans. They were totally different to the little blokes from southern Italy. All in all we did not have the trauma that the Japanese POWs had, nor the trauma that the Germans POWs had, but once you lost your liberty everything is a trauma.

"This camp was a notorious camp. In fact, the commandant, Colonel Kalkitera, was eventually on the list to be executed as a war criminal. However, the partisans got in first and disposed of

Executions carried out with a certain grim intensity. German officers felt a contempt for the Untermensch, the "sub-human" Slav

Soldiers at the start of the Bataab death march

the gallant colonel. He disliked Australians so much that he had a sign printed over his office saying that there was nothing worse than an Australian. However, we had different opinions."
Doug LeFevre, El Alamein, 1942

"This camp was very close to Auschwitz and death surrounded us daily. Some of the sights: trains (full) of naked bodies, men, women and children, black bodies. I could not explain the condition of those alive."

There were few cases of war crimes committed by German captors against Australian POWs. However, a great many Russian prisoners suffered the same fate as the six million Jews and Slavs in concentration camps. Many POWs witnessed these atrocities. Archie Whitehead, captured at Crete, recalls, "The Russians were in the camp next to us. Some of them were shot. They tried to get out. You see, they never got Red Cross support. We helped them a bit, not much though. They would try to get out and they were killed. You'd see some of them dead in the wire the next morning. There was an Australian shot, but I don't know what happened. He disobeyed a command and I heard he was given a lot of orders and he disobeyed them too and was shot. That was the one bloke I remember. I never saw it. But they were pretty annoyed about it, our boys that saw it."

In 1943 the German guards threatened POWs with Japanese-like reprisals – death for those that escaped, as well as for the POWs left behind. Most soldiers decided not to take the risk. But the threat of reprisals was in direct violation to the Geneva Convention. Ray Middleton remembers: "Following Allied successes in Sicily, the Italians changed sides – and we awoke to find German troops had ousted Italians round the wire. Those out working in many cases fared better, and many reached Switzerland and some fought with partisans. We became German propaganda, a 'British captured in Italy', and were given a rough time. In batches of 50 we were marched to trains, every exit guarded heavily, and warned that if one escaped, the rest of the group died."

Others POWs recall the crimes they witnessed or heard about:

"A transit camp was established for the Soviet prisoners in a

shed a few hundred metres from the railway station. According to members of our working parties in that area these Russians were in far worse condition – starved and scarcely able to walk. They were herded into already crowded sheds at bayonet point. There was one mess parade a day. At the meal point stood German NCOs with stock whips. The NCOs applied the whips and, as those in the front row broke away to avoid the blows, those following would receive the lashes. This was kept up for a few minutes then the prisoners were left to fight amongst themselves for the food. The mortality rate was horrific but the corpses presented no problem: huge pits were already dug on the hillside. Into these the bodies were thrown, sprinkled with lime and covered with earth but only lightly. The pits were intended to accept many layers of bodies. There was no medical treatment for the Russians, so all of those unable to work were left to die on the floor of the shed in which they were confined."
Ralph Churches, Greece, 1941

"As we approached the town of Kraljevo there was a strong smell of freshly baked bread. On pulling into the station, the local population thrust or threw still-hot loaves into the wagons. My own wagon accommodated 30 troops, and we received 36 loaves. They also threw wine, cakes, eggs and sugar, all of which was like manna from heaven. This station is 120 kilometres from Belgrade. It was very upsetting to learn after the war that some months after we had passed through Kraljevo, the Germans perpetrated horrific massacres upon these same people in revenge for the casualties inflicted on the occupying Germans by partisans. Their orders were to kill 100 Yugoslavs for every German killed in that fighting and 50 for every German wounded. These orders were carried out meticulously on several occasions during late 1941."
John Crooks, Greece, 1941

"One train went to Austria, we learnt later, to a big camp there. Ours unloaded us for a week in a siding deep in a valley in the Alps, with snow on peaks far above. It was in this transit camp where we first met bed bugs – and were they hungry! A mass grave beside the railway marked, we were told, a site where a locked trainload of Russians and Ukrainians arrived after three weeks without food or water, sometime in July or August."
Ray Middleton, El Alamein, 1942

"We were moved to Koningstadt (Glyweiz) to work in a factory. This camp was very close to Auschwitz and death surrounded us daily.

Some of the sights: trains (full) of naked bodies, men, women and children, black bodies. I could not explain the condition of those alive. It was here that we were issued with two cakes of green soap. At the Nuremberg trials it was revealed that the soap had been made from the residue fat of burnt bodies at Auschwitz. How do you clean that off?"
William Hoffman, El Alamein, 1942

As the end of the war drew near and the Russians pushed forward into Germany, the Nazis began to move POW slave labour and Allied prisoners from the east to the west. This labour force was estimated to be more than a million people. Moving such a large number of people was beyond Germany's capability at this late stage of the war. A number of these moves became known as the "Death Marches". William Hoffman, who was captured at El Alamein in 1942, remembers with horror the toll that was taken on him and the people around him:

"One day we returned from work and were told to be ready to march out the next morning. We did not know at the time where we would be marched to, but it was back into Germany and it became known as the 'Death March'. We joined other prisoners, such as Russians, political prisoners, those who were capable of walking from the notorious Auschwitz, plus civilians from many nationalities. We were escorted by Hitler Youth. It was winter and I was about 6.5 stone, but none of us Aussies were in top condition. But the condition of other people was horrific. Some, usually a civilian, died every 10 feet, or was shot if they fell. I had seen plenty of death but it was here that I saw the most horrific scenes and callous acts by a German.

"A Polish Jewish girl was heavily pregnant and in labour pain. She collapsed. Her stomach was slit open and the baby's head was crushed by the boot of a guard then she was shot. Not by the Gestapo but by Hitler Youth, who formed the guard on the Death March. I hope they were eventually captured by the Russians who gave Germans a serve, something that the Allies didn't do."

A significant number of Germans faced prosecution at the Nuremberg trials for some of the worst cases of war crimes. A number of cases related to the execution of Allied POWs (mainly British, French, Canadian and US soldiers) by Hitler's SS troops. A number of the perpetrators of some of the worst crimes against humanity – the Holocaust, the occupation of Poland, the annihilation of the Czech city of Lidice, the treatment of Soviet POWs, and the extermination of the Slavic population – were brought to justice.

After the war the new German government did stand up and take responsibility for the country's actions and ensured that the truth of this horrible time was published in the nation's history books. It listed more than 60,000 war criminals and provided their details to the Allies. Since that war Germany has paid more than $80 billion in reparations and compensation and has also apologised for the Holocaust.

During World War 1, some POWs were more concerned about disease than being worked to death. For prisoners in Turkish camps, disease and their captors' lack of care was distressing and life-threatening. One in four Australians held by the Turks died in captivity. George Handsley, who was captured at Romani in 1916, believed the Turks saved him from torture by the Bedouins soon after his capture. Prisoners were forced to march hundreds of kilometers with little food, water and no medical attention. These marches directly contributed to the extreme death rate.

Handsley recalled: "They looked very fierce (the Bedouins) and wanted to torture us, but our escort seemed to have influence over them and they departed, grumbling at being deprived of the opportunity to venge themselves on the hated infidel. When dawn came we resumed our march and all were feeling very hungry. Our appeals to the sentries for food were met with sneers and it sent us mad seeing our tormentors eat their fill while we poor wretches remained almost starving. This journey still lives in my memory as the most awful in all my experience. We were almost dead on arrival at Afyonkarahisar on the morning of 27 August, 23 days after my capture, during which time I can only recollect one square meal, namely the one in the hospital at Jerusalem."

Australian prisoners in German camps appear to have faced rough treatment and received little food, but there were few deliberate killings or war crimes. Of the 3,853 Australians captured by the Germans, 310 – about one in 12 – died in captivity. However, POWs were kept near military targets which was a direct breach of the Hague Convention. As a result, Australians were shelled and killed by their own men.

AWM Neg. 121782

Squadron Leader F. G. Birchall, interrogating Hosotani Naoji, Sandakan Kenpeitai (Japanese Military Police), with the assistance of an Allied translator. The Japanese prisoner confessed to shooting two Australians and five Chinese civilians

Labuan Island, North West Borneo 1945-12-20.
War crimes trials of Japanese officers of the
Borneo POWs
AWM Neg. 123170

"As I looked at the object I could see it was in the shape of a man. He turned his head and looked down at me and said, 'You'll be okay, mate.'"

During the Korean War, prisoners' rights under the Geneva Convention were again disregarded as they were subject to physical abuse, psychological torture and brainwashing by their Chinese and North Korean guards. Such breaches are by definition "war crimes", and yet the perpetrators never faced justice.

William "Slim" Madden died from the effects of his maltreatment and was posthumously awarded the George Cross. He bought food from civilians and shared it with his mates during a long and brutal winter march. His mate, Ron Guthrie, recalls him saying, "I won't become fertiliser for their rice fields" during the 300 kilometres march. Sadly, Madden was beaten and deprived of food for his defiance and non-compliance. To his mates, he died a hero.

His George Cross citation reads: "Testimonials have been provided by officers and men from many units of the Commonwealth and allied forces which showed that the heroism he displayed was outstanding. Despite repeated beatings and many other forms of ill-treatment inflicted because of his defiance to his captors, Private Madden remained cheerful and optimistic. Although deprived of food because of his behaviour, resulting in malnutrition, he was known to share his meagre supplies purchased from Koreans with other prisoners who were sick. This did not deter him and for six months, although becoming progressively weaker, he remained undaunted in his resistance. He would in no way co-operate with the enemy. This gallant soldier's outstanding heroism was an inspiration to all his fellow prisoners."

Another mate, Bob Parker, recalls a final "visit" from his mate while he was in a prison at the end of the march. "It was a cold day and I was in my room, lying flat on my back, wide awake because of the freezing cold. I was staring up at the ceiling when in through the place where the wall joined the ceiling floated this figure. It was moving from right to left, and some sort of glow surrounded it.

"As I looked at the object I could see it was in the shape of a man. He turned his head and looked down at me and said, 'You'll be okay, mate.' It was Slim Madden, and I can still see him to this day. It was a most spiritually moving experience, because I didn't know at the time that Slim had passed on."

As the end of the war came in sight the Chinese were determined to demonstrate to the United Nations that they had been honourable combatants not war criminals. They asked POWs, before their release, if they had had personal items taken from them and were at pains to return them before being repatriated. The night before Eric Donnelly was released, a Chinese officer visited him. "He asked me if I had lost any possessions while I had been a prisoner of the People's Liberation Army (PLA). I told him that I lost a Ronson cigarette lighter, a silver ring and my army belt. These items had been taken off me shortly after my capture by the soldiers in the front line bunker. The officer noted down what I had told him and said he would go and look for these items.

"He came back later in the night and told me that he had been unable to locate my Ronson lighter or my silver ring. He said that the army belt was a prize of war and I would not be getting that back. He also said that he would have to take me off the 'Exchange List' until they had been able to locate my possessions. This alarmed me, as I thought it might be a plan to have me taken off the Exchange List. I told the officer that the light and ring didn't matter to me and not to worry about trying to trace them. The Chinese officer said that it was very important that I get back my possessions as the People's Liberation Army were not thieves.

"He left me to continue his search for the missing items and I wished that I had never mentioned them to him. I was absolutely convinced I would be taken off the list and be left behind. The Chinese Possessions Officer came back about two hours later and said he had a proposition to put to me. By this time I kept breaking out in a cold sweat trying to think of plausible reasons for not wanting my gear back. I managed to ask him what his proposition was, without seeming too eager. He held out this beautiful silver lighter with dragons embossed all over its surface and asked me if I would accept it in place of my Ronson. He said a Chinese officer had donated his lighter to show how honest the PLA were in their dealings with the prisoners of war. I didn't hesitate in accepting his offer and left a message that when my Ronson lighter was found, as I had no doubt it would be, it was to be given to the officer who had given me his dragon lighter. The only thing that stood in the way of my release now was the damned ring I had reported missing."
Eric Donnelly, Korea, 1953

It would be wrong to claim that the Allies did not commit a single crime during the course of war. They did, and that was inexcusable. At Biscari airfield in Sicily, US soldiers massacred more than 70 German and Italian POWs. In the Asia Pacific region many Japanese dead were found to have been desecrated or mutilated. The Soviet Union's actions in expelling German troops and pursuing them back to Berlin involved some horrendous crimes against humanity. For such deplorable acts, only a small percentage of Allied personnel faced war crimes tribunals.

Gaining justice for crimes committed against POWs is important. POWs from all sides are vulnerable and almost always exist without people in support. Justice provides a sense of closure and can go some way to helping mend the scars of war. It provides an opportunity to air the facts and have the perpetrators reveal their reasons, however shocking, for inflicting such horror and pain on other human beings. Although justice will never completely answer the question: "Why?" it does enable us to gain a better understanding of circumstances. Hopefully with this knowledge comes wisdom which may bring us a few steps closer to a world where the term "war crime" is as redundant as the word "war".

Chapter 8
Freedom

"The following shall be repatriated directly:
(1) Incurably wounded and sick whose mental
or physical fitness seems to have been gravely
diminished. (2) Wounded and sick who, according
to medical opinion, are not likely to recover within
one year, whose condition requires treatment and
whose mental or physical fitness seems to have
been gravely diminished. (3) Wounded and sick who
have recovered, but whose mental or physical
fitness seems to have been gravely and permanently
diminished."

Article 110, third Geneva Convention

"Prisoners of war shall be released and repatriated
without delay after the cessation of active
hostilities."

Article 118, third Geneva Convention

Soldiers along
the Burma rail
camps wander free
after surrender of
Japanese, 1945
H98.103/3435

A soldier is trained to survive. The skills and drills learned in training and in the field help keep them alive on the battlefield. But there is no survival manual to consult if they are captured. To survive incarceration they must rely on what they've already learned and the values etched into their psyche. The glue holding the whole experience together is the individual's attitude and mental resilience – their determination to survive, their resolve to retain an intact spirit and the belief that one day they will be free again. All POWs dream of freedom. It occupies their day and their night. For some, hopes of making it through turned to dread as the war they had fought neared an end. In Europe during WW2, POWs were concerned that as the Allied air raids drew closer they might be killed by friendly fire. In the Asia Pacific, they feared the Japanese might slaughter them all in a final act of defiance. In fact, in August 1944, the Japanese government had ordered the execution of all POWs if the Allies came close to capturing a prison camp. In some cases, like the Sandakan death marches, this was carried out. Gerard Veitch recalls the fears he and his fellow prisoners had in early August, 1945. "We had our suspicions (or perhaps realised) that things were not going well for the Japs as they had working parties going over to Johor Bahru digging mass holes, which we presumed were to be our graves. The Japs had told us that no POWs were to be released alive." Fortunately for Gerard and his mates this did not eventuate.

"Dozens of jeeps and American tanks lined the road with the occupants tossing out cigarettes and chocolate."

Whether a war ends with surrender as it did in WW1 and WW2, or a stalemate as it did in Korea, freedom is one step closer. For prisoners, details of ceasefires, surrenders and the progress of war were hard to discover. Many only heard of the surrender the day before, or when their guards suddenly disappeared. Others remained oblivious to their change in status for days or weeks until news finally filtered through to their remote camps. Their freedom could arrive suddenly – when they walked out of a camp abandoned by guards, or if they were liberated by Allied forces. Sometimes the POWs took over the camp when the guards "surrendered". Realising that they had in fact survived was a moving moment. Nelson Short was one of only six men to survive the Sandakan death march. He was taken in by local inhabitants of the jungle. He recalled his relief when he heard footsteps coming towards him in the jungle and discovered they were friendly.

"We said, 'Hello, what's this? Is this Japs coming to get us? They've taken us to the Japs, or what?' But sure enough it was our blokes. We looked up and there are these big six-footers. Z Force. Boy, oh boy. All in greens. They had these stretchers and they shot them down. 'Have a cup of tea. Some biscuits'. You could see the state we were in. I cried, they all cried. It was wonderful. I'll never forget it. We all sat down and had a cup of tea together."

Nelson's story is not unusual. Many others experienced similar emotions.

"Ten days after our arrival the great day finally occurred and we heard the events leading up to 29th April, 1945 officially. The camp kommandant became uneasy with the arrival of a do-or-die SS unit that was to defend the town, which was a key road and rail centre. He called in a senior officer, whether American or British I do not recollect, and at midnight on 28th April they crossed the American lines under a flag of truce to see the American commander and so endeavour to arrange a surrender of the camp.

"The war was over with no hope of success for Germany, but the SS units were marked men for their support of the Nazi regime. Around 11.30 hours loud cheering came from the *Lagerstrasse* and we flocked out to see the cause. Dozens of jeeps and American tanks lined the road with the occupants tossing out cigarettes and chocolate. Again they appeared a scruffy lot, the jeeps only holding one or two at the most, the rest of the space taken up with kit and loot. We were not impressed, though deeply grateful for their part in freeing us. It was marvellous. We had won! Despite all the setbacks earlier in the war we always knew we were going to win. We just had to beat those bastards whatever happened."
Ron Lister, Crete, 1941

"We got up next morning and here's the two Red Cross flags flying out of the churchyard. We knew it was over."
Archie Whitehead, Crete, 1941

"At about 6pm on 26th August, 1945, I was in the hospital giving vitamin B powders to the patients. The next thing I heard was our adjutant, Captain Clive Newnham, running across the parade ground from the Japanese guardhouse shouting, 'It's over. The war has finished.' I threw the rest of the powders in the air and shouted, 'You won't need these.' The camp was in an uproar. Groups of friends were excitedly laughing and hugging one another.

I remember Neil McKeller, Allen Brownley and myself had a small green pumpkin growing, but it was soon in the cooking pot and eaten. I don't think anyone slept that night, as we were all planning what we would eat and do when we arrived home. Next day an American plane flew over and dropped three American soldiers by parachute but we never saw them till the next day as the Japs wouldn't allow them in. But they defied the Japs and came in and they sent planes down and dropped food, cigarettes, etc. and we were like kings smoking Camel cigarettes one after another."
Tom Pledger, Ambon, 1942

"When the British came within view of the barbed wire enclosures, the prisoners burst out cheering and during the next few hours were headed to safety, with the Boers shelling them and the 100 warders alike, and also a hospital train for the sick. The prisoners were too excited to assist in their own getting away, which lasted until after dark. Captain Nicholson and two troops of the NSW Lancers did good work in the fight of 400 of the brigade against 2,000 Boers."
Hugh Vernon, South Africa, 1900

"The war's end for us was an anticlimax. The Japs just seemed to disappear and we were told we were now free. It was a case of prisoner last night, free this morning."
Richard Armstrong, Singapore, 1942

"Then the news came. Emperor Hirohito had agreed to the terms of the Potsdam Convention (surrender treaty). The war with the Japanese had ceased, aided by the dropping of a bomb on both Hiroshima and Nagasaki. The almost overwhelming relief amongst all prisoners of war in Changi was clear to see. Even the 'Skinnies Hut' that housed those fellows whose weight was half their pre-POW weight was filled with excited conversation."
Bill Flowers, Singapore, 1942

"I considered myself free on 15th August, 1945, when I was with a work party near Changi collecting barbed wire to be used for fencing. The news came over a secret radio called a 'bird'. The truck driver with us told us the war was over. The barbed wire was then used to fence the Japanese in. They immediately became POWs and we no longer had to work for them. It was lovely."
Willoby "Bill" Wharton, Singapore, 1942

" I wanted to believe the news, I could not face the nerve-shattering disappointment which would have followed had I buoyed myself with hope, and then found the war was not over after all."

News of freedom came to POWs via leaflets, radio broadcasts or even just a change in their treatment. Gordon Nelson wasn't sure how the war was progressing but he suspected something was up when the attitude of the Japanese changed and supplies improved. "Early in August there was an obvious change in the attitude of the Japanese administration," he recalled. "Some clothes were issued and even medical supplies were said to be coming. By and large, bashings had ceased and a good deal more mail was distributed. In addition, food parcels were handed out in a more generous quantity than ever before."

Not surprisingly rumours of an end to the war would sweep through the camps. Many POWs simply would not let their hopes rise for fear they would be shattered if the rumour was found to be false. For self-preservation purposes many chose to wait for more concrete evidence. They knew they would be alerted by an air-drop of leaflets confirming the war was over and instructions about what to do. Below are the contents of a leaflet that was dropped in a Japanese-run POW camp in Korea in 1945 as well as some recollections of the POWs about what they felt when they realised they had probably made it.

Allied Prisoners of War & Civilian Internees, these are your orders and/or instructions in case there is a capitulation of the Japanese forces:

1. You are to remain in your camp area until you receive further instructions from this headquarters.

2. Law & order will be maintained in the camp area.

3. In case of a Japanese surrender there will be allied occupational forces sent into your camp to care for your needs and eventual evacuation to your homes. You must help by remaining in the area in which we now know you are located.

4. Camp leaders are charged with these responsibilities.

The end is near. Do not be disheartened. We are thinking of you. Plans are under way to assist you at the earliest possible moment.

Signed: Lieutenant General A.C. Wedemeyer, USA."

"Wednesday 15th August, 1945 was a day which will live forever in the memory of every prisoner of war in Siam. For us at Kanburi it was a day crammed with excitement and incident. In the morning while we were getting ready to pack, a rumour that the war had ended spread round the camp like wildfire. A few days before a friendly Korean had told us that Japan had asked for an armistice, but we had treated the information with reserve. We had been caught so often with false rumours that nothing short of an official announcement would convince us. So, when Lieutenant Meynell Davies came into our hut, did a war dance, and announced that the war was over, most of us just went on packing. I must confess to a tight feeling in the chest, due to suppressed excitement. I just could not bear to be disappointed, so I forced myself not to believe it. Desperately though I wanted to believe the news, I could not face the nerve-shattering disappointment which would have followed had I buoyed myself with hope, and then found the war was not over after all. I feverishly concentrated on my packing, and tried to think of other things. My efforts were not very successful, for all the time a little gremlin kept whispering to me: 'It must be true. It is true. Why don't you believe it? Don't you understand? You're free, free, free!'"
Jim Jacobs, Singapore, 1942

"I stayed on that party, 'P' party as it was called, working in town right through till the war finished. We came in one evening, went through the usual search, walked right down the side of the jail parallel with Changi Road and as we went round the corner 'Speed', Lieutenant Graham McKinnon, was there jumping up and down saying, 'The war is over, the war is over.' He was told in plain English where to go. We said we would find out when the work party lists come out. Sure enough that night the work party lists came out and there were still 200 men on 'P' party. Later on that night the details started to come through about the atomic bomb and everything else going on outside. The next day our mob dropped pamphlets, telling us that the Japanese had surrendered unconditionally."
Walter "Wally" Holding, Singapore, 1942

"Twelve large bags of medical supplies arrived on the 18th August, more than the total of what we had seen during the last three years. It was absolutely criminal the way they held onto that Red Cross stuff while men were dying through the lack of it. After lunch on the 18th, we all turned to look at one of our Liberators flying around. He came in very low and while we were all cheering and waving anything we could lay our hands on, all the Jap AA guns opened up all around us. Fortunately, he got away all right after dropping some leaflets, but it was very disconcerting to us. By evening, we had arranged to get one of the leaflets into the camp and learnt that the war was really over and that a Red Cross delegation was on its way to look after us. It also said that we must remain under Jap control until the Army authorities arrived and took over. We were officially told the war was over on the 19th. A Jap sergeant rushed into the camp and told us as though it had just happened."
Alfred Burkitt, Java, 1942

"Then the Americans arrived, I think they were Marines. It was a wonderful sight to see them come, to march into the camp, and they told us: 'We'll look after the buggers now.'"

Although they knew they would soon be free, the POWs still had a lot of work to do. Camp order and discipline had to be maintained and food and medical supplies gathered to ensure the prisoners remained fed and healthy while they waited for the repatriation force to arrive. Prisoners also had to make sure they did not over-indulge. Many had spent years on a limited diet and their bodies would not immediately cope with large quantities of food. Some of the leaflets dropped on camps spelled this out:

To all Allied prisoners of war

The Japanese forces have surrendered unconditionally and the war is over

We will get supplies to you as soon as is humanly possible and will make arrangements to get you out but, owing to the distances involved, it may be some time before we can achieve this.

YOU will help us and yourselves if you act as follows:

(1) Stay in your camp until you get further orders from us.

(2) Start preparing nominal rolls of personnel, giving fullest particulars.

(3) List your most urgent necessities.

(4) If you have been starved or underfed for long periods DO NOT eat large quantities of solid food, fruit or vegetables at first. It is dangerous for you to do so. Small quantities at frequent intervals are much safer and will strengthen you far more quickly. For those who are really ill or very weak, fluids such as broth and soup, making use of the water in which rice and other foods have been boiled, are the best. Gifts of food from the local population should be cooked. We want to get you back home quickly, safe and sound, and we do not want to risk your chances from diarrhoea, dysentery and cholera at this last stage.

(5) Local authorities and/or Allied officers will take charge of your affairs in a very short time. Be guided by their advice.

Finding food was made a little easier as Allied planes dropped critical supplies by parachute to those camps that repatriating forces would find hard to reach. The stronger men took the opportunity to get out of camp and see the sights or barter with the locals for food.

"Early in August 1945 you could tell that the war was just about over. Dozens and dozens of Flying Fortresses would fly over every day and you would rarely see a Japanese fighter plane. Then the news came that we did not have to go down into the mine and we thought that was very unusual. We would walk past a guard and never bow; they never said anything and looked real sad. I think about three days after that an American fighter plane flew over and dropped a message and we managed to retrieve it. The message told us that the war was over. It was from General Macarthur's headquarters. Eventually one fine day an American found an old mirror, a big old mirror in a house and he climbed up one of the barrack buildings and kept flashing it. He was a signaller in the United States Navy. Two or three B29s came over and they

dropped a lot of foodstuffs, footwear, clothing, cigarettes, chewing gum and K rations by parachute. That was a great day. That was nearly two weeks after the surrender. Then the Americans arrived, I think they were Marines. It was a wonderful sight to see them come, to march into the camp, and they told us: 'We'll look after the buggers now.'"
John Prosser, Timor, 1942

"The Padre held a thanksgiving service that evening. We sang the National Anthem for the first time in three and a half years. On the 21st, a Jap colonel came and inspected the camp and they were rushing food into the kitchen all day. We also got a packet of cigarettes per man. We shifted to the dock camp on the 23rd as the chaps from there had moved into large French barracks. We certainly had plenty of room but the place had been left filthy and it was quite a while before we could get it cleaned up decently. Typhoid fever had broken out in the camp and we had the sixth death on the 24th. We held a flag service on the 25th. We put up three flag poles and flew the Union Jack, the Australian and Dutch flags. I was up all night making ours. The Japs were rushing in all sorts of clothing, blankets, boots, mess tins, soap and tons of stuff that we really didn't need. Most of it was being 'flogged' to the natives over the back fence as fast as it came in the front. Quite a lot of our boys were going out through the fence at night. The Japs didn't worry very much but the Annamese (majority ethnic group in Vietnam) got a bit nasty about it and had even chased some of the boys with knives. On the 28th we got permission to have a route march for exercise and about 450 of us marched right through the city and French quarters. What a wonderful reception we got. All the French people lined the streets cheering and singing and they gave us everything they could lay their hands on. Everyone was loaded up with food, drink and cigarettes. Some of the boys even finished up with live poultry. We couldn't have got a greater reception nor had a better victory march if we had been home."
Alfred Burkitt, Java, 1942

"The next day our mob dropped pamphlets telling us that the Japanese had surrendered unconditionally. Instructions were not to leave camp which was as good as telling the boys to get going. Shortly after that other people started to come in. The Red Cross women came around. The first thing they did was give you a packet of cigarettes and a great big bar of chocolate, which was bloody stupid when you think about it. We would see some poor

After the Japanese surrender in 1945 the captors became the captives

Japanese
surrender

bloke, as skinny as a rake, get a great big block of chocolate and eat it quickly, then be violently sick. When we left Changi to get on the boat to come home I remember the sight of the Gurkhas, who came down with the 14th Army, wandering around with rifles over their shoulders standing guard over the Japs weeding the gardens and sweeping the streets – it was a bloody lovely sight."
Walter "Wally" Holding, Singapore, 1942

"The Yanks came in. And they were saying to us all the time on this radio: 'Stay put, stay put.' A lot of fellas didn't, they buzzed off. Some went down to Italy and some went all over the place, but I was mainly interested in getting home. So we stopped at this place and we weren't there that long when the Yanks came in with trucks and we were taken to Salzburg. We flew out from there and went across to Rheims in France. And we got there and the Yanks treated us like royalty and we were taken food and Yankee uniforms. The Germans were there and all cleaning your boots and things like that for you."
John Hawkes, El Alamein, 1942

Doug Nix and some mates were working near a dynamite factory in Austria when news of approaching Allied forces came through. Local residents thought they would be the ideal representatives to ensure the town was taken peacefully. Nix and his mates were given the use of a car.

"We got in the car and drove down the road, and come around the corner, and there sitting in the middle of the road was a big old Matilda (tank), and she's waving the gun-piece around. Any rate, next minute the turret opened and this lieutenant got up and said, 'Who are you blokes? You've got a British ensign on you.' 'We're ex-prisoners of war from the dynamite factory up the road.' He said, 'We're looking for that.' Now these blokes had a list of everything they were after, right? They were British field security police, and they could come into an area and they could reel off the names of people they were after. He said, 'Well, you turn around and we'll follow you.' And away we went back to the place, and we handed it to them. All the people were standing near the gate of the dynamite factory when they came up in their tank and I went and was doing a bit of interrogation with the field security police before the British Army put up notices everywhere stating all ex-prisoners of war that are on the loose in this area have to report to a British unit."

When Germany surrendered in April 1945 more Allied forces were free to take the fight to the Japanese. British forces defeated the Japanese in Burma and moved on to Rangoon at the same time as the Americans took Iwo Jima and Okinawa in their drive to Japan. On July 11th, the Allied leaders met in Potsdam, Germany. They confirmed earlier agreements on Germany and reiterated the demand for unconditional surrender by Japan, specifically stating that "the alternative for Japan is prompt and utter destruction". Yet Japan still would not surrender. In response, the US dropped atomic bombs on the Japanese cities of Hiroshima and Nagasaki in early August. On August 15th, 1945 Japan surrendered. WW2 was over.

"I shouted to them to leave their rifles on the back of the truck and line up on the side of the road - and blow me down if they didn't do just that! They were terribly frightened."

Jack Thorpe and his POW mates witnessed the devastation wreaked by the second atomic bomb on Nagasaki. Previously, some of them had seen flames on the night horizon as Thorpe finished a shift down a mine. One mate commented that Tojo (the Japanese Prime Minister) must have been copping a hiding that day. Shortly after their guards lined them up in front of machineguns and argued about murdering them. Later the guards dismissed the POWs and then left the camp for good. Were they avoiding war crime recriminations or did they simply wish to go back to their families? Certainly, it would have been difficult to carry out such a crime after the Emperor had officially ordered the surrender. The reprisals on Japanese soil would have been dramatic and the guards must have known this.

No longer underguard, Jack and his mates decided to commandeer a truck to go in search of some food. What were his chances? Unarmed and in Japan a couple of days after more than 80,000 people had been vaporised in Nagasaki, he was lucky to stay a free man, as he recalls:

"I was the one designated to stop the vehicle and talk to the driver as my Japanese was better than the others. I walked out into the middle of the road to stop it and as it got closer I realised that it was a Japanese Army truck. It was too late to change our minds, so I went straight up to the driver and told him and his co-driver

Atomic
bomb at
Nagasaki

Nagasaki after
atomic bomb

to get out and stand on the edge of the road. Then I realised there were six armed Japanese soldiers in the back. I shouted to them to leave their rifles on the back of the truck and line up on the side of the road – and blow me down if they didn't do just that! They were terribly frightened. We took their watches off them – after all the Japanese Imperial Army hadn't yet returned ours – and what money they had. Then we hopped in the truck and headed for the camp, laughing all the way about how three unarmed Aussie POWs each weighing seven stone (44 kilograms) had bluffed eight Japanese soldiers. It looked as if the war was definitely over.

"On the way back we saw a camp much the same as ours and we thought we might call in and see who was there – it might have other POWs. So I turned into the road leading to the camp and as I got closer I saw that there was a Japanese soldier on duty at the guardhouse. I couldn't turn around as there were two deep drains and then swampy paddy fields on either side of the road. The guard saw the Japanese Army truck coming and shouldered his rifle to salute the truck. Suddenly he realised that it was being driven by either POWs or foreign soldiers. He let out an enormous yell and threw his rifle away. After that, there were soldiers running everywhere. The camp was surrounded by paddy fields and soon it didn't matter where you looked there were Jap soldiers running through the paddy fields. We went through the huts to see what we could find. Some of the officers in the camp had left their swords behind and we each collected three as souvenirs.

"This great plane lumbered over our hut. You could see the crew looking out and waving. It did a turn and then came back and started dropping food in 44 gallon drums with parachutes attached. The parachutes were all different colours and gave the event a note of festivity. I brought back a piece of a yellow one as a souvenir. Unfortunately, half the parachutes didn't open and the drums smashed on hitting the ground. Included in that first food drop, along with the vitamins and the spam and tinned fruit, were cigarettes and matches. And so what did a man do? He got hold of a packet of cigarettes and a box of matches and promptly started smoking again – after not having been near a cigarette for three years!

"One morning soon after this an American parachutist walked into the camp. We hadn't been aware of a plane in the area and I don't know where he dropped. We'd never seen anything like him – not even in comics or the movies. He was over six feet tall, had a machinegun strapped across his back, two revolvers in his belt, two big knives in his socks or puttees and a radio on his hat. He wanted to see the camp commander and we all stood around for the next hour or so to hear what he had to say. The conversation got around to Nagasaki and Captain Moore told him what we'd seen on our trip there a day or so earlier and our opinion that it would have taken hundreds of planes to have delivered that amount of devastation. The paratrooper said: 'No, that was only one bomb. It killed over a hundred thousand people.' We all laughed and told each other he was another bullshitting Yank.

"So we stayed three or four more days and then we were told we were going down to Nagasaki. So we left on a train fairly early in the morning and it took a long, long while to get down to Nagasaki. They'd repaired the line fairly well. (Where there) used to be suburbs of Nagasaki, there was nothing, it was just flattened. Even the pine trees on the hills surrounding the city were scorched. Anyhow, the train took us right into the port area. Fortunately, whether it was planned that way when they dropped the bomb I would not know, but that area wasn't so badly damaged. It still had a few port facilities. There was a band (that) played the American national anthem and then it played 'Waltzing Matilda', and an American Army girl with doughnuts and hot coffee. So we had that when we got off the train which was good. We were told not to walk into the city."

Captured at El Alamein in 1942, Ray Middleton and other POWs were being herded away from American troops advancing through southern Germany. Conditions near the end of the German winter were harsh and some POWs died of exhaustion and lack of food. Sensing that their liberators were near, Middleton and two mates decided to break away from the march and hide.

"On April 24, 1945 all prisoners were 'roused' at dawn and put on the road without even a count. I dived into the haystack, as did two Tommies, and waited there quietly for several hours, watching a convoy of tanks, sandbagged at the turrets against rockets, manned by fit-looking types in coal scuttle helmets. We three (were) wondering where Jerry got all this equipment when I saw US and a white star on each gun-barrel. 'It's the Yanks!' I called out and ran downstairs, realising they'd changed from the British-style steel helmet. We were greeted with, 'Hiya! Have a carton of smokes, fellas. Any of you want to come along and interpret for us?' We declined – German not up to required standard – and set out along the line of the incoming column, a continuous line of trucks and men. First, we stopped and asked a German hausfrau to prepare a meal for us. This she did, and while we ate, an alert Yank with Tommy gun burst in, searching for hiding troops. Our paybooks, accents and uniforms convinced him we weren't escaping Nazis. Before long we found a jeep going against the traffic, with space for us, and heading for Nuremburg, so grabbed it at once."

" To see us freshly shaven, with manicured hands and fresh clean pyjamas and wearing little blue caps, you would be excused for thinking that we had been released from a rest camp."

Some soldiers taken prisoner during the Korean War returned home thanks to POW exchanges like Operation "Little Switch". For others freedom came after the armistice in 1953. Eric Donnelly was exchanged as a wounded POW after being captured in January 1953. He saw the People's Liberation Army (PLA) trying to get propaganda mileage out of the exercise. Just as the Japanese suddenly "found" Red Cross parcels after surrendering in 1945, the PLA abruptly began handing over articles to the POWs that were required under the Geneva Conventions just before the exchange. While cynical of the whole charade, he was happy just to get home.

"We were taken from Freedom Hall and put into a big and shiny ambulance that was a lot easier to ride in than the steel floor of a five-ton truck," Donnelly recalled. "No more breakages for my plaster cast at their conveyance. The communists left our side for dead, in the show they put on, for the world's press waiting at Panmunjon to record the changeover of the wounded and sick.

"To see us freshly shaven, with manicured hands and fresh clean pyjamas and wearing little blue caps, you would be excused for thinking that we had been released from a rest camp. The big ambulances and all the goodies such as cigarettes, chocolates, soap, toothpaste and little mirrors all piled on top of the blankets that covered us, added to the great illusion that was recorded by the world's press covering this historic event.

"From Panmunjon I was flown encased in a plastic bubble attached to the landing skid of an army helicopter to Seoul where American doctors gave us a thorough going over. My plaster was cut off and the colony of body lice which had eaten their way into the flesh above my right knee seemed to number in the thousands. An American nurse who had helped take off the plaster cast became quite ill when she saw the lice and the damage they had done. They were quickly dealt with and the terrible creepy crawly feeling that I had put up with for the last couple of months became a memory. I was wounded and taken prisoner of war on 14th January, 1953 and released three months later on 23rd April, 1953. I had lost five stone in weight during this period of imprisonment."

George Handsley, captured at Romani in 1916, knew that World War 1 was coming to an end when his captors' behaviour towards him verged on pleasant. Turkey signed for peace before Germany, due in no small part, to Australia's own Light Horse Brigades spearhead in Beersheeba, Jerusalem and Damascus. The efforts of Handsley's Light Horse "brothers" helped secure Turkey's surrender and his early release. "We stayed at Ushak until about 1st November, 1918; and as soon as word came through that the Turks had given in, we were allowed to roam around town as we pleased. But things were so bad in Turkey, shortage of food and money, that we did not have a very good time waiting to be repatriated."

Captured in France in 1917, Justin Dawson learned of his liberation from the workers and sailors in Kiel who joined the KPD (Communist Party of Germany) and took over the city. The German government ordered the Baltic high seas fleet based at Kiel to sea for one final attack on the Allies in the English Channel. The sailors decided to stay and mutinied. Although Dawson was a POW, he was considered a comrade rather than the enemy, a worker forced to fight for the bourgeoisie. As a comrade he was treated well. The Kiel mutiny was crushed by discharged German soldiers returning home in December 1918 and January 1919. These Freikorps (free corps) soldiers were still armed with their front line weapons. Luckily Dawson had left in December just before the fighting began.

"On November 5th, four days before the general revolution took place, the navy mutinied and our little *lager* (camp) came under the red flag. From that time we did no work and were allowed out without sentries. We promenaded all over the countryside and into Kiel and generally enjoyed ourselves. After 10 months inside the barbed wire, never out of sight of sentries with rifles, it was unbridled joy to get out at last. We inundated Kiel and were treated as friends by the populace, chatted to the girls in vile German and invaded the postcard shops and pub, which all had music. As one person said to me, 'That is one thing we have plenty of in Germany, if nothing else.' There was much misery to be seen in Kiel, poor little pinched kiddies, who followed us about in the hope of getting a biscuit. All round the district the youngsters looked upon us as sort of fairy godfathers who sometimes had food to give away.

"We quite took charge of Kiel and nobody minded. I saw a crowd of our fellows marching through one of the main streets singing, of all the jingo songs, 'Sons of the Sea', and the Germans who understood only laughed. A very short while before this, we got orders to pack up and go to Gustrow for transportation. Of course, we thought that we were bound for Blighty straightaway, but we were doomed to disappointment. We spent a beastly, tedious month marching about the camp, and the town of Gustrow. A nice old-fashioned town, but being so fed up with everything German, we were not interested."

"Their reaction was a studied calmness, accompanied by quiet smiles, born of long waiting and many disappointments."

At the end of WW2, John Crooks was hoping his and other POWs' liberation from Stalag VIIIA would pass without incident. He had already seen prisoners killed by Allied air attacks in Bavaria. To try and prevent it happening again the POWs arranged permission to display a Red Cross flag.

"On 27th and 28th April, the bombing in the vicinity of the camp increased and on the morning of the 28th the Americans could be seen with the aid of some binoculars produced by somebody; they were setting up some guns on a distant hillside. At this stage, discipline vis-à-vis the Germans had all but disappeared, except as regards any attempt to escape. For example, most of the supports of the inter-compound fences had disappeared for use as firewood, as had a good deal of the flooring in some of the buildings.

"This particular day had started, for me, by being detailed with Fergie Ferguson to find some civilians to attend the water supply pumping station, which seemed to have stopped working. But no one was there, nor was a soul to be seen anywhere nearby. I reported that it seemed that the locals had been warned to make themselves scarce before the arrival of the advancing American forces, which we knew were very close, and because of the probability of the hostilities that would follow their appearance.

"As soon as I had reported this and as though someone above had heard me, a voice from Heaven, per medium of a loudhailer on an American spotter plane, advised us to 'stay inside, and keep your heads down'. There followed the sound of guns and small-arms fire for about an hour then the first sign of our liberation – the tank which rolled through the gates. It was immediately set upon by a crowd of noisy and highly excited American POWs anxious to greet their countrymen. Their reaction was in marked contrast to that of the long-time prisoners, particularly the Brits, who had been captive for up to five years. Their reaction was a studied calmness, accompanied by quiet smiles, born of long waiting and many disappointments. The Americans had for the most part endured a small fraction of the length of confinement of these former captives."

Even as the end of the war drew closer, prisoners were still willing to try to escape. After five failed attempts Keith Hooper was ready for one more. He didn't expect an encounter with the "enemy" which would highlight the futility of war for him.

"I think that was the sixth time I tried to escape. I remember we got through the wire and there was a German guard there and he took no notice. I think the guards knew by that time that they'd had it. So we set off down through the woods. We ran into the spearhead of a tank unit, the American tank unit of the 83rd Division and I always remember we thought at first they were Germans and then we saw the white star on the tank and we thought, *Nah, can't be Germans*. We got down there and Frankie, who was much older than me – he'd be in his 40s, I suppose, I was about 23 then – got hold of this tank commander. The tank commander was a lieutenant and Frankie got hold of his hand. He wouldn't let the hand go and he's trying to talk and he can't get a word out and the tears were streaming out of his eyes.

"We said to the Americans, 'Now, where do we go to be repatriated?'

" A nine-year-old Japanese boy's drawing of American planes dropping food to us POWS at Izuka. He copied the English writing on the plane with impressive accuracy, as well as the fact that some drums broke free of their parachutes." Given to Jack Thorpe in Japan on liberation

Camp 22 at Iizuka. This photo was taken after the Japanese surrender. Note the PW painted on the roof in lime according to instruction pamphlets dropped by a US bomber

And this lieutenant said, 'Oh, our boys are about 20 or 25 miles behind us, we're the spearhead.' So we went along the road and damn it all if we didn't run into a German battalion falling back. We had no way of getting out, so we just sat down on the side of the road. And this German sergeant came up and we're smoking, you see, and he said, 'Who are you blokes with?' I said, 'Oh, we're a couple of escaped prisoners of war.' He asked, 'Can you spare one of those (cigarettes)?' I said, 'Yeah, sure.' I could speak German so I asked, 'How are things going?' 'Oh, bloody terrible,' he said. 'And what about your mates, all these fellows falling back?' He said, 'Tonight they will all vanish into the dark, take off their uniforms, throw them away and go for their lives.' That was the stage of war in April 1945. They let us be and we eventually got back to the Allied barracks."

"The officer there was a big bearded bloke with bandoliers on him and grenades and all this. They were all strapped up these partisans with whatever they could get hold of."

Ernest Brough was captured in 1942 at El Alamein and escaped from Austria in April 1944 with two mates. They decided to cross into Croatia and join up with partisans from where they hoped to be repatriated to England. They lost their food crossing a river and were very cold and hungry by the time they made it to the Croatian border. Ernest and his mates spent 60 days moving south before making contact with Allied forces and being flown to North Africa. As Brough recalls, it was quite a journey.

"We got through and on the other side, on the Croatian side, there was a creek or it might have been a channel dug for defence, I don't know, but it was full of water. The first thing, we got a big stick and we tested it, and we didn't want the New Zealander to get in it, because he had a big cold and if he got wet again it would probably kill him. I was as good as gold. Anyway, we decided to walk along it. We had a bit of a chat and we thought, *Righto, we'll walk along as far as we can and see if we can find a way across it*. We must have gone about 100 metres or so and there was a bridge across it. It was about eight or ten-feet high and it was all wired up like that, right down to the apron wire to stop anybody from getting across to the other side. So we thought we'd climb up it, so we climbed up the wire, right over the top and over the side and the Kiwi says: 'You better take your boots off, there might be an echo in the bridge.'

"So we take our boots off and there was a guardhouse about 50 yards further on which had a light on inside. We'd never seen any movement there. We did it all nice and quiet, but little did we know that they weren't in there, they were out scouting around. We tip-toed across the bridge and sat on the other side and we're doing our boots up nice and quiet and Allan says, 'I think there's some guards out there.' The two guards, you could see them out under the trees on the Croatian side with rifles on their shoulders. You can see in the dark if you spend a fair bit of time in it! Around the corner were these two soldiers with their rifles and when we saw the red caps we said, 'You partisans, you bloody beauty.' They took us away to another house and there was an Austrian fellow there, he was in the partisans, he could speak English. He was sitting behind the desk and he had a Luger on the desk. He said: 'If you're not telling the truth, you're dead. You'll be interrogated and we want your name and numbers and next of kin, who your parents are and what your name is and everything else.' It was all tapped out and went to Australia House in London.

"Within three or four hours they knew who we were. They gave us a little bit of a stew and an apple I think it was. It was bloody lovely though. They had some straw laid out on the ground and we slept on the straw. The officer there was a big bearded bloke with bandoliers on him and grenades and all this. They were all strapped up these partisans with whatever they could get hold of. They were wearing German uniforms and then they wanted to know how we got through the wire. They said, 'Did you have to shoot anybody?' 'No.' 'Well, when we get short of clothes we go down along the wire there and shoot them through the head so it doesn't destroy the uniform so we can get some more clothes'."

Jim Connor was being transported on a POW ship from Singapore to Japan in September 1944 when it was destroyed by the Allies. For him there was no euphoria at being rescued after four days adrift. Instead he felt only relief that he had survived his POW experience and the sinking of his ship.

"Any man who jumped into the water and didn't have a life jacket, he soon took one off a dead Jap as there was hundreds of dead Japs in the water," Connor recalled. "We tied two rafts together and there were 18 of us, but when we got rescued four days later there was only seven alive. Well, we were floating and the sea was calm but there was a big swell and you'd come up on the top of the swell and you could see this little black, (what) looked like a fishing boat in the distance. And we'd say, 'Yes it's coming,' and of course we're waving every time we come up on top of the swell. Eventually we saw it coming close to us and then we realised it was a submarine and then when it got closer to us the sailors were diving in with ropes and tying them onto our rafts to pull us over, because we were that black with oil and that greasy we were slipping everywhere, plus the water was choppy.

"They pulled us over and I can remember the sailor that rescued me, his name was Bob Bennett, and he pulled us over with the rope and then when he got on board the submarine he stuck his leg out for me to hang onto and when the other sailors took my hands I pleaded with them not to grab my arms as they were that badly burnt. Then we got on board. We were still black with oil. They said, 'Drop your clothes.' The seven of us were on the second-last raft rescued that day. They picked up one lone man after that on a raft. You went down below and they give you a bit of wadding to suck or a bit of rag to suck and then give you a teaspoon of water to drink. Then after that they gave us pineapple juice and orange juice galore to drink but you hadn't had any sleep for four days and of course you didn't know where you were but you knew you were free and that was all."

" The Yanks were marvellous and took us to a huge building in Paris where we saw doctors, dentists, had showers, got new uniforms and plenty of food (but no girls)."

According to Les Manning, for many liberated POWs in Europe, there was a party atmosphere. Many headed off to France and Paris. Their thinking was: What are they going to do, charge me AWOL and put me in prison? Tragically, though, they were sometimes reminded that the war still had not ended.

"News of the war was getting through and we knew it was only a matter of time before it would be over. It was 31st March when the Yankee tanks rolled up the road. Our guards took off and we were finally free! We ran out to meet Patton's 3rd Armoured Division and they greeted us with rifles to guard a few hundred prisoners they'd taken. On that day one of our boys called out, 'See you' as he jumped onto a tank headed out of town. A sniper got him with a shot and there wasn't a dry eye amongst us.

"The Yanks were marvellous and took us to a huge building in Paris where we saw doctors, dentists, had showers, got new uniforms and plenty of food (but no girls). At Le-Havre we caught flights with the RAF boys to High Wycombe and then on to Gowrie House in London. There, while on leave, I had a set of teeth made and met the Duchess of Kent when I was sitting in the dentist chair with my mouth wide open. On 8th May, 1945 the war was declared over in Europe and we all went crazy in the streets of Brighton. The Poms really knew how to throw a party."

Jim Jacobs' priority was to seek justice for crimes committed. He went straight to work once his Japanese guards had become his prisoner. He was determined to see these men tried for war crimes and worked hard in his first month of freedom to do so. At the time, he wrote about collecting the information needed along with a team of others: "We have collected hundreds and hundreds of atrocity stories from prison camps in Burma, Siam, Java, Sumatra, Malaya and French Indo-China. I now have seven clerks assisting me to copy and index the reports. Among them are several from the area where Johnny Stringer was sent nearly a month ago. They make pretty grim reading. It's a gruesome business reading story after story of Japanese inhumanity and cruelty."

Elsewhere in the world, some soldiers took justice into their own hands but most simply went about preparing to return home.

"After war's end in mid-August, many people who worked on Changi airfield had time on their hands and waited impatiently to go home. Some were not very happy with the way the really brutal Japanese were to go free after the harsh treatment that was given to prisoners of war. Several Englishmen, with Australians, sought and found out where some 'Nips' were camped, so they visited their barracks and dealt with them, showing no mercy."
Max Venables, Singapore, 1942

"'Blue' and I found a young Digger from the hospital trying to get six Japanese to carry a piano up the stairs to the second floor to be used in a concert and these lazy 'Sons of Nippon' were not going to do the job. How wrong could they be? The Digger was carrying a pick handle as we were in a military hospital and weapons were not allowed so the soldier was issued a pick handle to protect himself. Blue quietly took it from him and asked him to stand back

a little. The pick handle rose and fell once and the first Jap went out like a light. Blue roared *'Kura, Bakero'* (probably meaning; warehouse, idiot) and the piano went up the first flight of stairs like a shot. Then the sons of Nippon paused for a breather without permission and again the pick handle went to work. The piano went the rest of the way without another rest and only four Japs finished the job. Blue handed the young Digger his pick handle back and offered the advice, 'Don't just hold the bloody thing mate, use it the way they expect it to be used'. This young Digger did not have the benefit of experience, such as we had enjoyed from our honourable hosts. This single episode was the only time I personally saw, or heard of any Australian ex-prisoner raising his hand to our former task masters, I never heard of any other mob trying to take the law into their own hands."
Richard Armstrong, Singapore, 1942

In many different lands and circumstances, freedom was restored to thousands of Australians prisoners across four wars. The POWs who survived incarceration would forever more remember their mates who did not make it. The prisoners who died in captivity are a tragic reflection of the enemy's failing morality combined with government policy.

War/Captured by	Australians captured	Died in captivity
Boer War	200 approx	4
World War 1, Turkish	217	62
World War 1, German	3,853	310
World War 2, Japanese	22,376	8,031
World War 2, Europe	8,591	265
Korean War	30	1
Total	35,267	8,673

Freedom for these 8,673 men and women was not found in this life. For those who did return, their struggle to readjust into Australian society had only just begun. But at least they were struggling as free men and women and could take strength in their good fortune. Perhaps more importantly they had beaten their enemy by living to tell their stories, shining light on the fate of their mates and preserving the memories of those who did not make it home.

Jack Thorpe's telegram to his Mum,
telling her he had been freed

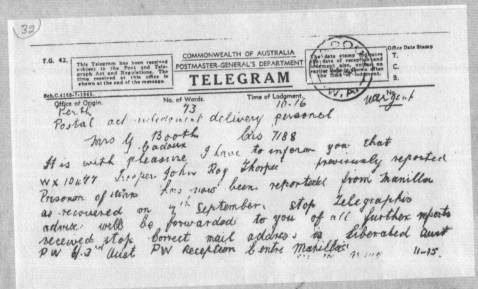

COMMONWEALTH OF AUSTRALIA
POSTMASTER-GENERAL'S DEPARTMENT

TELEGRAM

The date stamp indicates
the date of reception and
lodgement also, unless an
earlier time is shown after
the time of lodgment.

Office Date Stamp

T.
C.
B.

Sch.C.4168-7-1943.

Office of Origin	No. of Words.	Time of Lodgment.	No.
Perth	73	10.16	urgent

Postal act enforcement delivery personel

Mrs G. Booth   Lns 7/88
G. Ladoux

It is with pleasure I have to inform you that
WX 10477 Trooper John Roy Thorpe previously reported
Prisoner of War has now been reported from Manilla
as recovered on 7th September. stop Telegraphic
advice will be forwarded to you of all further reports
received stop Correct mail address is Liberated aust
PW H.3rd Aust PW Reception Centre Manilla   11-15.

View of Hiroshima about
eight months after the
atomic explosion

Chapter 9

Coming Home

"We were taken down to the docks and there was this great ship there, a great white ship, the Oranje with red crosses all over it. There was a gangway going up to it. We who were the walking wounded had to face this great long gangway. I stood at the bottom of the gangway and I thought to myself, I'll never get up there. Just then there was this Kiwi nurse. She came racing down this gangway that I was afraid to face. She put my arm around her shoulder and lugged me up. She said to me, with tears streaming down her face, 'Come on soldier you're going home.' And that was my therapy, she took me up and I came home. It was a beautiful trip home."

Jim Connor, Singapore, 1942

Bob Parker and
Don Buck released from
incarceration in Korea

A soldier heads off to war knowing he or she will be away from home and loved ones for as long as the Army requires. During WW1 and WW2 this could be as long as five years. Contact with home was sporadic, but at least it was possible. For some POWs, however, it was often impossible. Re-establishing ties after being liberated could be an emotional rollercoaster that, for some, would only stop when they were settled at home once more.

For most POWs in this book repatriation came when the war ended. But this was not the case for everyone. Those freed from the Boer camp at Waterval went straight back into battle, while others were repatriated as the war raged. Under the Geneva Conventions non-combatants, like medical staff and chaplains, should not be taken prisoner. If such personnel were captured they were to be repatriated at the earliest opportunity. The Conventions also state that the severely sick and wounded should be repatriated to a neutral country. Such exchanges occurred in World War 1 through Switzerland and the Netherlands in 1917 and 1918. In Korea, badly wounded prisoners were exchanged in an operation called "Little Switch". These soldiers, such as Eric Donnelly who had a severely wounded leg, were not supposed to participate in the war again.

When Leslie "Brick" Edmunds was captured in Crete in 1941 he told his captors that he knew first aid. The Germans over-estimated Edmunds's qualifications and made him a medic in the prison camp. He wasn't about to complain, although his mates were very sceptical about his medical skills. Classed as a medical orderly by the Red Cross, he was repatriated back to Australia as a non-combatant. He wasn't free for long. "I went straight back to war and got stuck into the Japanese," he recalled. Edmunds reckoned that technically he had not breached the Geneva Conventions. It was not his fault the Germans and Italians had him recorded as a non-combatant!

"When we asked what had taken them so long to come and get us they said they'd had to wait for the radiation to clear. We said, 'What's that?'"

The first steps in the journey home for most liberated POWs in World War Two were medical treatment, hot showers, clean clothes, good food and then some R&R. The repatriation process of former prisoners by boat or plane was organised by American,

British or Russian personnel depending on where they had been incarcerated. The process may have been slow but it was far more civilised than forced marches, crammed cattle trains or fetid prison ships without food and water. Those POWs who were held near to atomic bomb targets Hiroshima and Nagasaki, like John Prosser, had to be decontaminated before they could be moved. Captured at Timor in 1942, Prosser's clothes were removed to ensure nuclear fallout was not carried out of the area. Like most Australians at the time, he knew almost nothing about the hazards of radiation.

"They didn't tell us anything about the bomb," he recalled. "They just said it was dangerous. We just thought the old buildings might collapse. We had a bit of a walk round; they had removed most of the bodies by then. It was still a nasty sight to see, really. They took us to a place nearby; we had showers and got rid of our old clothes. We were fumigated to get rid of the lice and fleas and bugs and so on. We were sprayed – they didn't tell us with what – and were given a new set of American clothes, under clothes, the lot. Then we were taken aboard the United States destroyer *Greene* which had seen action at Okinawa. The American crew gave us their bed bunks. They slept on deck in hammocks. It was very good of them. That's what I called the first part of getting into real freedom.

"When we got to Okinawa we could see where the marines had fought that big battle. There were ships as far as I could see. If they hadn't dropped the atom bomb they would have been on their way to the island we had just left. In that way we were fortunate the bomb was dropped. It saved our lives and it saved all those Americans. And maybe Australians would have gone in there too. We stayed on the destroyer for a day and the next day we were transferred to a British aircraft carrier, the *Speaker*. By the time I got off the ship I had over-indulged in good food."

Jack Thorpe was also decontaminated after Nagasaki and described the experience as similar to going through a sheep dip. When he set eyes on the fit-looking Americans, Thorpe realised just how thin and close to death he and his mates must have appeared.

"When we asked what had taken them so long to come and get us they said they'd had to wait for the radiation to clear. We said, 'What's that?' The troop ship was waiting for us down on the wharf but before we could go on board we had to line up in single file outside a decontamination chamber to be cleansed of any radiation we were carrying on our skin and clothing. The chamber consisted of a series of small rooms. In the first one we had to strip off and drop our clothes into a chute. Things like wallets went into a case that went through the different sections of the chamber with you. Next came the decontamination procedure, which began when we were checked for radiation in the second room.

"The next step in the process occurred in what looked like a mobile sheep dip, with water sprays and soapsuds coming from all angles. From there we went into a drying room and after that we went to the Quartermaster to be kitted out in brand new US Army uniforms. There were a hundred men in our camp – No.22 at Iizuka – and the average weight of the men before boarding ship for Manila was 100lbs (45kg). This was five weeks after the war ended and the Americans had been dropping good food to us for about five weeks. However, I must say that after having been deloused, decontaminated, washed and polished, some of the old blokes didn't look too bad in their new clothes which concealed much of our emaciated bodies."

" It was wonderful to get under the first hot shower since our captivity three and a half years earlier. There was plenty of soap and we scrubbed ourselves as if to wash away the grime of a lifetime."

After being consumed by thoughts and dreams of hot showers and food while in captivity, the liberated POWs made sure they enjoyed these little luxuries on their journey home. The main drawback was that food, long dreamed of, was often difficult to keep down. Most POWs had lost enormous amounts of weight and their stomachs had shrunk. They had been deprived of nutrients and rich foods for so long that going from famine to feast could be harmful. Thankfully the journey home gave them the opportunity to regain some of their former health and weight. For Ernest Brough that first meal was truly special. "Oh, it was bloody beautiful," he recalled. "It was lovely food." He was not alone.

"I was due to board the troop ship *Largs Bay* to come back to Australia on 20th September, 1945 as I had turned down a trip home by plane earlier. I wanted time to get used to eating proper

food again after so long on starvation rations. Even so I was sick on the ship every night for the first six nights. Not seasick as the water was as calm as a millpond, it was just customising my stomach to good wholesome food."
Gerard Harvey Veitch, Singapore, 1942

"It was wonderful to get under the first hot shower since our captivity three and a half years earlier. There was plenty of soap and we scrubbed ourselves as if to wash away the grime of a lifetime. Our bodies were tanned down to the waist after long exposure to the sun and it took several years before normal Australian living left me with natural white skin all over."
Gordon Nelson, Singapore, 1942

"Eventually, after being fattened up a bit, I got to 6 stone 13lbs and we boarded the *Highland Brigade* to come home. Freedom still really hadn't become a realisation to me."
Milton "Snow" Fairclough, Java, 1942

"The RAAF were doing the run to Singapore so we had a very nice air hostess to look after us. It took seven hours to get to Singapore but it was an excellent trip. We had some wonderful views. At the airport we were handed over to the Red Cross and given a very nice afternoon tea, cigarettes and chocolates. We were then taken to a large house near Changi where we were issued with a blanket and a bit of clothing plus quite a lot of Red Cross toilet gear, cigarettes and chocolate. A few Sisters came down on the 22nd and made me quite sick with fruit cake and chocolate. It took me four days to recover."
Alfred Burkitt, Java, 1942

"The sea voyage did wonders in restoring me to my former good health. I landed back in Brisbane on 1st April, 1919 little the worse for my terrible experiences while prisoner of war in Turkey."
George Handsley, Romani, 1916

"We boarded our ship out of Poland on 8th March, 1945. It was wonderful after not seeing the sea for four years. The Russian band played us down to the ship. The food on board was very nice, the first good food for four years. They fed us up well."
Reginald Lindley, Crete, 1941

"Most of the blokes broke into a trot to get to the flag pole and kiss it, some got down on their knees and prayed, while others pumped the air with a clenched fist, saying, 'You bloody beauty!'"

For these men freedom meant having the Australian flag flying above them again. As prisoners they were often forbidden to fly or salute their national symbol. Occasionally the Germans allowed a flag to be draped on the coffins of dead POWs during burial, but the Japanese did not even allow that. "On our arrival in Manila there were buses waiting to take us to a huge tent city on the outskirts of Manila," recalled Jack Thorpe. "At the entrance was a big tent that looked like headquarters and had our beautiful Australian flag flying out in front. Most of the blokes broke into a trot to get to the flag pole and kiss it, some got down on their knees and prayed, while others pumped the air with a clenched fist, saying, 'You bloody beauty!' It is very heart-wrenching to see a display of patriotism such as that. Those men may have had haggard faces and emaciated bodies but their hearts were as big as lions and they sprang into action at the sight of our national emblem, the Australian flag. We were transformed, everyone with happy, smiling faces. And ill though most of us still were, we all seemed to suddenly have a spring in our step. It was an amazing sight and experience. One that I will never forget."

In post-WW2 Europe, POWs were repatriated back to Australia via Britain. To get there many flew over the white cliffs at Dover. Made famous by a Vera Lynn song in the 1940s, the cliffs had an impact on more than one soldier. Even to Australian soldiers they symbolised the endurance of the British Empire which had stood up to the fascists. Remember that in 1945 many Australians considered themselves to be British subjects as well as fiercely independent Aussies. The cliffs had been a sign of hope for Empire and Commonwealth airmen following raids into Axis territory. Seeing the cliffs meant they had survived a mission over enemy territory and were nearly home.

"We came back in Lancaster bombers and I worked my position in the plane so that I could see the white cliffs of Dover over the navigator's shoulder – that was my aim. We landed at Oxford and we were taken down to Eastbourne pretty quickly. And we had six weeks or so in London and in England, and went up as far as

Scotland and then caught the *Mauritania* home."
John Hawkes, El Alamein, 1942

"I managed to scramble to a position near the astrodome at the top of the Lancaster bomber and contrived with some difficulty to see just a little of the famous white cliffs of Dover as we approached the coast of Kent. The flight had lasted an hour and a half, so we arrived at Westcott Aerodrome at 1300 hours. As my foot touched English soil for the first time, a strange feeling came over me. It was probably brought about by having imagined the moment for so long and so often, added to the warm kindly reception given us by the young uniformed lass from one of the services – probably the RAF or the Red Cross, I can't remember which – who helped us down from the flying giant. This was indeed a very emotional moment for us all. More than one native of the UK bent down and kissed the ground of his homeland. I wasn't the only one who had to wipe away a tear or two of relief from the eye. One became aware of a sudden falling away of an extreme tension and a conscious relaxing of every muscle at the realisation that we were now really free, and with all our trials behind us. Nevertheless, there was more to be done and after a wonderful reception, including a cup of tea and eats, we were taken to a temporary camp 45 kilometres from London at 1520 hours. Here we were fed and registered, and were able to write a letter and send a cable home."
John Crooks, Greece, 1941

Despite what seemed to be a lack of co-ordination, the Australian government was working hard to manage the mammoth logistical task of getting the POWs home. However, many spent several weeks in the UK awaiting their embarkation orders. The British, well aware of the Australian soldiers' antics while on leave during the Great War, tried to round them up. With money in their pocket and years of captivity under their belt, many took this time to travel the countryside and play tourist.

"As there was no transport available at the time to get back to Australia, the Army gave us more leave which I spent in London seeing all the sights. Fifty of us Australians were invited to a garden party at Buckingham Palace where we were introduced to the King and Queen, Princess Margaret and Princess Elizabeth. It was all very informal with cups of tea and sandwiches. It was quite an experience considering it wasn't that long since I had been in a POW camp living in squalor and eating next to nothing.

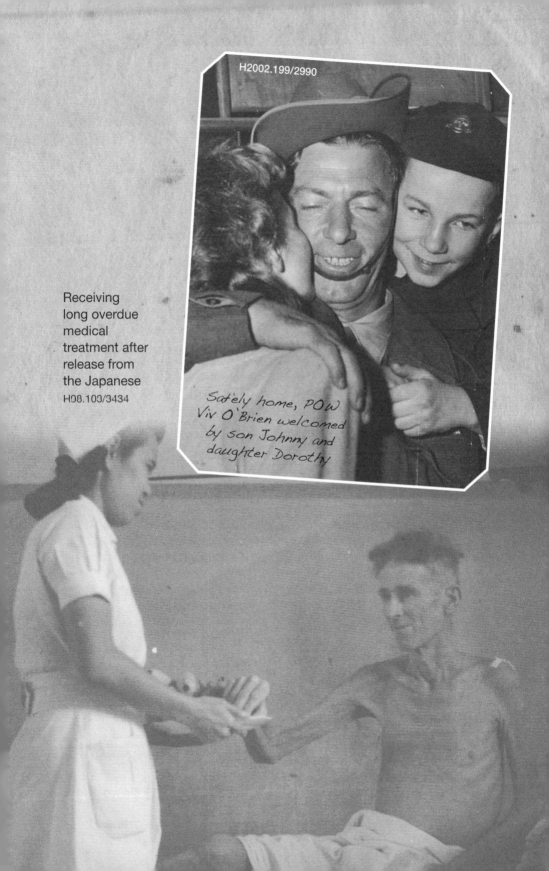

H2002.199/2990

Receiving
long overdue
medical
treatment after
release from
the Japanese
H08.100/3434

Safely home, POW
Viv O'Brien welcomed
by son Johnny and
daughter Dorothy

I finally returned to Eastbourne and on 18th June, 1945, we were moved to Liverpool where we went aboard the troop ship *Stirling Castle* bound for Sydney via the Panama Canal, Wellington in New Zealand and then to Australia. We were transported by train from Sydney to Melbourne, arriving July 25th, where I was granted more leave."
Jack Calder, El Alamein, 1942

"We went down to Aldingen airfield and damn it all, who should we run into but Marlene Dietrich. They had just arrived by plane in one of the DC3s, they call them Dakotas, and we were going off in a Dakota to Brussels. One of the blokes said, 'I dare you to kiss her.' I did and I've got a photo of it in a book by a fellow who did a biography of Dietrich, and I saw it once on television. They then flew us to Brussels and it was bloody cold too. We flew out over Cologne and that's the first time I had seen any of the German damage. We got to Brussels and we went and enjoyed ourselves for a couple of nights and then flew on to Britain in a Lancaster. They flew in all different routes. We went out over Holland where there were still Germans and they were firing at us with their anti-aircraft guns. The plane in front of ours flew out over France and hit a hill and killed every bloke in it. It's just the luck of the draw.

"They again had trouble with transport to Australia, as they did in the First World War when they started a scheme where you could take up your trade for six months, because they needed the ships for taking troops over to France and so on. So I stayed on for six months. I worked on several newspapers there and at the BBC in Bristol. I got a telegram from Sir Keith Murdoch congratulating me on my successful repatriation and I left in November 1945."
Keith Hooper, Crete, 1941

" It was a wonderful sight sailing into the harbour. It was all very quiet and peaceful. Just as it had been four and a half years before when we sailed out about the same time of day."

Once home there were other issues to be resolved. Some former POWs were reunited with children they barely knew or had never met. Many still needed medical attention. Others just wanted to enjoy life again. The Army decided to ration the back pay owed to these soldiers as a way of stopping them spending it all at once. But that didn't stop some of them having a good time. Mostly, though, they were just glad to see their homeland again.

"The *Dominion Monarch* left London with us aboard in May and we arrived at Sydney Harbour in early July. It was the first time on Aussie soil for over six long years. What a feeling!"
Les Manning, Crete, 1941

"We weren't allowed leave so a few of us sneaked off with the girls to try and ring up home. Unfortunately, I couldn't get through. We got a naval launch to take us back on board about 10pm that night. We left for Brisbane early on the 2nd and had quite a good trip. Very calm and plenty of sun, arriving there about 8am on the 9th. A few of us raced into town to have a look around and I managed to ring Mum. Brisbane was quite a nice quiet place, very much like one of our large country towns. We got back on board by 2.30 pm and were on our way to Sydney by 3pm. We had come all the way down the east coast inside the Barrier Reef and there were some wonderful sights as we weaved our way between some of the islands. After leaving Brisbane, we ran into a bit of a storm and had some quite rough weather but the old *Highland Chieftain* rode it out very well. It was surprising just how steady the old tub was. On the morning of the 11th we were all up about 4.30am looking for the big lights. And with the first light of dawn we saw the top of the Sydney Harbour Bridge. It was a wonderful sight sailing into the harbour. It was all very quiet and peaceful. Just as it had been four and a half years before when we sailed out about the same time of day."
Alfred Burkitt, Java, 1942

"Most of the well chaps left by destroyer for home, but the medical staff stayed with the sick and were picked up by the English hospital ship *Jerusalem* and taken to Hong Kong and there transferred to the British aircraft carrier *Striker* and returned via Manila and Manus Island to Sydney. Don't ask me what day we arrived because I can't remember. It now seems so long ago, but I married my sweetheart, Jessie, the day after I was discharged and we had a very happy life, having twins Paul and Nan of whom we were both very proud."
Tom Pledger, Ambon, 1942

"At last (we) passed through Sydney Heads into the harbour on a beautiful, warm, sunny morning. Our reception made a fantastic spectacle from the flight deck of the Speaker. There were warships,

ferries and boats of all sizes, many of them with the name of a particular POW painted on the side or on a big cloth sign."
Jack Thorpe, Java, 1942

"Arrived at Fremantle and there was a bloody huge crowd on the wharf. Looked for my parents and saw my cousin Lela Fairclough holding up a big banner with FAIRCLOUGH on it. Mum and others were with her. A tearful reunion all round."
Milton "Snow" Fairclough, Java, 1942

"Actually, from the wharf I saw my brother and my mother, but then we got into these cars to take us to Greenslopes. Then the car broke down in blooming Queen Street. When we went to get out the men on the outside said, 'Stop where you are.' And they raced in and grabbed a beer out of the pub and brought it to us in the car. We made it into Greenslopes after that. It was an emotional home coming. I couldn't get enough to eat. I used to have breakfast at home, morning tea, lunch, afternoon tea, evening meal, supper, and then I'd be walking round the house looking for something to eat. When we got home we had the best of food but we hit the grog, of course. In those days it was only two beers per person when you went to get a beer, it was rationed. We would go into the 12 'til two session, about seven or eight of us."
Cyril Gilbert, Singapore, 1942

"We got into cars and were met by a group of Red Cross ladies with blankets. If we got cold they would put them round us. It was wonderful. We got ourselves into a convoy, a few people waved to us, too, and we got to the repatriation hospital at Heidelberg. We got leave one night to go into Melbourne and we got on the train and it was so strange. People reading this can't imagine how strange it would be. We had gone away young men, we were 19 or 20, and come back, some of us in our twenty-fifth or twenty-sixth year.

"About two days later we were transported by car to Port Melbourne and there a group of us we got on the old steamer *Nirana* and the next morning we arrived off Tamar Heads, the first sight of Tasmania after five years. We eventually arrived in Launceston, tied up and got off the ship. There was my mum and my three sisters. They had a banner across Mulgrave Street. It had on it 'Welcome home John our loved one', and then I knew we were home free.

"The next thing to happen was we went down to get our discharge. We went to Hobart, Teddy and myself and Dave Lewis stayed at the Y.M.C.A., a few shillings a night. We had a good time. Met a couple of girls and spent a considerable amount of money. We decided we had five years taken out of our lives from 19 until when we came back. We had a bit of time to make up. And we made it up too."
John Prosser, Timor, 1942

"I will not attempt to describe my emotions on seeing the Victorian coast this morning. The *Highland Brigade* sailed up Port Phillip Bay in perfect weather and berthed at Port Melbourne soon after lunch. They then took us to the show grounds where our loved ones were waiting for us, and here I met Dorothy, Joan, Raymond and my mother. A Red Cross car took us home to Essendon, and the most eventful period of my life had ended. We look forward to the future with new hope and confidence."
Jim Jacobs, Singapore, 1942

"After arriving in Melbourne we were herded into tramway buses and taken out to the show grounds at Ascot Vale where we were given a very cursory medical examination, some money – three months pay to cover the three months leave – ration tickets, etc. and then were allowed to meet our next of kin. My mother and sisters had been waiting all this time. We were then allowed to go home. On the trip out on the buses they moved very slowly so that we could see other friends and relatives who had come to Spencer Street Station to welcome us home."
Gerard Harvey Veitch, Singapore, 1942

"I received a call to go to the pay depot at Karrakatta. When I got there this man came out and he asked me who I was and I told him. 'Oh,' he said and he brought out his file. 'You were missing from 27th July, 1942 until 20th January, 1944.' He said, 'You are entitled to X amount of days' subsistence at three and ninepence per day.' I have forgotten what it came to but I took the money and I went down to my wife and I said, 'Berta, we are off on our second honeymoon'."
Doug LeFevre, El Alamein, 1942

H98.103/4150

POWs on their way home

Repatriates from German
POW camps reach Australia
H98.103/4705

" Over the years I have often wondered how many of my mates had rice for their first meal after getting home. I would venture to say, some perhaps, but not too many."

Prisoners of the Japanese had survived for years on a staple diet of rice or over-boiled pap. In Australia rice was in short supply and rationed. For everyone except the returning POWs, rice pudding was a treat made only on special occasions. Many of them could not stomach it, although the irony did not escape them.

"They drove us through Melbourne and we had quite a show there. Then we boarded the *Strathmore* which took us to Perth via Tasmania. We had about 300 Tasmanians on board. They were members of the 40th Battalion. They had been caught on Timor and came through with the Java party. We got on board in the afternoon and the first night out a beautiful start to a beautiful meal. And then they brought the sweets out - rice custard. That nearly caused a bloody riot. The chef came out and he was very, very apologetic and he said, 'Rice is rationed in Australia and we saved this up as a special treat for you people!' We had had three and a half years of rice so there was nothing very special about it to us. Some ate it and some did not."
Walter "Wally" Holding, Singapore, 1942

"I was dropped at the front gate of my sister's home and made my way to the backyard where two of my nephews, each about nine years old, were playing and as I stopped to watch them they looked at me in wonderment and asked each other who I was. The other finally said, 'I know, it's Uncle Dick.' He then yelled his head off with, 'Mum! Mum! Uncle Dick's here.' To this my sister replied from inside the house, 'Uncle Dick won't be here until tomorrow.'

"As the boys raced to me and hugged me, my brother-in-law looked out the window and said, 'It's Dick all right.' The humour of my homecoming was that my sister and brother-in-law were spring cleaning when I arrived at the house and I unexpectedly caught them at sixes and sevens working like galley slaves. However, after things quietened down for a while we sorted ourselves out. I explained the mix-up to the family and all was well until teatime. That's when matters came unstuck. My brother-in-law was a driver for the shell oil company and only the previous Thursday he had made bulk deliveries to the Botany area where some of his customers were the Chinese market gardeners who abounded in that area in those years. When Bill made his delivery to one Chinese place, the boss of the garden had given him about two pounds of rice which was a basic diet item to the Chinese but a luxury item for other folks.

"The instructions given to Bill along with the rice was, 'You take this home to Missy.' Sis had decided on the strength of my telegram on the Saturday to have baked rice pudding for tea on Sunday and a special sweet for Monday for my first meal home. That night after we had eaten our meal my nephew asked, 'Mum are we having any sweets tonight?' Here Sis broke down and cried like rain and when I asked, 'What's wrong?' her reply was: 'You're going to hate me.'

"I finally got from her the problem of the rice pudding. I then told her not to be silly but to get the pudding out of the oven and we would eat it. Which we did. And very nice it was too. I then explained to Sis that there was a vast difference between baked rice pudding at home and the muck we so often ate during our years of captivity. Over the years I have often wondered how many of my mates had rice for their first meal after getting home. I would venture to say, some perhaps, but not too many."
Richard Armstrong, Singapore, 1942

> "We said, 'Well, we have just come back having been POWs.' And the lady turned around and said we should be ashamed of ourselves, living a life of luxury in a POW camp while the boys were fighting for Australia up in the islands."

Jack Thorpe arrived in Perth and was keen to have a beer on Aussie soil with some fellow POWs. Two were amputees and the other, Arthur "Snow White" Morrison, was an Aboriginal soldier who at the time under Western Australian law could not be served in "white" pubs. Nothing breaks down prejudice more than shared experiences and suffering. Thorpe was prepared to take on the entire WA police force single-handed. After all, what could they do to him and his mates that the Japanese hadn't already tried?

"We got to the Alhambra Bars and I fronted the bar and ordered four beers. The barmaid told me that she couldn't serve me with 'that Aboriginal'. 'You must serve him,' I told her. 'He's wearing the King's uniform, he's been overseas fighting for this country for the last four and a half years, plus he's been a prisoner of war of the Japanese for three and a half years!'

"She said, 'No, I can't serve you if you have him in your company. If you don't go I will call the police.' 'Good idea. Call the police!' I told her. And I walked over to the foot of the stairs to wait for them to come down. When they arrived I asked them if they were here for the purpose of ejecting an Aboriginal. They said they were, so I told them all about 'Snow White' and that we had been POWs together and that this was going to be our first drink in Australia for four and a half years.

"They asked where he was and I was taking them over when one of the police said, 'Is that him talking to those two men with their legs off?' I said it was, and they walked over to the three of them and shook their hands. Then they went to the bar, put down a pound and told the barmaid, 'Serve them all, and the drinks are on us!'

"Words cannot describe my personal feelings on arriving back into Western Australia and driving along Mounts Bay Road. That was the first time, but the second time I went round with the late Frank McKay. We were travelling on the bus and at that time we had not been fully kitted out and I still had a safari suit on which I had purchased in Bombay in India and the lady in the seat in front of us was talking to her companion, another lady, and they turned around and they said, 'Which unit are you from?' We said, 'The 2/28th.' And she said, 'They are up in the islands, why aren't you there?'

"We said, 'Well, we have just come back having been POWs.' And the lady turned around and said we should be ashamed of ourselves, living a life of luxury in a POW camp while the boys were fighting for Australia up in the islands. This was too much for Frank. He got up to leave and I said I wasn't leaving. I told the woman to mind her own business. But apart from that little hiccup, we had a most welcome homecoming. There were no bands, we just hopped off the station and I found my way down to Cottesloe where my wife lived. No one had bothered to notify her that I was coming back. So I guess she was surprised."
Jack Thorpe, Java, 1942

" I was not the only one who came back to find that I felt something of an outsider in my own country, which had changed and moved on while we were away."

Despite the best intentions of the armed forces, demobilisation in 1945 and 1946 meant numerous personnel were discharged with undetected health problems. It was inexcusable that so many people were allowed to slip through the cracks. It didn't help that conditions like post-traumatic stress disorder (a name coined in the 1970s to describe what had previously been called "shell shock" or "battle fatigue") was not treated as seriously as it should have been in 1945, let alone 1918 or 1901.

"The interesting thing that has always stuck in my mind is when the fellows came out of Japanese hands, including my kid brother, who was lucky enough to come home, and all the fellows from Korea later, they were all shoved into hospital. When we came home from Germany we never got any of that. I remember the bloke in Melbourne saying, 'How do you feel?' What are you going to say? 'Oh, not bad?' Then later on you get these various problems that come on. I'm a disabled veteran and now I'm starting to get depression and insomnia."
Keith Hooper, Crete, 1941

"There was no counselling or emotional therapy then for people who had been through what we had. The Army patched up our bodies and sent us on our way, to cope with post-POW life as best we could. And many of us couldn't. I wasn't the only one who had returned home to discover that a grateful nation had not kept our jobs available for us, despite promises. I was not the only one who came back to find that I felt something of an outsider in my own country, which had changed and moved on while we were away."
Jack Thorpe, Java, 1942

"After discharge from the Army the hardest thing was to settle down to civilian life. You felt you were unwanted. You had done nothing during the war and you just wanted to keep moving all the time. This was the attitude of the ex-POW; after his release from captivity, after so many lost years, there was so much that one had to do to make up. We didn't want to be paraded through the streets to cheering crowds we wanted just to get out of the Army, come home unnoticed, meet our loved ones, and try to settle

down. For us, the war was over the day we were taken prisoner."
Jim McCauley, Libya, 1941

"We saw quite a lot of doctors there and they tried to give us this crap psychology to see whether we were troppo or not. Everyone started feeling better in themselves and getting to know their family again, which was hard. You know, awkward. Going into the city of Launceston and getting used to things again, it was all heavy going. Still we got through that all right with the help of our family and loved ones. Everyone helped, all the ex-servicemen around Launceston, didn't matter what service they were in at that time they helped one another. If someone wanted a car touched up, well I would do that. If someone wanted a bit of carpentry, well Monty would do that and vice versa. We all worked in that way."
John Prosser, Timor, 1942

" Please tell me, someone, how can anyone close his or her mind to three and a half years of their existence as if it had never happened?"

Richard Armstrong is adamant that soldiers were discouraged from talking about their experiences onto friends and family. World War One veterans with "shell shock" were often prescribed two tots of rum. World War Two POWs were advised to simply forget the whole experience. This approach has proved to be wrong.

"One of the first groups we saw was a group of army psychologists and psychiatrists. The utter garbage they fed us was sickening to say the least. One of the first – and most emphatic – instructions we were given was never to tell any one of our family or friends anything about our experiences, under any circumstances. We were not to tell of the Japanese brutality, the slavery, the starvation, the murder of our mates, the killing of native civilians. In fact, we were ordered to say absolutely nothing of our three and a half years of hell.

"The next instructions issued by these medical officers were that we had to put all our experiences as prisoners completely out of our minds as if it were only a bad dream. Then, according to these psychologists and psychiatrists, in a short time we would forget it all as if it really had been a bad dream. Please tell me, someone, how can anyone close his or her mind to three and a half years of their existence as if it had never happened?"
Richard Armstrong, Singapore, 1942

"The average prisoner became an expert at holding back his feelings of rage, fear and utter disgust at having to be bashed by ugly ape-like guards and of seeing his mates suffer the same indignations, when his normal reaction would have been to retaliate in no uncertain manner. For many these feelings are still inside us and it has been our wives who have, during the past 44 years, borne the brunt of their husband's erratic behaviour.

"The inability to express their feelings to their wives was perhaps the most damaging part of the post-war years. Inside them still existed the code of survival, to not let anyone know the unforgettable fears and stress built up during their years of captivity. Fortunately, the majority of the wives realised that their husband's outlook on the outside world was unpredictable. Their personalities had changed to such an extent that their attitude towards the family, employment and life itself could change within minutes. Despite all this, these women stuck to the task of rearing a family and trying to understand what years of captivity can do to not only the body but the mind of a loved one. Our wives – the unsung heroines."
Walter "Wally" Holding, Singapore, 1942

" I decided that I would not harbour bitterness for the rest of my life because, if I did, I would be the only one who would be affected."

"When we returned, many people thought we had come through our many years of imprisonment very well, but they didn't know about what we call 'the survival code' that we had acquired to use to control our emotions. Many personalities have changed and unpredictable behaviour is common. Most of us only discuss the funny or humorous side of our captivity. The bond between us survivors is so strong that many marriage partnerships have broken up, I believe, because the partner considered she was second in line to the POW bond. Personally, the bond with me is as strong as steel, come what may."
Milton "Snow" Fairclough, Java, 1942

For some POWs life went on. They even said they were better for the experience. For others the memories were locked away, never to be revealed. Others simply tried to delete that part of their life from their thoughts. But by all reports, all returned home with a

AUSTRALIAN MILITARY FORCES

His Majesty
King George VI

has instructed that the following message
from himself and Her Majesty the Queen
be conveyed to every ex Prisoner
of War on disembarkation
in Australia.

The Queen and I bid you a very warm welcome home. Through all the great trials and sufferings which you have undergone at the hands of the Japanese you have been constantly in our thoughts. We know from the accounts we have already received how heavy those sufferings have been. We know also that these have been endured by you with the highest courage. We mourn with you the death of so many of your gallant comrades. With all our heart we hope your return from captivity will bring you and your families a full measure of happiness which you may long enjoy together.

6-10-1945
Perth, W.A.

George R.I.

Each POW received this message from the king
and Queen on his return to Australia. 1945

special bond of mateship and shared experiences. It came, Ken Gray captured in Singapore believes, from the knowledge that they would not have survived without their mates' support.

"My experience as a POW definitely changed my outlook on life. It made me aware how precious life was, and how easily lost. I saw thousands of men's lives treated as rubbish by the Japanese. I survived the cholera outbreaks in Burma where you might say goodnight to the man lying next to you and find him dead beside you in the morning. I have valued each day since coming home. I know how lucky I am to have made it. My experience as a POW also made me aware of just how much can be achieved by people working together and helping each other and I have tried to put what I learned into practice over many long years as an active member of the RSL and other community organisations."
Jack Thorpe, Java, 1942

"I decided that I would not harbour bitterness for the rest of my life because, if I did, I would be the only one who would be affected. No one in Japan was going to lose any sleep over my carrying that bitterness."
Neil MacPherson, Java, 1942

"War is painful not only for the soldiers fighting on the front line but for the ones who are left behind. Consider the worry they must go through and the anxiety they must suffer. You take our wives when they heard we were prisoners of war. What they must have gone through. It's unbelievable. They suffered just as much in their own way as we suffered in our way wondering are we ever going to meet again."
Owen Campbell, Singapore, 1942

"When we look back over those troubled times is it any wonder that we thank the good Lord for his provision of steadfast mates, and above all for the doctors and medical staff who overcame incredible difficulties to return so many men to their loved ones at home."
Bill Haskell, Java, 1942

"My experience as a POW has made me appreciate food more and has probably made me more resourceful. For the first few years after my release, I felt animosity towards the Japanese and the hairs on the back of my neck would rise if I heard Japanese spoken. As the years have passed these feelings have subsided

and I have come to realise that the Nippon troops were simply obeying orders, as we were. However they were needlessly cruel and often sadistic."
Willoby "Bill" Wharton, Singapore, 1942

"To me it was totally different to come back. I went away a very insecure young man, I had a speech impediment, I was against everybody, I was against authority. I went away, as the saying goes, a snotty-nosed kid and I came back a man."
Doug LeFevre, El Alamein, 1942

" It will be a bad thing to pay these men this money. If there is ever another war, it would induce men to become prisoners of war."

It is unfortunate that so many veterans had to fight the government for what was rightfully owed to them for serving their country. The POWs who returned after WW2 had to fight for a sustenance allowance for their days of war service when the Defence Force did not provide them a meal (they were eligible for all the days of their incarceration). They also had to fight for their pensions. The ignorance and penny-pinching of the politicians of the day was an embarrassment that took too long to correct. Robert Sproull, a prisoner of the Japanese, recalls a remark made by a Federal politician at the time that greatly disappointed him: "It will be a bad thing to pay these men this money. If there is ever another war, it would induce men to become prisoners of war."

On the 50th anniversary of the Sandakan death march, Owen Campbell said, "The Sandakan story has got to be brought out into the light. That's what I reckon. Bring it to their (young people's) notice and then they'll start to talk and that will bring it further into the minds of the younger generation that is coming up. That's the only way I can do it. When you realise it's got to be told then you don't mind the personal anguish, as long as it does some good somewhere along the line and opens people's eyes." This sentiment holds true today. We must keep these stories and memories alive. As difficult as it is to tell and to hear such stories of horror, pain and cruelty, we must talk and listen, for those that do not learn from the past are destined to make the same mistakes.

What can be said about being a POW and how it impacts on a man or woman? How can we really understand what these incredible men and women have been through? We weren't there and we can't pretend to know. Sometimes part of us doesn't want to know because we fear that we would fail such a test of character. Perhaps we fear that we would not live up to their examples of strength and honour. Perhaps we think we would not find the determination to make numerous escapes attempts like Doug Nix, or take beatings like Jim Jacobs or defy the enemy like Archie Whitehead.

Maybe we would fail. But at least we know that the strength is there in our national character, toughened by the examples of these men and women. And hopefully, if we were in their position, we could also honour their sacrifice and mateship. Maybe we could show our gratitude and respect by living our lives in freedom, because they sacrificed theirs for ours.

Perhaps the final words should go to all the soldiers and prisoners who were not able to taste that freedom again. The dedication plaque to one of Australia's most famous POWs, Sir Ernest Edward "Weary" Dunlop AC, CMG, OBE, KStJ, is at the Hellfire Pass Memorial in Thailand. The words on it read:

"When you go home, tell them of us and say we gave our tomorrow for your today."

POWs on their
way home
H98.103/4185

Chapter 10
POW Camps

"Mum said Dad would often wake suddenly in the night in a sweat. Winter or summer Dad always slept with the window open; he was claustrophobic.

"Growing up we became aware that Dad had had a hard time but we were encouraged not to ask him about his experiences as it might upset him. I understand that this approach was not unusual as there were suggestions by the then government that this approach to reintegration was preferable. He did however open up to my wife, who had not been brought up with the 'don't ask' attitude. He told her some things that Mum didn't even know.

"Dad was more forgiving of the Japanese than Mum, she is still very bitter. Dad said he didn't like what they did but went on to repeat a saying from the era: 'A bayonet is a weapon with a worker at either end'. I think Dad was more bitter about their desertion by the British.

"At the age of 17, I joined the army and in 1971, at 19, I went to Vietnam. It was one of the few times I saw Dad upset. It must have been hard for him. When I came home Dad and I related to each other quite differently – as peers and fellow veterans. In 1987 Dad died from respiratory complications along with heart failure. I'm now on a Totally and Permanently Incapacitated pension and understand Dad even more, especially in the context of post-traumatic stress disorder.

"I know that Dad wore the scars of his POW experience all his life and that had some impact on how he related to the rest of the family. He didn't tolerate fools gladly and was a hard taskmaster. When I was in my early teens, he and I clashed as I rebelled. I don't view those years in a negative light, as I think that thanks to Dad's high expectations there weren't too many new experiences I shied away from."

Ken Gregson talking about his father,
Robert George Gregson, and his experiences
as a POW at the hands of the Japanese.

This chapter, "POW Camps", summarises key aspects of some of the prison camps in which the main contributors to this book were held. The seven POW camps are a very small sample of the hundreds of camps in which Australian soldiers have been incarcerated since the Boer war. The chapter is designed to convey a sense of the daily routines and conditions in these camps, which spanned several continents and cover the nations of our captors throughout our history.

POWs return home
H98.103/4221

Camp: Waterval

Conflict: Boer War/Second Anglo-Boer War

Location: Waterval, South Africa, 1900

Prisoners: 4,000 British enlisted men were held 24 kilometres north of Pretoria in the first half of 1900. Amongst these prisoners were over 100 Australians who had been captured as part of Colonial contingents sent to assist the Mother Country. There were also volunteers from Canada, New Zealand and India. All were classed as British soldiers.

Daily routines and camp conditions: Whilst officers were sent to Pretoria where there were bathrooms, servants and cooks, enlisted men were sent to less salubrious, yet still satisfactory accommodation. Men were housed in galvanised iron sheds and parades and exercise were conducted to maintain discipline. Diaries written by these men indicate that the autumn of 1900 was uncomfortable at night due to the lack of heating. Food was of a reasonable quality, with bread and tea supplied every day and 500 grams of meat constituting a week's ration.

Boer guards had Maxim machineguns mounted in towers to prevent mass escapes, and the prisoners were confined by fences made of newly invented barbed wire up to two metres high. The guards themselves were older soldiers and many lacked uniforms. They were however good shots so few chanced it and tried to escape.

Prisoners were allowed to supplement their diet with goods they bought with money sent to them. The Transvaal government was happy to do this and expected the same treatment from the British, so similar funds were sent through to their men in British prisons. Food was not an issue, in that although it was bland, there was sufficient quantity. The main concern was water purification. The concentration of so many men in such close proximity led to breakouts of diseases like typhus and enteric fever. Fortunately the prisoners were only in the camp for a couple of months before they were rescued. The outbreaks in the civilian concentration camps run by the British in 1901, however, were far worse and caused great hardship and thousands of deaths amongst civilians.

As General Lord Roberts invaded Boer Territory, one of his aims was to release the officers held at a school house in Pretoria, as well as the men in Waterval. His advance in June 1900 was so rapid that not only did the whole Boer government have to quickly evacuate, but only one quarter of the British prisoners at Waterval were successfully withdrawn by the retreating Boers. The remaining 3,200 prisoners were freed with only one casualty from a Boer artillery piece. The release of these prisoners effectively gave a brigade's worth of troops back to the British. The remaining British prisoners were handed back soon after the Boer government capitulated.

Camp: Holzminden, Germany

Conflict: World War 1

Location: North-west Germany, 1917—1918

Prisoners: This was a purpose built officer POW camp, designed to hold officers from the western portion of the Allied forces. As a result it held French, Belgian and Commonwealth commissioned officers. 550 officers and 100 orderlies were imprisoned inside its wire.

Daily routines and camp conditions: The commandant, Niemeyer, was harsh in his punishments. He singled out prisoners he considered high risk for escape attempts. He spent many years in the United States and was given the posting due to his command of English. He used solitary confinement and the restriction of privileges liberally. He used detectives from Berlin to ferret out escape attempts and he continuously searched barracks. The officers in particular disliked the strip searches on arrival. In some respects his precautions were warranted as the "Great Escape" of 1918 had occurred under on his watch.

Within the first month of Holzminden being set up there were 17 escape attempts. This was the camp that had the largest mass escape from Germany in the Great War and Australian officers were in the thick of it. A tunnel was created in November 1917 and 29 officers escaped. Ten made it to neutral Holland by July 1918.

The camp was reasonably comfortable for the officers; enlisted men were assigned as their orderlies and batmen. They organised uniforms, made beds and prepared meals for the officers. Although the food was sparse, Red Cross parcels made for a reasonable fare. Officers were entitled to mattresses instead of straw sacks and had a designated mess for meals which were served by orderlies. The initial complaint raised by a senior British officer within weeks of the camp being opened was the lack of a library, common room and restricted sports area. While these complaints may seem minor, many officers had been used to such conditions in other camps and as officers they were exempt from work and had plenty of time to fill. If one asked whether this was a punishment camp, the answer was "*Ja*".

There were 12 men to a room and each room had a stove. The prisoners were entitled to a German soldier's food and fuel ration each day. The fuel ration was rarely delivered so some men bought fuel from the canteen when there were trees for potential firewood only metres away through the barbed wire. Others burnt stools and bedding slats. The rate was 40 Marks a cubic metre of wood, when a day's pay for a working POW was 30 Pfennig. Officers were paid 60 Marks a month, but they were charged most of that for their meals and board. When the Red Cross parcels arrived, some officers provoked their guards by burning their German bread ration in front of them. Hauptmann Niemeyer soon put an end to this waste. Some officers also used a neutral country to draw cheques, but the charges were exorbitant. They used this money to buy extra food. Imagine what it was like for the Diggers in the enlisted camps!

In the end the mass escape from an "escape proof camp", which had a neurotic commandant who conducted random and intense searches, was a victory for our Aussie soldiers.

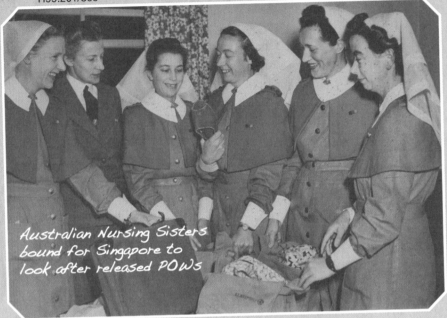

Australian Nursing Sisters
bound for Singapore to
look after released POWs

Propaganda
photograph of
POWs eating
apples at camp,
Pyoktong, in the
winter of 1952-53

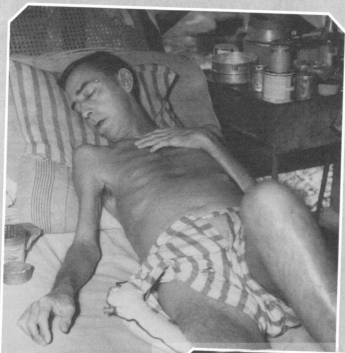

H98.103/4085

H98.103/4080

Released POWs
at Kranji Camp,
Singapore

Camp: Campo PG 57 ('Campo PG' is short for '*campo concentramento di prigioneri di guerra*', meaning 'permanent camp')

Conflict: World War 2

Location: Gruppigano, Udine Northern Italy, 1941—43

Prisoners: Initially designed for Greek and Yugoslav prisoners, Campo PG 57 was built near the ruined chapel of San Martino or Gruppignano. The chapel was removed in 1940 and work began on the camp. By 1942 it had two compounds each housing 1,000 prisoners. Australians taken at Tobruk and some from the Greek campaign were sent here. Greek and Yugoslav prisoners, taken in 1940 and 1941, were moved out by June 1942. After the battles of El Alamein in 1942 the camp was to hold 4,000 ANZAC prisoners. Campo PG 57 housed 'other ranks' with the officers being sent to Campo PG 78, Sulmona.

Daily routines and camp conditions: Each compound had 20 huts that held 50 men and a hut leader. The huts were on concrete foundations to prevent tunnelling and the walls were composed of two layers of wood. There was a heating stove in each hut, but very little fuel was supplied for them. Each compound also had a cookhouse, sanitation facilities and a recreation area. Prisoners who claimed to be farmers were made to work on farms near the camp or in camps nearby. These work farms provided great opportunities for escape, often with the support of the farmers or partisans throughout Italy.

The 'boob' was the disciplinary compound where prisoners were sent for breaches of discipline. Unfortunately breaches of discipline might include not standing to attention when a guard entered a hut. It is not hard to imagine how many Australians found themselves on bread and water and in isolation for 10 or 20 days. As with most camps, Red Cross parcels sustained life when deaths from malnutrition could have taken their toll. Ten Australians were recorded as having died in the camp. Unsanitary water and pneumonia were the two gravest threats to the POWs in Campo PG 57.

The escape of nineteen ANZACs in October 1942 through a tunnel in the new compound was a great boost to the spirits of those in the camp. They had organised the escape with just a small pick and a helmet. They dug four metres down then more than 40 metres out to the wire. Although all of the escapees were recaptured and dealt with harshly, they insulted the claim of the commandant, Lieutenant Colonel Calcaterra, that his camp was escape proof. The sign in his office read, "THE ENGLISH ARE CURSED – BUT MORE CURSED ARE THOSE ITALIANS WHO TREAT THEM WELL" and it sums up the brutality of the man. He was later indicted for war crimes, but his own countrymen caught up with him first. He suffered the same fate as his leader, Mussolini, and was executed by partisans. The attitude of the prisoners towards him is summed up by "Bluey" Rymer, a British wireless operator/air gunner. He called Calcaterra "a short-arsed, fat-gutted little shit".

When Italy capitulated in 1943, some Australians fled to either Yugoslavia, which was fifty kilometres away, or to Switzerland. Italian farmers helped several to escape the Germans, but most found themselves prisoners of the Third Reich and were transported north to Greater Germany.

The local cemetery holds the bodies of 11 ANZAC prisoners of war and a plaque in Italian. *"The land on which this cemetery stands is the gift of the Italian people for the perpetual resting place of the sailors, soldiers and airmen who are honoured here"*.

Camp: Stalag 18a

Conflict: World War 2

Location: Wolfsberg, Austria, 1941—1945

Prisoners: 48,000 Allied, Soviet and Italian prisoners of war

History: Stalag 18a was the main base camp for a variety of smaller work camps or work assignments in Austria and the Greater German territory. It had held internees in the Great War and was enlarged to take in Polish, French and Belgian prisoners in 1939 and 1940. The prisoners from France comprised over half the prisoners at the camp.

Stalag 18a took in a large number of Commonwealth troops after the fall of Greece and Crete in 1941. Around 10,000 Commonwealth troops were held within its walls or controlled from it. After Italy capitulated in 1943, the Germans moved thousands of prisoners north, and Stalag 18a was one of the camps that took the extra prisoners. Italian prisoners who fought against the Germans after Italy changed sides were also incarcerated there for a while before becoming "workers" in 1944.

Soviet prisoners numbered over 8,000 and suffered a higher, but unknown, death rate. Their deaths were caused by a lack of food and harsh working conditions rather than mass executions. Their treatment at the hands of the Nazis was very similar to the treatment given to prisoners of the Japanese in the Pacific at the same time.

Daily routines and camp conditions: Each hut in the camp was designed to house 300 men in double bunks. Soviet prisoners had triple bunks. The mattresses were stuffed with straw so they provided ideal conditions for lice and other parasites to breed. The French had access to six doctors and two dentists as well as the Commonwealth's six doctors. X-ray equipment was available until it was discovered that it was being used to take photos for escape plans. Roll calls were held routinely and unscheduled snap inspections occurred on a regular basis.

Clothes and prisoners were deloused when they entered the camp. They were segregated into compounds based on their nationality, which were separated by barbed wire. Then they waited to be allocated a work party. Different German companies or individuals could request a work party for a period of time provided they could meet certain living and feeding requirements. These mini camps were called *Arbeitskommando*. Prisoners generally preferred agricultural work as they were often fed by the farmer. Others had to work on dams, in mines or factories. The most common factories in the area produced paper and glass. Under the Geneva Conventions, prisoners were meant to be protected and paid more for harder work. Extra rations were given for work in the mines near Steyr or for putting in 10½ hours work a day on a local dam.

For the prisoners waiting for jobs in the main camp, there were several ways to kill their boredom. Both Commonwealth and French sections had formed orchestras and constructed theatres; although the British one was destroyed during a bombing raid in 1944. Sport was popular, especially soccer, table tennis, bowls, hockey and cricket. Some of the prisoners were post-graduates so they held university type courses. The Commonwealth library had 15,000 volumes alone.

French and Commonwealth prisoners were officially allowed access to newspapers, which had been strictly censored by the Germans first. These included two Commonwealth papers published fortnightly by the Anglican and Roman Catholic clergy, as well as a Commonwealth monthly publication called *POW WOW*. The Commonwealth troops had a hidden radio and would spread any news they heard verbatim from barrack to barrack. Later, they actually relayed parts of the news in the theatre.

The men who escaped often did so while they were in transit to the camp or on work parties. By the end of the war many of those who escaped joined Yugoslavian partisans near the border either to continue fighting or to be repatriated.

The camp was liberated by the British in May 1945. Several British parachuted nearby to arrange the surrender. The Germans surrendered to the senior British officer and were disarmed. The last remaining building in Stalag 18a was finally demolished in 1998 thereby destroying what was left of a centre that once commanded the lives of 50,000 men.

Portrait of POWs at German
Camp Stuttgart, Germany, 1917

Medical evacuation on
The Kwai Noi River 1943

Drawing by Fred Ransome Smith

Small Fortress survivors

Camp: Changi

Conflict: World War 2

Location: Singapore 1941—5

Prisoners: Over 15,000 Australian prisoners were confined in the area known as Changi in February 1942. Changi was a series of seven confinement camps on the Eastern peninsular of the geographical area, also called Changi. Australians generally found themselves at Selarang Barracks, although by 1944 they were located in the actual civilian Changi gaol.

The camp was a concentration point where prisoners were brought together to form work parties across Asia. As a result, the camp's numbers fluctuated as work tasks were filled. For example, the Australian population dropped to 2,500 in the middle of 1943 but climbed back up to 5,000 in 1944. The camp held up to 50,000 Empire, Commonwealth and Allied prisoners at its peak. The deaths at Changi amounted to less than 1,000, whereas more than 7,000 Australians died in other camps.

Daily routines and camp conditions: At first life in Changi was misleadingly benign. Once the prisoners realised they had to take care of themselves, they organised water, sanitation and living quarters in the three former army barracks on the peninsular. Things changed in March when barbed wire separated the barracks and compounds and again in August when all officers above the rank of lieutenant-colonel were removed to Taiwan. The Australians were then under the "command" of LTCOL "Black Jack" Galleghan; of whom former POWs noted in this book have the greatest respect for.

The camp began a university-style training scheme, similar to those in European prison camps, and musical and literary societies were also established. Contact with the Japanese was sometimes limited as orders for working on the wharves, roads or loading stores were issued through the senior officers. Punishment for disobeying orders could result in anything from beatings, to torture to summary execution. That said, the proximity to "civilisation" meant that the death penalty was generally limited to attempted escapes and violence towards guards. Most of these executions were illegal under both the Hague and Geneva Conventions. The guards were often Indian soldiers who had changed sides. A number of beatings were at the hands of former Allies, not just the

Japanese. For example, the execution of two attempted escapees in early 1942 was performed by former Indian soldiers.

Rations in 1942 could be supplemented by trade with civilians or by buying goods at the canteens, which were run by local Singaporeans or Chinese at highly inflated prices. Prisoners were paid for work in the Singapore area and they supplemented their diet with these wages. This meant these POWs were generally better fed than their mates in German and Italian camps in 1942/3. That said, by the end of 1942, several "forces" of Australians were sent to work around Asia by the Japanese. These men were starved and worked to death; they had a one in three chance of perishing. In addition, by 1945, prisoners found themselves in overcrowded and unsanitary conditions in Changi and with meagre rations. This was mainly due to a lack of supply caused by effective Allied submarine operations against convoys which sent supplies to Singapore.

The forces that Australians either volunteered to be part of, or were forced to be involved with, were as follows:

Force	Location	Date of departure from Changi
A Force	Burma	15th May, 1942
B Force	Borneo	8th July, 1942
C Force	Japan	28th November, 1942
D Force	Thailand	14th–18th March, 1943
E Force	Borneo	29th May, 1943
F Force	Thailand	April, 1943
G Force	Japan	26th April, 1943
H Force	Thailand	May, 1943
J Force	Japan	16th May, 1943
K Force	Thailand	June, 1943
L Force	Thailand	23rd August, 1943

Those who survived these forces and were lucky enough to be sent back to Changi, found the food and conditions in Singapore a life-saving relief compared to the horrors of their labour.

Camp: Burma-Thai Railway

Conflict: World War 2

Location: Camps scattered over 414 kilometre strip of rail and road in Burma and Thailand, 1942—3

Prisoners: Over 60,000 prisoners worked on the railway from a variety of countries including the United Kingdom, Australia, New Zealand, the Netherlands, India and the US. Over 170,000 civilian slave labourers also worked on the railway including Thais, Burmese, Javanese and Singaporeans

Of the total number of prisoners of war sent to work on the railway, over 12,000 died – a ratio of one in five. Australians numbered around 9,500 and workers died at a ratio of one in four. The civilian slave labour died at a rate of one in two. Deaths were predominantly due to overwork, malnutrition and a lack of medical equipment and antibiotics.

Daily routines and camp conditions: The first camps in Burma were set up in May 1942 with 3,000 prisoners drawn from Brigadier Varely's brigade in Singapore as well as soldiers and sailors captured in Java. This main force was called "A" Force, with smaller groups sent to specific tasks and named after their commander, such as Black or Anderson. Prisoners were made to construct airfields, prepare materials for the railway, build new camps along the route and, of course, construct the railway.

Each of the camps along the railway where the prisoners laboured were called "kilo" camps, that is, a distance in kilometres from the Burmese camp at Thanbyuzayat. For example, 55 Kilo Camp where Colonel Coates acted as a surgeon was 55 kilometres from the start of the railway in Burma. The appalling conditions on this part of the railway meant that 479 Australians lost their lives here.

The vast majority of Australians sent to work on the railway began in Thailand at Nong Pladuk and worked north to eventually meet up with their comrades coming down from Burma. The forces here were D, F, H, K and L. They were marched or trucked to various camps along the route. Marching would be the norm, and it would not be unusual to cover a distance of 40 kilometres or more a day on foot. Weary Dunlop's force was on this part of the railway and it was his ingenuity as a doctor, especially with respect to distilling saline for intravenous injections administered to dehydrated cholera patients, that saved so many lives. Despite this effort, F Force, for example, began with 7,000 British and Australian men. Of the 3,600

Australians, 29 percent, or more then 1,000 soldiers, perished. The 3,300 British soldiers suffered a death rate of 61 percent or more then 2,000 soldiers.

The camps themselves did not require fences. The rugged terrain and death penalty for attempting to escape was a deterrent for most. Those few who thought they could make it to the British lines in India were quickly rounded up and executed. Food became more and more difficult to obtain the further prisoners moved from the coast. Everything had to be transported inland and that usually meant on foot. As the priority was equipment to build the rail there was little room for transporting food. Japanese guards did not miss out on food so it was the prisoners who suffered.

Often there were only one or two meals a day. It was generally a cup or two of over-boiled rice which came to be known as "pap". The best way to describe pap is starch sludge. Occasionally vegetables or a small portion of meat were added. It is hardly surprising that disease soon took its toll. The problem here was that sick men received half or no rations, as rations were part of their "pay". No work, no food. This burden was increased when mates gave their food to sick friends so they themselves went on to become ill.

The diseases that caused so many deaths were dysentery, cholera, malaria and beri-beri. With adequate food, anti-malarial drugs and good sanitation, these diseases would never have taken hold. Weaknesses in immune systems also led to a susceptibility to ulcers; especially on the legs. Tropical ulcers are caused by a bacterial infection that eats the flesh. A healthy person's immune system will generally cope. A sick person would also cope if they were given antibiotics. A man on two cups of rice sludge a day would need to be very lucky and have mates scoop the dying flesh out regularly or have his leg amputated. The alternative was to die from gangrene.

The engineering feat of this man-made hell stands as an ironic homage to those who died. Six hundred and sixty-eight bridges were built with the most primitive equipment and 1,400 sleepers were laid every kilometre – a total of almost 600,000 sleepers. The steepness of the gradients and the 12-hour plus working day made this an incredible feat. It also cost the lives of at least 100,000 people, some say up to 150,000.

The railway was completed at the end of 1943. It ran six trains a day, far below the expectations of Tokyo. Following the completion of the railway, most of the surviving Australians were sent back to Changi for redeployment in Japan and other work camps.

Camp: Bean Camp

Conflict: Korean War

Location: Suan, North Korea, January—April 1951

Prisoners: Bean Camp was the nickname given to a former "workers" barracks that was controlled by the Japanese. Korean labourers worked the local mines until the Japanese defeat in 1945. The Democratic People's Republic of Korea (North Korea) used these facilities to incarcerate United Nations prisoners during the Korean War before they were taken to other camps. Its proximity to the capital made it an important central location for POWs. Around 1,000 prisoners moved through the camp, including Australians, British, Americans, Turks and Canadians. The camp was moved to the nearby mine complex to escape potential air raids and was abandoned after only a few months' operation. Australians captured in early 1951 where processed through this camp.

Daily routines and camp conditions: Conditions at Bean Camp were harsh for the POWs held there. A quarter of the prisoners died in the camp; most from either wounds received prior to arrival, the torturous march north without proper food or the lack of adequate medical facilities. Fortunately no Australians died at Bean Camp, although our only prisoner to die in captivity, "Slim" Madden, died on the march up north.

Bean Camp had no barbed wire or walls and didn't need any. It was set in a valley with huts on either side of a dirt road for a couple of hundred metres. Guards were posted at each end of the road and there were constant roving patrols around the camp. The North Korean and Chinese guards did not see the need to confine prisoners with barriers. The harshness of the terrain, the distance to the Republic of Korea's (South Korean) border and the fact that non-Asians moving through enemy territory would be easily discovered, made blockades unnecessary.

The huts were 15 metres by 5 metres and had smaller rooms inside that held 15 prisoners each. Lice were rife and the washing facility in the middle of winter was a single well. This also provided the camp's drinking water and diseases were contracted if the water was not boiled before drinking.

From this camp, near the Capital Pyongyang, prisoners were split up into camps numbered 1—12 as well as other temporary camps.

Australians found themselves in camps such as "Camp 1" on the Yau River or "Camp 5" near Pyoktong. At these camps prisoners were treated to programmes of "re-education" and Marxist philosophy. Sometimes they were subject to food, water and sleep deprivation and at other times they were seemingly ignored for weeks. None of the 29 Australians who survived internment and these torturous processes cracked. Unfortunately, a small number of our United Nations brothers did, and were used for propaganda purposes by the Chinese and North Koreans.

The permanent numbered camps had better conditions than Bean Camp. As negotiations to end the war began in Vienna, the Chinese and North Koreans needed to prove their "humanity" to the world. They staged photos and films showing good food and recreation facilities, especially towards the end of the war, but they did not fool the international community. From an Australian perspective, the Chinese and North Koreans were only moderately "better" captors than the Japanese in World War Two, and they were inferior to the treatment delivered by Germans to their POWs. Unlike the Australian prisoners, 38 percent of the 7,000 United States POWs, or more then 2,660 soldiers, did not make it home alive. This was the same POW death rate the Americans received at the hand of the Japanese in WW2. Statistics indicate that the Germans singled out Soviet prisoners to brutalise, while the communists chose the Americans.

Chapter 11

Battle Book

You know there is a saying
That sunshine follows rain,
And sure enough you'll realise
That joy will follow pain;
Let courage be your password
Make fortitude your guide,
And then instead of grousing
Remember those who died.

Written by an unknown prisoner
during WWII found on the wall
of a solitary confinement cell,
in a German POW Camp

The four campaign summaries in this "Battle Book" (Greece, Crete, Malaya/Singapore and El Alamein) were selected not because they were more important than others but simply because they represent the battles where the majority of Australia's prisoners of war were captured. Almost 80 percent of Australia's 35,000 or so POWs were captured in these campaigns.

Stalag Luft 1 snow-covered tower

Battle: Defence of Greece

Date: 6th March 1941—29th April 1941

Mission: Defend Greece's central border in order to deny Axis occupation

Units: Australian: 6th Australian Division, 2nd New Zealand Division, 1st British Armoured Brigade, up to four under-strength Greek divisions. Commonwealth forces: around 60,000 men

Enemy: Von List's 12th Army with three Panzer armoured divisions, two mountain and five infantry divisions with two infantry divisions in reserve

Casualties: Australia: KIA: 320, WIA: 494, PW: 2,030. Total Commonwealth: KIA: 900, WIA: 1,260, PW: 14,000.German forces, KIA: 1,160, WIA: 3,755, MIA: 345 (official German Records)

Significant features: At Tempe Gorge the ANZAC Corps once again fought as brothers against overwhelming odds to delay German armour

Synopsis: The Greek campaign ended in a painful defeat for the Australians. The 6th Division, so victorious after its 1,000 kilometre rout of Mussolini's army from December 1940 to February 1941, faced an almost impossible task when it landed in Greece in March. While historians have debated the wisdom of sending Commonwealth forces to Greece, especially without air cover and little armour, it did help delay Operation Barbarossa by one month and also influenced the German outcome against the Soviets.

In October 1940, Italy invaded Greece from Albania and was thrown back. Hitler was not consulted and demanded a "please explain". However, he was more concerned that his plans for the Soviet invasion were forcibly delayed. Italy refused German support as they feared Germany would occupy Albania, even though Albania had been invaded by the Greeks.

There seemed to be no threats to Hitler's larger plans, however, as Yugoslavia stood between Greece and Germany and it would soon (like Rumania and Bulgaria) join the Tripartite treaty with Germany. Rumania had permitted a German build up of troops for the Russian invasion and Bulgaria allowed German troops to prepare to invade Greece if Allied forces arrived.

The Commonwealth forces landed in Greece almost as a deliberate goad. Three weeks after Commonwealth forces landed to take up the centre of the Greek defensive line of Albania-Yugoslavia-Bulgaria, Yugoslavia experienced a coup and the new government declared its intentions to seek Allied support. The panzers rolled on 6th April and 50 divisions moved into Yugoslavia and Greece. Two Allied and four Greek divisions fell back under von Lists 12th Army. The Australians, Kiwis and Poms fought rearguard actions that were forceful and, to some extent, effective. The fighting at Thermopylae Line and Pinios Gorge both surprised and frustrated the Germans. Many Greeks survived because the Allied forces fought so hard and, under General Blamey, leapfrogged back in good order and with a vicious bite. The main anti-tank weapon, however, was a Boyes anti-tank rifle. This was a very effective weapon against Italian light vehicles, but useless against Panzerkampfwagens, the German tanks.

The Greeks kept the bulk of their forces against the Italians. In fact they may have inflicted 100,000 casualties in the Italians. The Greeks in the centre, however, were poorly trained and led and capitulated early.

This armour advantage and the air superiority of the Axis, meant hard day defences and rapid night withdrawals. In an Anzac Day speech in 1989, one of the COs of the 6th Division explained that his men had held a river crossing against German Infantry. Panzers kept coming and tried to cross it. Several sank. Eventually it was forded. At this point he told his men to withdraw as a ".303 does little against a tank." He said to his men, "You have done enough, get to the coast as best you can."

A withdrawal to Crete and Egypt was called by mid-April. On Anzac Day 1941, Aussies and Kiwis, exhausted but with heads held high, were delaying the enemy or embarking for the next battles; together as their fathers had done at Gallipoli back in 1915. As at Gallipoli, this defeat did not end the war. It primed our men to fight harder and fiercer. They were as much ANZACs as their fathers, and they were going to show it later in the war; in New Guinea for the Australians and in Italy for the New Zealanders.

In the short term, the campaign cost more than it was worth. The delay to the Axis, however, was telling as this campaign, along with the one in Crete, delayed the Axis invasion of the Soviet Union by up to six weeks. This meant the Russian winter held the Nazis just short of Moscow.

Battle: Defence of Crete

Date: April—May 1941

Mission: Defend Crete in order to maintain an Allied presence in the Eastern Mediterranean.

Units: 16th and 17th Australian Infantry Brigades (composite less than 1,000 men from 2/2, 2/3, 2/5 and 2/6 Battalions) in addition to 2/1, 2/4, 2/7, 2/8, 2/11 Battalions (most under 19th Brigade), 2nd NZ Division and British 14th Brigade. Total Australian Infantry was eight under-strength battalions. Total numbers: Allied 40,000 of which 6,500 were Australian

Enemy: Major General Student's Fliegerkorps XI, 7th Flieger Division, 5th Gebirgs Division. Total: 30,000—35,000

Casualties: Commonwealth losses: KIA: 1,742, WIA: 2,225, PW: 11,370. Greek losses: In excess of 5,000 casualties. Australian losses: KIA: 274, WIA: 507, PW: 3,000. Axis losses: KIA: 5,000—7,000, WIA: 3,000—6,000 (based on official Axis media releases and war graves/reports from Crete)

Significant features: The Allies had the German battle plans and were defeated. The German paratroopers suffered such losses that they never attempted drops of this scale again

Synopsis: Crete was the Wehrmacht's Pyrrhic victory. Numbers killed in action and wounded in action on the Axis side were about three times those of the defeated Allies. The German official figure of 2,000 dead does not tally with the 4,000 graves on the island. The Allied defeat was not caused by a lack of courage, skill or determination on the Australians part. In fact it is testament to the 6th Division soldiers that those who survived the retreat from Greece and the subsequent retreat from Crete then drew on their ANZAC roots to drive the Japanese invaders from the South Pacific.

The battle was lost due to lack of air superiority and communication. Although the decision to send the men, who brilliantly took Bardia and Tobruk, to a doomed Greece in March 1941 has often been criticised as a waste of resources and good men, it inadvertently set in motion a series of events that caused Hitler's invasion of the USSR to stall at Moscow. The Commonwealth presence in Greece, and Italy's defeat by the Greeks, forced the German Army to be directed into Greece. The ensuing stunning German victory against a Commonwealth Corps, which lacked armour or air support, forced Commonwealth forces to withdraw to Egypt. A larger than division-sized force, under

New Zealand command, evacuated to Crete to maintain a British naval presence in the eastern Mediterranean.

This force threatened Axis supply lines as well their staging ground for a future invasion; especially with the planned Axis invasion of the USSR set for May 1941. It had to be removed. British naval vessels threatened to destroy a seaborne invasion fleet off Crete and the Commonwealth forces were spread out to cover all possible landing zones from the sea and air if the enemy got through.

The use of the Enigma/Ultra code-breaking machine by the British gave Kiwi General Freyberg the summary of the German battle plan, including 12,000 airborne troops (and their three airfield targets) with 600 aircraft and 10,000 seaborne landing troops. This was General Student's own battle plan and the Allies had their very own copy! Freyberg took the gamble of protecting both sea and air zones and this decision led to the fall of Maleme airfield and consequently the loss of the island. The seaborne troops were never part of the original invasion force and were to be follow-up troops. In fact the Royal Navy sank one of the fleets. The message Freyberg received was misinterpreted.

After daily air raids over three weeks, the Australians heard the *thrum* of a different type of engine on 20th May. It was predicted that 600 Junkers would be dropping the first brigade of the 7th Flieger Division by air. Up to half of these men died before they hit the ground. The other half, however, fought back hard. They had three main objectives: the Maleme, Candia and Retimo airfields.

While the Australians contained the Germans at the centre and to the west of the battle area, the Kiwis were unable to hold Maleme airfield to the west. Once the Germans held the strip, more soldiers and supplies arrived by air. German troops and planes were shot as they disembarked (over 100 aircraft littered the field by 26th May), but the continual volume of soldiers, combined with a continual supply of ammunition, gave the Germans the foothold with which to conquer the island.

After a week or more of fighting and defeating the enemy at a unit level, the Australians retreated and regrouped to Egypt. Many, however, were to spend the rest of the war in a POW camp. Six hundred hid from the Germans and escaped by boat over the following year.

The defence of Crete caused delays to Germany's invasion of the USSR until June 1941 and this arguably led to its failure at the gates of Moscow, as the Germans were forced to struggle through the Russian winter.

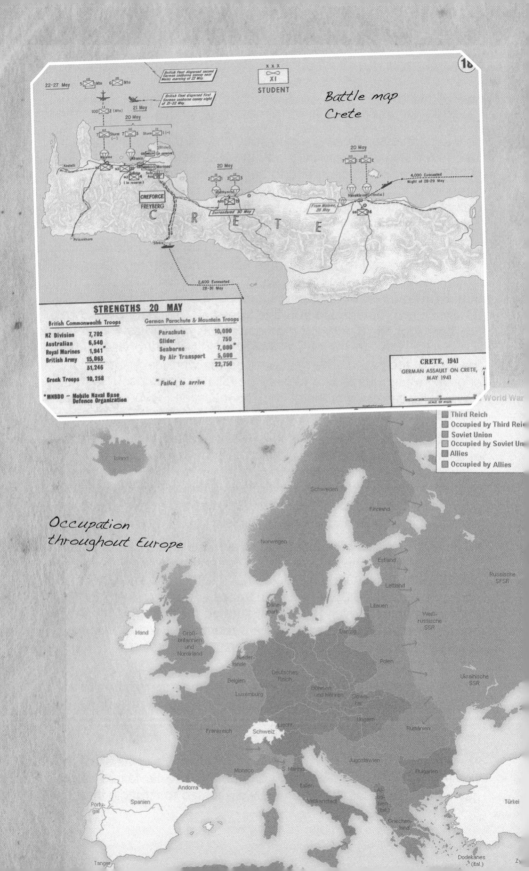

Battle map
Crete

XXX
XI
STUDENT

CREFORCE
FREYBERG
C

CRETE

STRENGTHS 20 MAY

British Commonwealth Troops		German Parachute & Mountain Troops	
NZ Division	7,702	Parachute	10,000
Australian	6,540	Glider	750
Royal Marines	1,941*	Seaborne	7,000*
British Army	15,063	By Air Transport	5,000
	31,246		22,750
Greek Troops	10,258	*Failed to arrive	

*MNBDO — Mobile Naval Base Defence Organization

CRETE, 1941
GERMAN ASSAULT ON CRETE,
MAY 1941

Occupation
throughout Europe

Third Reich
Occupied by Third Reich
Soviet Union
Occupied by Soviet Union
Allies
Occupied by Allies

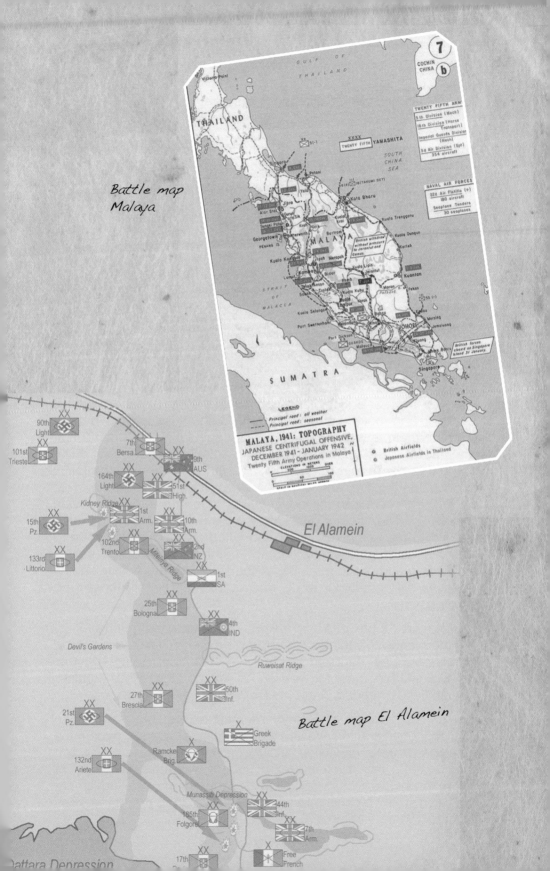

Battle map
Malaya

Malaya map labels

7
b

COCHIN
CHINA

GULF OF
THAILAND

THAILAND

TWENTY FIFTH YAMASHITA

SOUTH
CHINA
SEA

TWENTY FIFTH ARMY

5th Division (Mech)
(6th Division (Horse)
Transport)
Imperial Guards Division
(Mech)
3d Air Division (Spt)
554 aircraft

NAVAL AIR FORCES

22d Air Flotilla (+)
180 aircraft
Seaplane Tenders
30 seaplanes

Victoria Point

Singora

Patani

Kota Bharu

(TAKUMI DET)

Yala

Kuala Trengganu

Jitra

Alor Star

Kroh
Kroi

Kuala Dungun

Kuala Kedah

Betong

Kuala Lipis
Jerantut

Kerteh

Georgetown
PENANG IS.

Butterworth

Ipoh

Raub

MALAYA

Kuantan

Kuala Kangsar

Tapah

Bidor

Maran

Pekan

Lumut

Telok
Anson

Tanjong Malim

Pahang

Kuala Kubu

STRAIT
OF
MALACCA

Kuala Selangor

Seremban

Port Swettenham

Malacca

JOHORE

Mersing

British withdrew
without pressure to
Jerantut and
Gemas.

British forces
closed on Singapore
Island 31 January.

Port Dickson

GUARDS

Muar

Kluang

Batu Pahat

Singapore

Jemaluang

S U M A T R A

LEGEND

Principal road: all weather
Principal road: seasonal

○ British Airfields
● Japanese Airfields in Thailand

ELEVATIONS IN METERS
200   OVER

MALAYA, 1941: TOPOGRAPHY
JAPANESE CENTRIFUGAL OFFENSIVE,
DECEMBER 1941 - JANUARY 1942
Twenty Fifth Army Operations in Malaya

ELEVATIONS IN METERS
50   200   OVER

SCALE IN NAUTICAL MILES

El Alamein map labels

90th
Light

101st
Trieste

7th
Bersa

9th
AUS

164th
Light

51st
High.

Kidney Ridge

1st
Arm.

10th
Arm.

15th
Pz.

102nd
Trento

2nd
NZ

Miteirya Ridge

El Alamein

133rd
Littorio

1st
SA

25th
Bologna

4th
IND

Devil's Gardens

Ruweisat Ridge

27th
Brescia

50th
Inf.

21st
Pz.

Greek
Brigade

Battle map El Alamein

132nd
Ariete

Ramcke
Brig

Munassib Depression

185th
Folgore

44th
Inf.

7th
Arm.

Qattara Depression

17th

Free
French

Battle: Defences of Malaya and Singapore

Date: 8th December 1941—15th February 1942

Mission: Defend Malaya and Singapore in order to halt Japanese expansion in the south-west Pacific

Units: Allied: Australian 8th Division, Indian 9th and 11th Divisions, British 18th Division, 4 independent brigades (140,000)

Enemy: 25th Imperial Army (three divisions, plus one in reserve in Japan)

Casualties: Allies: KIA/WIA: 9,000, PW: 130,000. Nearly 22,000 Australians captured at Singapore, Malaya, Java, Timor, Ambon and Rabaul. Japan: KIA/WIA: 9,000

Significant features: British Prime Minister Winston Churchill described the fall of Singapore as "the worst disaster and largest capitulation in British history"

Synopsis: Often when analysing the fall of Singapore, we either point the finger at British planning or claim that the Japanese martial prowess had been underestimated. Both these claims detract from the main reason for Singapore's capitulation. You can't fight without water and you can't, as a civilised culture, leave one million civilians to die of thirst or hunger. The 8th Division did a fantastic job considering the lack of supply lines, food and water, as well as having to shoulder the additional burden of a suffering civilian population. Their needs and safety were the major consideration that led to the Allies' surrender and withdrawal. This was done to preserve life of combatants and non-combatants alike and serves as a strong and proud reminder of the sacrifices the Aussie soldier makes in his endeavour to do what is just and fair for those who solicit our help.

The tin and rubber of Malaya were vital resources for the Allies. The thousands of vehicles to supply divisions in North Africa relied heavily on rubber supplied by Malaya for the manufacture of tyres. Tin was vital for solder for welding, as well as other alloys required for war. Japan needed it and the Commonwealth had it.

The British defence of Malaya seemed sound: there were two divisions forward in Malaya and the Australians in depth. Two British warships, *Prince of Wales* and *Repulse*, were sunk by aircraft two days into the invasion. Pearl Harbour was attacked 24 hours beforehand. The British ability to destroy enemy sea movement had been sunk. Japanese forces landed with armour and the Allies had little to throw against it.

The Indian divisions withdrew down the Malay peninsular. Some claim that this was the result of the Indian Nationalist movement (thousands were later recruited to fight the British), but it was more likely to have been caused by the ferocity of the Japanese attack and inferior numbers. As the Indians withdrew, the Australians waited at Jahore, about 100 kilometres from Singapore Island. Here the Japanese encountered a strong defence and a series of cunning Aussie ambushes.

Over 1,000 Japanese casualties fell for a comparatively light loss of Australians. The Australians used the environment to fight the enemy on their own terms until the eventual withdrawal to the relative safety of Singapore. The myth of the guns pointing south causing Singapore to fall is a fallacy. The vitality of the defence of Singapore lay in its food and water supply. Tobruk had sea resupply and desalination plants. Leningrad and Stalingrad also had a resupply line. So did Gallipoli. Singapore was totally cut off but was home to one million civilians. It has also been argued that the Japanese had only 30,000 fighting men from their force able to storm Singapore. This also seems credible, but without air reconnaissance the Allied command had little to support this theory. What they did know was that the Japanese were relentless and that Singapore's civilians were suffering.

In addition, the water supply from Jahore had been cut. The Japanese were on the outskirts of the city and no supplies, ammunition or reinforcements were forthcoming.

Surrender on the 15th was the best option available if they were to limit the loss of innocent civilian lives. The surrendering force expected a civilised response from the Japanese however they were not aware of the massacre at Alexander Hospital a couple of days earlier. Doctors and patients had been brutally bayoneted and although the Allied command was not aware of this, it is difficult to say whether it would have altered their decision given that there were no other options available.

If these brave Commonwealth men had continued fighting to the last, the devastation to the Singaporeans would have been greater than it was. Singapore would have been razed to a slag heap by unopposed bombers.

During the battle the 8th Division proved their worth and by their surrender, saved the lives of many innocent civilians.

Battle: El Alamein

Date: July—November 1942

Mission:
July: Defend in order to prevent the capture of the Suez Canal
November: Attack Afrika Korps' positions in order to draw his reserve and allow a Commonwealth armour breakthrough

Units: October: 8th Army including the 9th Australian (220,000 men and 1,100 tanks)

Enemy: October: Panzer Armee Afrika (180,000 men and 600 tanks)

Casualties: Australian: Oct/Nov KIA: 620, WIA: 1,944, PW: 130 (nearly 2,000 throughout North Africa). Allied: total 13,000

Enemy: Oct/Nov: KIA/WIA: up to 30,000, PW: 27,000. Loss of 450 tanks

Significant features: Field Marshall Montgomery wrote, "We could not have won the battle in 12 days without the magnificent Australian Division." The 9th Division suffered 6,000 casualties between July and November

Synopsis: There were three major battles at El Alamein, although they are often broken down into the First Battle in July 1942 and the Second Battle in October/November.

1942 was the last throw of the dice for the Axis forces to win the war. Hitler desperately needed to capture the Volga River and the Caucus mountains. By doing so the Axis forces would not only gain vital oil reserves but, more importantly, cut both Moscow and the factories in the Ural Mountains off from its own oil supplies. Iraq was close to civil war and a link up with pro-German Iraqi forces would deny British oil reserves and prepare an invasion gateway to India. All that was needed was the capture of the Suez Canal and a push through Syria to meet up with the German troops that were invading southern Russia. The man given the task was Field Marshall Erwin Rommel. The division that was to once more defeat him and force his retreat from Egypt and Libya was the Australian 9th Division, the "Rats of Tobruk".

As was the case in North Africa, the side on the offensive stretched supply lines to the point that the defender could regain the initiative. After the Allies relieved Tobruk in late 1941, Rommel regathered his strength and advanced. Tobruk, the port that resisted Rommel for

242 days, fell in two days when the South Africans surrendered in June 1942. The 9th Division was livid. They wanted another crack at Rommel and were given one in October that year when newly appointed commander, General Bernard Montgomery, devised a plan to destroy Rommel's armour and finally secure the vital Suez Canal and oil supplies for the duration of the war.

Most of July saw the 9th Division hold their line near the railway stop of El Alamein. To the south was the Qattara Depression; terrain impassable for an army. This corridor between the Depression and the Mediterranean was vital and Rommel's men pounded themselves against the wall of Australians. Air superiority and intense artillery support bolstered the men who once again defeated Rommel.

While the 8th Army, under Montgomery's command, built up for the offence, Rommel was once again defeated in August and September as he tried to force his way through to the Suez, south of the Australian lines.

On 23rd October, over 1,000 artillery pieces opened up and the 30th Corps advanced, with Australians in the lead. British armour in the south met heavy opposition, but the Australians and Kiwis met their objectives further north. It was in some ways a repeat of the Great War, whereby Australian units took their objectives while their Allies were left behind. An entire German infantry division was pressed against the Mediterranean, so Rommel sent in his armour to save them. This is what Montgomery wanted. While the 9th Division was mauled by the bulk of Rommel's armour, British armour broke through in the south and hit the rear Axis echelons. It was the German's first taste of Blitzkrieg from the receiving end.

Hitler naturally ordered Rommel to stay and fight, but Rommel pulled back and in doing so lost most of his armour.

Australians, making up less than 10 percent of the Army took about 25 percent of its casualties. Rommel suffered his third defeat at the hand of the 9th Division and now he was on the run. It is testimony to the respect the British had for the toughness of the 9th that Major-General Francis de Guingaund, Montgomery's Chief of Staff, Allied Land-Forces, was alleged to have said on the eve of D-Day in 1944, "My God, I wish we had 9th Australian Division with us this morning".

Many in the 9th would have preferred to have been in Tunis in May 1943 when the Afrika Korps surrendered, but they had another mission: the Japanese were still threatening Australia and the boys were needed at home.

The Small Fortress of Terezín

By Paul Rea, author of "Voices from the Fortress," the story of Walter Steilberg an Australian ex-prisoner of war illegally thrown into a Nazi concentration camp called the "Small Fortress of Terezín" in Czechoslovakia.

Walter and other allied POWs were stripped of any protection offered by their national and military status and punished for escaping from a POW camp. Because the army had no record of their detention, successive Australian governments refused to believe the survivors' ordeal at the hands of the Gestapo. Their application for war crimes compensation was denied for 40 years.

Small Fortress, Terezín
Photo courtesy Terezín Memorial

The stories told in these pages deserve to be heard. Many returned prisoners-of-war never tell their stories: they carry a life-long silence covering deep personal hurt that forces loved ones to move gently around all the things not spoken about.

Some POW stories have a sharp political edge that leads to recognition and change. This is the case with a small handful of Australian and New Zealand prisoners whose experiences were denied and dismissed by their governments for more than 40 years after World War 2.

These are the concentration camp men who slipped through the POW system into the hands of the Nazi security apparatus – the Gestapo and the SS – and were stripped of their military and national status and thrown into camps for political prisoners. Many of these men returned from Europe highly traumatised by cruelties unimaginable to most of us and then had to fight hard to have their stories heard.

Walter Steilberg, 2/1 Field Company, Royal Australian Engineers, is a central figure in this remarkable story. Steilberg was told his war was over in Greece on 6th May 1941. He was then a strapping 21-year-old from Sydney's Freshwater who had joined up not for any patriotic reason, but because the Army offered him a paid job – his first permanent job. Like many others he felt humiliated by capture.

"That really stuck in my craw," he recalls. "I made up my mind then that I would beat them in the end and that I'd be a free man by the end of the war …and I bloody was, too."

Steilberg escaped from POW camps and work parties seven times, often in the company of his little Pommy mate from Nottingham, Bob Slater, 2nd Battalion, Coldstream Guards, who had been taken near Tobruk in June 1942.

Together they were a handful, always looking to break out and get on the road and under the stars for a few weeks at least. Then, usually, it was back to the camp for 30 days' punishment. In fact, Steilberg got as far west as Hungary and down into Yugoslavia. He was always trying to get back into the fight.

But in late 1944 they had the bad luck to be picked up in Czechoslovakia and were handed over to the Gestapo. From Prague they travelled 60 miles north to a place called the "Small

Fortress of Terezín" where, against Geneva Conventions on the treatment of POWs, they were stripped of their uniforms and issued with the striped burlap we now associate with Jewish prisoners.

Terezín, known as the "Living Grave", was a Gestapo prison for political prisoners, mainly civilians, and this was something different. Gloating guards told the new arrivals to get up early in the morning to see what passed for sport in Terezín.

"We got up at first light and in the courtyard a few yards away was a pile of corpses and body parts," Steilberg recalls. "It looked like someone had gone mad with an axe. Some of the bodies were missing limbs, some were headless, and other prisoners in vertically striped garments, like the ones they were wearing, were hurriedly sewing these remains into big hessian bags."

Steilberg and Slater spent the winter of 1944-45 in an icy concrete cell in the IV Yard with several British prisoners, a Belgian and an American. In 1945 came other Allied POWs picked up by security forces in Bohemia. A war crimes prosecutor later described the Small Fortress as the "cruelest Nazi jail" where several thousand prisoners died from starvation, disease and hardship.

And many prisoners were sent there to be murdered. The guards shot them summarily or made them fight to the death in a section of moat they called "The Coliseum" or buried them alive or whipped them with weighted truncheons and leather thongs tipped with nails. Killings took place in the IV Yard and in Slater's words, "something Satanic had descended on this place".

With the Russians approaching in March 1945, Steilberg and Slater were among several thousand prisoners taken out to work on an anti-tank ditch. This scene resembled an ants' nest with prisoners digging with their bare hands and scurrying up to the lip of the ditch, hurried along by guards and kapos, (trusted prisoners working in concentration camps).

"Oh, they used all sorts of ways of killing them," says Steilberg. "I saw this one old chap, he'd fallen on his knees and couldn't get up. I saw a kapo pick up a spade and split his head open straight down the middle with the edge of it. This chap's head just sort of fell apart onto his shoulders. Oh, it was horrible, you couldn't imagine anything like it. I saw another chap fall down and this SS guard started shooting him and went up his legs, just shot him in the ankle and then the knees and finally killed him.

"Just around us in our part of the ditch there were so many killed. Just around where I was working I saw 27 people killed," he said.

Steilberg lost half his bodyweight in six months in Terezín. The enduring companionship of Bob Slater helped save him. They were always at each other's side, urging each other along. They staggered out of the fortress with about 170 Allied men in early April and fearing being used as hostages they decided to break free from that group.

When Steilberg encountered the Americans at Weiden, Bavaria, on Anzac Day 1945, he had been a prisoner a few days short of four years. Ahead was a British Empire Medal in recognition of his many escapes. He had also fulfilled his pledge to end the war as a free man.

Back home in Australia, Steilberg felt anything but free.

Terezín had wrecked him. His marriage fell to pieces, he rejoined the Army briefly and was immobilised by depression and unable to work. These were the days before acceptance of post-traumatic stress disorder (or its treatment) and like everyone else he was expected to put the war behind him and get on with his life. For Steilberg, and other survivors of the Nazi concentration camps, this was impossible.

"I just couldn't settle down after the war," said Steilberg. "I couldn't talk about it. Nobody wants to listen to that stuff, nobody wants to know. People just don't want to believe that things like that can go on, it's too horrific to think that people can do these things to other people. For a couple of years after I got out of Terezín there were large blanks in my memory, I just couldn't recall things that happened in those years. And after that, I've been sick most of the time with stomach ulcers, hypertension and now these heart attacks. And I was affected mentally more than I'd really imagined. There were two British soldiers, one of them from the Coldstream Guards, a huge chap, and when they came out of Terezín they went stark raving mad because of what they'd witnessed and what they'd experienced. It's taken me my whole life to get rid of the smell of that place."

The British government understood that its concentration camp men needed special help and in 1964 it pressed their case as victims of war crimes and obtained compensation on their behalf from West Germany.

When the Australians learned of this they approached their own government only to be told that the Army had no record of their detention in Terezín. No papers, no POW questionnaires attached to their files, nothing to say they were there. Therefore, the government would not recognise their ordeal and would certainly not make any approach to West Germany for war crimes compensation.

This denial continued through successive Australian governments from Menzies through to Fraser – they were all aware of the men's claims but never acted, never inquired. Government officials dismissed the concentration camp men and told them it never happened, they were never in this place called Terezín…it was all in their minds.

But the men couldn't let it rest. Most could not recall other Australians and New Zealanders from the camp so a call was put out in 1978 through the RSL and the media. Walter Steilberg finally got to tell his story. So did Alexander McClelland, 2/1 Infantry Battalion, Sixth Division, a Terezín survivor who fled to England in self-imposed exile after suffering nervous collapse brought on by government rejection. Word travels fast on the POW grapevine. Other Terezín men came forward to add their testimonies: Herb Cullen (2/1 Battalion), Walter Wise (2/12 Battalion) Walter Riley (3 Anti Tank Regiment). Each man held part of the puzzle, each telling a story that added weight to the claims of others, each liberating himself in the service of his comrades by uttering things he had never before divulged, not to anyone.

The New Zealanders soon came on board and began making calls, writing letters and getting in the ears of their politicians. They were tireless. The story captured something of the ANZAC myth – individual courage and endurance against a backdrop of official blindness and incompetence. Compensation didn't drive these men, it was their growing need to be acknowledged as telling the truth about their war.

Finally in 1987, almost a decade after Steilberg first told his story and more than 40 years after the end of the war, the governments of both countries officially recognised the experiences of the men and offered modest ex-gratia compensation. Up to 20 Australians and New Zealanders were held in Terezín. These men were soon joined by POW survivors of Buchenwald and the government finally called on all of the concentration camp men to come forward with their claims. Their only weapon had been the power of the word and their stories of personal experience. But looking back now, no government could prevail forever in denying their extraordinary and terrible truths.

Officialdom, however, remained unmoved on an astonishing allegation thrown up by the Terezín story. This was a claim that up to 40 Allied prisoners, including Australians and New Zealanders, may have been massacred at the anti-tank ditch near Terezín in March 1945.

A Czech witness alleged in several statements that a newly arrived group of POWs refused to get down into the ditch, citing Geneva Conventions protecting them from work on military installations. This witness said that supervisors from the Small Fortress and Waffen SS guards stationed nearby formed a semi-circle around the prisoners and fired wildly into them.

To this day no Australian government has investigated this claim, other than to obtain a 1963 court transcript that describes it. If there is any truth to this allegation and Australians were shot at Terezín, their stories may have gone to the grave forever.

Bob Slater migrated to Australia after the war. Before he died in 1993 he described "Digger" Steilberg as a man of great dignity. "The Gypsies have a word that's been watered down a lot in modern slang," Slater said. "It's a Romany word, pal, and it has a deep meaning. It means someone who is your comrade or brother in spirit, thought and feeling and in some ways it goes deeper than blood. I am very proud to call Digger my pal."

Another British cellmate at Terezín, Jim Ilott, a tough professional from the 1st Parachute Brigade, deserves the last word on Walter Steilberg. "If ever a man honoured his country with courage and loyalty, it was Wally, he was a great son of Australia," Ilott said. "Wally was our mainstay, he was the backbone of us all."

Walter Steilberg lives on the north coast of NSW and turns 90 this year (2009). He doesn't talk much about the war these days. Like many of the POWs in these pages, he has told his story. What is extraordinary about the man is that he told it when no one wanted to listen, even his own government.

And each time he told his story he faced the terrible demons of Terezín, an act of inspirational courage he repeated time and time again.

Glossary

2/:	Indicates a unit of the 2nd AIF in WW2.
2IC:	Second-in-Command – from a section to a whole Army. Usually responsible for administration.
2LT:	Second Lieutenant, usually a platoon commander of 30–45 men.
2nd AIF:	Second Australian Imperial Force, Australian Army of WW2.
AC:	Companion of the Order of Australia.
ADF:	Australian Defence Force.
AIF:	Australian Imperial Force, Australian Army of WW1.
AK:	Knight of the Order of Australia.
AM:	Member of the Order of Australia.
AMF:	Australian Military Forces.
ANZAC:	Australian and New Zealand Army Corps.
Appel:	German roll call.
ARA:	Australian Regular Army.
ATF:	Australian Task Force.
Attap:	Palm used on traditional village huts.
BDE:	Brigade, 3–4,000 men.
BDR:	Bombardier, corporal equivalent in artillery.
BEM:	British Empire Medal.
Benjo:	Japanese meaning "toilet".
BHQ:	Battalion headquarters.
Bn:	Battalion, 600–1,000 men.
Boob:	POW term for detention facility or lock up inside POW camps.
Bren Gun:	Light machinegun of WW2 and Korea.
BRIG:	Brigadier, commands a Brigade.
Bty:	Battery, 4–6 pieces of artillery.
Bty HQ:	Battery headquarters.
Bunker:	POW term for detention facility or lock up inside POW camps.
Burp Gun:	Type 50 Chinese sub-machinegun.
Byoke:	Japanese meaning "stick".
Campo di concentramento:	Italian meaning "main POW camp".
Campo di lavoro:	Italian meaning "work camp".
CAPT:	Captain, commanded a company in WW1, Company 2ICs thereafter.

CASEVAC:	Casualty evacuation.
CB:	The Order of the Bath – Companion.
CBE:	The Order of the British Empire – Commander.
CdeG:	Croix de Guerre.
CStG:	Cross of Saint George.
Chocko:	A conscripted militia soldier of WW2. Derived either from the derogatory term "chocolate soldier" (melts in battle) or the colour of the pugaree on their slouch hat.
CHQ:	Company headquarters.
CO:	Commanding Officer of a Battalion. Usually a LTCOL.
COL:	Colonel, generally a staff rank in a headquarters.
Coolies:	Asian conscripted laborers on the Burma-Thai railway.
COY:	Company, between 180 (WW1) and 120 men, commanded by a captain or major.
CORPS:	A formation of army troops with a common functionality, for example infantry, artillery, armour, engineers and signals.
CPL:	Corporal, usually commands a Section of 9–18 soldiers.
CQMS:	Company Quartermaster Sergeant, who provides logistic support to a company.
CSC:	Conspicuous Service Cross.
CSM:	Company Sergeant Major, a Warrant Officer Class Two responsible for supporting a company commander in relation to discipline, administration and personnel.
CSM:	Conspicuous Service Medal.
CVO:	The Royal Victorian Order – Commander.
D-Day:	D-Day is the day on which an operation is to be initiated. D-Day often represents a variable, designating the day upon which some significant event will occur or has occurred, for example, D-3 is three days prior, D+1 is one day after, and so on. The most commonly known D-Day was 6th June, 1944, when British, Canadian and United States troops landed along the Normandy coast of France. They landed by air and sea on five codenamed beaches – the Americans on "Utah" and "Omaha", the British on "Gold" and "Sword", and the Canadians on "Juno".
DCM:	Distinguished Conduct Medal.
DET:	Detachment, a small group of soldiers.
DIV:	Division, 15,000–20,000 men commanded by a major general.
Dixie:	A soldier's eating plate consisting of two metal containers. A smaller one fits inside a larger one to conserve space.
Doover:	An old/alternative term for "hutchie".
DSM:	Distinguished Service Medal.
DSO:	Distinguished Service Order.

Durry/Durrie:	Slang for cigarette.
DVR:	Driver.
ENG:	Engineers, responsible for providing mobility to a unit or depriving mobility from the enemy.
Esprit de corps:	Morale of a group, unit or body of soldiers.
FO:	Forward observer.
Fritz:	Derogatory term for Germans, from Frederick the Great.
Geneva Convention:	A series of international laws on the conduct expected towards captured and wounded soldiers and non-combatants. The Conventions have been revised between 1864 and 1949 with four Conventions defining the treatment of these particular "protected peoples".
GESTAPO:	Geheim Staats Polizei (Nazi secret police).
Ghurka:	(also Gorkha) People from Nepal and parts of North India, who take their name from the eighth century Hindu warrior-saint Guru Gorakhnath. Gurkhas are best known for their history of bravery and strength in the British Army's Brigade of Gurkhas and the Indian Army's Gorkha regiments.
GNR:	Gunner, Artillery Soldier.
GOC:	General Officer Commanding.
Godown:	Slang term for warehouse.
Goons:	Term for German guards in a POW camp.
Hague Convention:	A series of international laws involved primarily with the conduct of a war and rules of engagement. Two versions were created: one in 1899 and the other in 1907.
Hausfrau:	German housewife.
Heinkel:	German plane – bomber.
HMAS:	Her (or His) Majesty's Australian ships.
Hoochie/Hutchie:	A soldier's tent in the field consisting of a waterproof sheet which can be joined together to form a larger tent.
Hun:	Derogatory term for Germans, from the 452 sacking of Rome by Barbarians.
Itais:	Slang for Italian soldier.
Japs:	Slang for Japanese soldier.
Jerry:	German soldier. A WW1 English term used to describe either a common German first name, or the shape of the German helmet that looked like a chamber pot, which was commonly called a "Jerry".
KBE:	The Order of the British Empire – Knight Commander.
KCMG:	The Order of St Michael and St George – Knight Commander.
KCVO:	The Royal Victorian Order – Knight Commander.
Kempetai:	Japanese secret police.

KIA:	Killed in action, killed by direct enemy action.
Kriesgefangener:	German for POW.
KStJ:	Knight of the Most Venerable Order of St John of Jerusalem.
Lager:	German term for a POW camp.
LCPL:	Lance Corporal, Section 2IC. Second-in-command.
LOCSTAT:	Grid reference of troops.
LST:	Landing ship tank.
LT:	Lieutenant, usually a platoon commander commanding 30–45 men.
LTCOL:	Lieutenant Colonel, usually commands a battalion of 600–1,000 men.
Luftag:	German POW camp for airmen.
LVO:	The Royal Victorian Order – Lieutenant.
MAJ:	Major, commands a company (post-WW1) of 120 men.
MAJGEN:	Major General, commands a division of 15,000–20,000 men.
Mangelwurst:	Meaning "lack sausage". Colloquial term used by prisoners in German camps to describe sausages made of sawdust, fat and meal.
Mauser:	German bolt action rifle.
MBE:	Member of the British Empire.
MC:	Military Cross.
Messerschmitt:	From the German company that produced fighters, like the Me-109, or jet fighter, like the Me-262.
MG:	Machinegun.
MIA:	Missing in action. Cannot be accounted for after enemy action, as either dead, wounded or captured.
MID:	Mention In Dispatches.
Mini-Warfa:	German mortar of WW1.
MM:	Military Medal.
MO:	Medical Officer. A doctor working in a battalion or regiment. Technically an MO was a non-combatant and could choose to be repatriated under the Geneva Convention.
MP:	Military police.
Nasho:	National Servicemen, a conscript between 1951 and 1972.
NATO:	North Atlantic Treaty Organisation is a military alliance formed on 4th April, 1949. There are currently 26 countries within the Alliance.
NCO:	Non-commissioned officer, LCPL-WO1.
Nippon:	Term used for Japanese, derived from Dai Nippon, meaning "Great Japan".
NZ:	New Zealand.

OAM:	Medal of the Order of Australia.
OC:	Officer Commanding. Commands a company of 120–180 men.
Oflag/ Offizierslager:	German POW camp for officers.
OP:	Observation post.
Owen Gun:	Sub-machinegun of WW2.
Pap:	Rice and water mixture that is both glutinous and very unappetising.
Panzer:	Panzerkampfwagen, German tanks.
PF:	Police force.
PLA:	Peoples Liberation Army (China).
POGO/POG(S):	The acronym given to any service corps soldiers (non-combatants) or "posted on garrison duty" soldiers.
Pommy:	Slang for British soldier.
POW/PW:	Prisoner of war.
Prigioneri di guerra:	Italian meaning "POW".
PTE:	Private, soldier…The Aussie Digger.
RAA:	Royal Australian Artillery.
RAASC:	Royal Australian Army Service Corps.
RAE:	Royal Australian Engineers.
RAEME:	Royal Australian Electrical and Mechanical Engineers.
RAINF:	Royal Australian Infantry.
RAP:	Regimental aid post.
RAR:	Royal Australian Regiment.
Reg:	Regular (full-time) Soldier.
Regt:	Regiment. Either a general term for a group of units, an armoured battalion-sized unit or 3 batteries of guns (12–18 pieces of artillery).
RNSWR:	Royal New South Wales Regiment.
RNZA:	Royal New Zealand Army.
ROE:	Rules of engagement.
RPG:	Rocket propelled grenade.
RSM:	Regimental Sergeant Major, a WO1 who supports a CO in matters of discipline, and personnel. It is the most senior rank of the non-commissioned officers. In addition, the senior Warrant Officer in the Australian Army holds the unique rank of Warrant Officer and the appointment of Regimental Sergeant Major of the Army (RSM-A).
RV:	Rendezvous point.
SASR:	Special Air Service Regiment.
Section:	9–18 men, commanded by a corporal.

SGT:	Sergeant, generally a second in command of a platoon.
SLR:	Self-loading rifle. Semi-automatic rifle, 7.62mm in caliber.
SM:	Sergeant-Major.
Spandau:	German light machinegun
"Speedo":	Period when work on the Burma-Thai railway line sped up as it was behind schedule.
SPR:	Sapper, engineering equivalent of a private.
SS – *Schutzstaffel:*	"Protection squad", Hitler's elite troops.
Stalag/ Stammlager:	German POW camp for non-commissioned soldiers.
Stuka:	German plane – bomber.
TAOR:	Tactical area of responsibility.
Tenko:	Japanese meaning "parade".
Tommy:	British soldier. The origins of the name go back to a sample pay book in the 18th century where the name Thomas Atkins appeared. In many ways it is the equivalent of having John Citizen on a sample credit card.
Tommy gun:	Term for either a Thompson sub machinegun, or any sub-machinegun in general.
TPR:	Trooper, SAS or armoured corps, equivalent of a private.
Troop:	A platoon-sized unit of the SAS or armour/cavalry.
Turk:	Turkish soldier, WW1.
UN:	United Nations.
Unit:	A group of soldiers of battalion, battery or armoured regiment size. Around 600–1,000 men.
VC:	Victoria Cross.
Vino:	Italian for wine.
Wehrmacht:	German Army.
WO1:	Warrant Officer First Class, generally a Regimental Sergeant Major.
WO2:	Warrant Officer Second Class, generally a Company Sergeant Major.
WWI/WW1:	World War One.
WWII/WW2:	World War Two.
Yank:	Slang for American soldier.

Contributors

Anderson, Charles, Singapore, 1942

Anderton, Norman, Singapore, 1942

Armstrong, Richard, Singapore, 1942

Ashby, Lindley, Crete, 1941

Benoit, Max, Singapore, 1942

Botterill, Keith, Singapore, 1942

Bourne, Alexander, Singapore, 1942

Braithwaite, Dick, Singapore, 1942

Brough, Ernest, El Alamein, 1942

Brown, Ray, Singapore, 1942

Bullwinkel, Vivian, Bangka Island, 1942

Burkitt, Alfred, Java, 1942

Calder, Jack, El Alamein, 1942

Campbell, Owen, Singapore, 1942

Churches, Ralph, Greece, 1941

Condon, Denis, Korea, 1952

Connor, Jim, Singapore, 1942

Cornford, Roydon, Java, 1942

Crawford, Doug, Greece, 1941

Crooks, John, Greece, 1941

Daff, Frank, Pretoria, 1900

Davis, Richard Harding, Pretoria, 1900

Dawson, Justin, France, 1917

Dodd, Keith, Mediterranean Sea, 1941

Doddy, Don, Singapore, 1942

Donnelly, Eric, Korea, 1953

Drower, Bill, Singapore, 1942

Dumbrell, Ken, Singapore, 1942

Edmunds, Leslie 'Brick', Crete, 1941

Fairbairn, Terry, Crete, 1941

Fairclough, Milton 'Snow', Java, 1942

Flanagan, Arch, Singapore, 1942

Flowers, Bill, Singapore, 1942

Gafney, Gordon, Singapore, 1942

Ganson, Horace, France, 1917

Gilbert, Cyril, Singapore, 1942

Gooley, Len, Singapore, 1942

Gray, Ken, Singapore, 1942

Greer, Lanny, Thailand, 1942

Gregson, Robert 'George', Singapore, 1942

Greville, Phil, Korea, 1952

Griffin, David, Singapore, 1942

Guthrie, Ron, Korea, 1951

Hackney, Ben, Singapore, 1942

Handsley, George, Romani, 1916

Harnett, Hal, Pretoria, 1900

Haskell, Bill, Java, 1942

Hawkes, John, El Alamein, 1942

Hendry, Peter, Singapore, 1942

Heron, 'Blue', Germany, 1941

Hodel, Fred, Singapore, 1942

Hoffman, William, El Alamein, 1942

Holding, Walter 'Wally', Singapore, 1942

Hollis, Tom, Korea, 1951

Hooper, Keith, Crete, 1941

Hunter, Rick, Crete, 1941

Jacobs, Jim, Singapore, 1942

Jamieson, Gordon, Singapore, 1942

Kerr, Jim, Singapore, 1942

Kidley, Mick, Singapore, 1942

LeFevre, Doug, El Alamein, 1942

Lindley, Reginald, Crete, 1941

Ling, Jim, Singapore, 1942

Lister, Ron, Crete, 1941

MacPherson, Neil, Java, 1942

Manly, Bill, Somme, 1916

Manning, Les, Crete, 1941

McCauley, Jim, Libya, 1941

McCracken, James, North Africa, 1942

McDonald, Murray, Greece, 1941

McDonald, Stan, Greece, 1941

McLaren, Don, Singapore, 1942

McWilliams, John, El Alamein, 1942

Merrigan, Neville, Singapore, 1942

Mettam, Bert, Singapore, 1942

Middleton, Ray, El Alamein, 1942

Morgan, George, Singapore, 1942

Morley, George, Crete, 1941

Moxham, William 'Dick', Singapore, 1942

Nelson, Gordon, Singapore, 1942

Nix, Doug, Greece, 1941

O'Donnell, Jack, Singapore, 1942

Parker, Jim, Singapore, 1942

Parker, Robert 'Bob', Korea, 1951

Pledger, Tom, Ambon, 1942

Prosser, John, Timor, 1942

Richardson, Leslie, Suez Canal, 1916

Rowe, Bill, Singapore, 1942

Rudd, Bill, El Alamein, 1942

Short, Nelson, Singapore, 1942

Smith, Fred Ransome, Singapore,1942

Smith, George, Korea, 1953

Smith, L.H, Palestine, 1917

Smith, Thomas, Singapore, 1942

Sproull, Robert, Singapore, 1942

Steilberg, Walter, Greece, 1941

Sticpewich, Hector 'Bill', Singapore, 1942

Stone, Alfred, Greece, 1941

Stone, Eric, Singapore, 1942

Taylor, Tommy, Bullecourt, 1917

Thorpe, Jack, Java, 1942

Underwood, Geoffrey, Singapore, 1942

Veitch, Gerard Harvey, Singapore, 1942

Venables, Max, Singapore, 1942

Vernon, Hugh, South Africa, 1900

Walsh, Paddy, Singapore, 1942

Webster, Malcolm, Crete, 1941

West, Lansell, Crete, 1941

Wharton, Willoby 'Bill', Singapore, 1942

Wheeler, Jim, Bullecourt, 1917

Wheeler, Ray, Singapore, 1942

White, Thomas, Mesopotamia, 1915

Whitehead, Archie, Crete, 1941

Whitmore, Ted, Singapore, 1942

Wood, Ken, Singapore, 1942

Yacopetti, Charlie, Korea, 1953

Young, Bill, Singapore, 1942

Zeeno, Joe, Singapore, 1942

Note: Some soldier's names have been withheld over the years for reasons of security or medical confidentiality. These contributors appear as "Unnamed Soldier", "Anonymous Soldier", "Boer Prisoner" or "Unnamed Officer"

Bibliography

Books and Periodicals

Davis, R.H., *With Both Armies in South Africa*, Charles Scribner's Sons, New York, 1901.

Dennis, P., Grey, J., Morris, E., Prior, R., & Connor, J., *The Oxford Companion to Australian Military History*, Oxford University Press, Melbourne, 1997.

Department of Defence, *How Germans treated Australian Prisoners of War*, Department of Defence, Melbourne, 1919.

Dornan, P., *Nicky Barr, An Australian Air Ace: a story of courage and adventure*, Allen & Unwin, Sydney, 2005.

Dunlop, E.E., *The war diaries of Weary Dunlop: Java and the Burma-Thailand*, Penguin, Melbourne, 1990.

Johnston, Dr. M., *The Japanese Advance 1941—1942 Australians in the Pacific War*, Department of Veterans' Affairs, Canberra, 2007.

McDonald, M., (ed.), *Changi*, ABC Books, Sydney, 1992.

Moremon, Dr. J., *Burma and India 1941—1945 Australians in the Pacific War*, Department of Veterans' Affairs, Canberra, 2006.

Morley, G., *Escape From Stalag 18a*, Meni Publishing, Cranbourne, Australia, 2007.

Nelson, G., *Men of the Line Building the Burma–Thai Railway 1942—1945*, Australian Military History Publications, Loftus, Australia, 2005.

Nelson, Professor H., *Australian Prisoners of War 1941—1945 Australians in the Pacific War*, Department of Veterans' Affairs, Canberra, 2007.

Newton, R.W., *The Grim Glory, The Official History of 2/19 Battalion AIF*, 1/19 RNSWR Association, NSW, 2006.

Pierce, M. and Kirkland, F., *Korea Remembered*, Department of Defence, Canberra, 1998.

Rea, P., *Voices from the Fortress*, ABC Books, Sydney, 2007.

Reid, Dr. R., *Sandakan 1942–1945*, Department of Veterans' Affairs, Canberra, 2008.

Reid, Dr. R., *Stolen Years: Australian prisoners of war*, Department of Veterans' Affairs, Canberra, 2002.

Silver, L.R., *Sandakan: A Conspiracy of Silence*, Sally Milner, Binda, Australia, 1998.

Sissons, D.C.S., *The Australian War Crimes Trials and Investigations (1942—51), research paper*, Australian National University, Canberra, n.d.

Smith, K., *Borneo, Australia's Proud But Tragic Heritage*, K.Smith, Armidale, Australia, 1999.

Stanley, Dr. P., *Borneo 1942—1945 Australians in the Pacific War*, Department of Veterans' Affairs, Canberra, 2007.

The Royal Air Force's ex-Prisoners of War Association (Australian Division), WA, *Silk and Barbed Wire*, Sage Pages, Perth, 2000.

Wall, D., *The Heroes of F Force*, D. Wall, Sydney, 1993.

White, T., *Guests of the Unspeakable*, Hamilton, London, 1928.

Wood-Higgs, S., *Bamboo and Barbed Wire*, Roman Press, Bournemouth, UK, 1988.

Wright, P., *The Men Of The Line, Stories of the Thai—Burma Railway Survivors*, Miegunyah Press, Melbourne, 2008.

Private Manuscripts, Journals and Diaries

Armstrong, R., *Return from the land of milk and honey, a true story of living hell*.

Burkitt, R., *The Diary of Sergeant A.J.E. Burkitt, 2/2 Pioneer Battalion, 1941—1945*.

Churches, R., *A Hundred Miles as the Crow Flies*.

Crooks, J., *My Little War*.

Flowers, W., *A Recollection by Bill Flowers of his time with 2/9th Field Ambulance, 8th Division, AIF*.

Hoffman, W., *Prisoner of War Account.*

Holding, W., *World War Two experiences of Walter Holding.*

Jacobs, J., *The Burma Railway. One Man's Story.*

Layton, K., *Don's Story–Personal Memoir of Don Doddy.*

Lister, R., *I Missed the Boat.*

Manning, L., *The Wrong Boat.*

Middleton, R., *My War.*

Smith, David F, *Memoirs of F Force, Thai—Burma Railway.*

Thorpe, J., *Bloody Lucky.*

Veitch, G., *War Diary and recollections whilst overseas with the 2nd AIF.*

Interview Extracts

Extract of interviews with Sir David Griffin, Lady Griffin and Jim Connor from *Compass*, "Changi Days", first published by ABC Online, 27 April 2003, is reproduced by permission of the Australian Broadcasting Corporation and ABC Online. (c) 2003 ABC. All rights reserved.

Extract of interviews with Fred Hodel, Ray Brown, Bill Young and Roydon Cornford from *Four Corners*, "No Prisoners", first broadcast by ABC, 11 March 2002, is reproduced by permission of the Australian Broadcasting Corporation and ABC Online. (c) 2002 ABC. All rights reserved.

Extract of interview with Ralph Churches from *Lateline*, "100 POWs make Great Escape", first published by ABC Online, 13 October 2003, is reproduced by permission of the Australian Broadcasting Corporation and ABC Online. (c) 2003 ABC. All rights reserved.

Websites

ANZAC – A Grateful State Remembers, WA:
www.anzac.dpc.wa.gov.au

AIF POW Freemen in Europe: www.aifpow.com

Australian Army: www.army.gov.au

Australian Army newspaper: www.army.gov.au/news/armynews

Australians At War: www.australiansatwar.gov.au

Australians At War film archive:
www.australiansatwarfilmarchive.gov.au

Australian Boer War Memorial: www.bwm.org.au

Australian Broadcasting Commission – *Four Corners*:
www.abc.net.au/4corners

Australian Broadcasting Commission – *Compass*:
www.abc.net.au/compass/s841311.htm

Australia's War 1939—1945: www.ww2australia.gov.au

Australian War Memorial: www.awm.gov.au

Burma Thailand Railway Memorial: www.btrma.org.au

Department of Defence: www.defence.gov.au

Department of Defence, Army History Unit:
www.defence.gov.au/army/ahu

Digger history: www.diggerhistory.info

Geneva Conventions: www.genevaconventions.org

Hague Conference on Private International Law: www.hcch.net

International Federation of Red Cross: www.ifrc.org

International humanitarian law treaties and documents:
www.icrc.org/ihl.nsf

Kingston Historical Website – Boer War:
www.localhistory.kingston.vic.gov.au

Korea Veterans' Association of Australia Inc:
www.austkoreavets.asn.au

Korean war site: www.rt66.com/~korteng/SmallArms

National Archives of Australia: www.naa.gov.au

Prisoners of War of the Japanese 1942—1945:
www.pows-of-japan.net

Red Cross: www.redcross.int

South Australians at war: www.slsa.sa.gov.au/saatwar

South Australian State Library, SA Memory: www.samemory.sa.gov.au

Stalag 18A: www.stalag18a.org.uk

Thailand—Burma Railway Centre: www.tbrconline.com

Tom Pledger's Prisoner of War Diary 1940—45: http://members.ozemail.com.au/~pledgerp/PLEPOW.HTM

United Nations Human Rights: www.ohchr.org

Victorians at war: www.victoriansatwar.net

Visit Gallipoli: www.anzacsite.gov.au/

War and identity education: www.warandidentity.com.au

Wikipedia: www.wikipedia.org

World War Two Nominal Role: www.ww2roll.gov.au

Photos Courtesy of:

Australian War Memorial
Photos courtesy of the Australian War Memorial.
AWM Negative Number 133913
AWM Negative Number 101099
AWM Negative Number 121782
AWM Negative Number 123170
AWM Negative Number ART25107
AWM Negative Number P03960.001
AWM Negative Number P01981.022
AWM Negative Number P00866.001
AWM Negative Number P03236.004
AWM Negative Number P00305.001
AWM Negative Number P03473.006
AWM Negative Number RELAWM16875
AWM Negative Number 116061 (back cover image)
POWs released from Changi camp were evacuated from Singapore by the Australian Hospital Ship *Manunda*. A Red Cross worker handing out cakes to ex-prisoners of war waiting on stretchers to be carried aboard the *Manunda*.

National Library of Australia
Photos courtesy of the National Library of Australia.
VNA4227532
AN615200
VN3107073
VN4227531
VN3585436 photo also courtesy of artist,
Ward O'Neill and the *Sydney Morning Herald*

State Library of South Australia
Photos courtesy of the State Library of South Australia.
PRG1300/15/5
PRG1300/15/16
SRG770/40/179
PRG1300/15/17
PRG1300/15/12
PRG1300/15/9
PRG1300/15/4

State Library of Victoria
Photos courtesy of the State Library of Victoria,
Argus newspaper collection of photographs.
H.98.103/4690
H.98.103/4705
H.99.201/809
H.98.103/4080
H.98.103/4085
H.98.103/4150
H.98.103/4185
H.98.103/4205
H.98.103/4221
H.98.103/3434
H.98.103/3435
H.98.103/3437
H.2002.199/2990

Private Collections
Doug Nix
Fred Ransome Smith
Jack Calder
Jack Thorpe
Les Manning
Malcolm Campbell
Reginald Lindley
Richard Leggo

Index

Index

Index

"He is the raw steel whose spirit has been forged in the furnace of war from the Boer campaign and Gallipoli to the present day conflicts. It has hardened under fire in difficult situations during the desert and jungle campaigns of WW2, Korea, Borneo and Vietnam. It was then tempered under modern conflicts which have been far different, where compassion, understanding and patience are as much a part of the soldier's kitbag as his war fighting skills."

Warrant Officer Arthur Francis, CSC, OAM, ex-RSM Army

Compassion, Mateship, Courage, Initiative, Loyalty, Integrity and Trust.

These core values are the backbone of the soldier and are highlighted in the personal anecdotes and stories recounted in *Aussie Soldier up close and personal.*

From World War One to the modern day conflict, Australian soldiers young and old provide an up close and personal perspective on the Army's core values and how being a soldier is more then just putting on a uniform.

With anecdotes and excerpts from diaries that have never been published, plus stories and personal perspectives from the battle grounds of Europe, the jungles of New Guinea and Vietnam, the desert sands of Iraq, the complexities of Afghanistan as well as the peace keeping missions in Rwanda, Timor and Somalia, our soldiers' honest and thoughtful accounts run the gamut of emotions.

In addition *Aussie Soldier* includes stories about the Larrikin, Close Calls in Battle, extracts of Diaries and Letters as well as a Battle Book that summarises some of Australia's most famous battles.

Confronting, thoughtful and with a sense of humour the collection of stories featured in *Aussie Soldier* provide an insight into the human side of a high profile and often misconstrued field of expertise.

Available at all good bookstores or purchase online at www.bigskypublishing.com.au
Postage within Australia is free. PO Box 303, Newport NSW 2106 Australia Ph: +61 2 9918 2168 Fx: +61 2 9918 2396

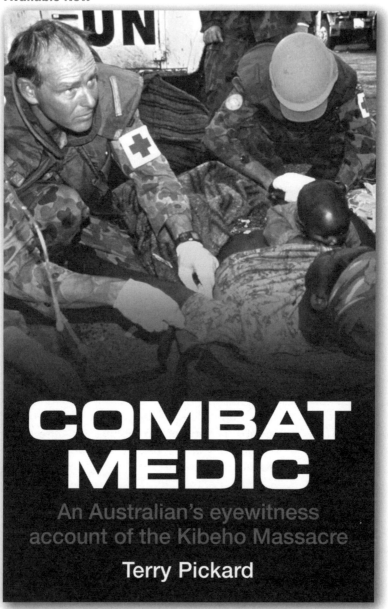

COMBAT MEDIC

An Australian's eyewitness account of the Kibeho Massacre

Terry Pickard

The Kibeho Massacare. Living With The Scars.

"I was one of 32 Australian soldiers in the area. We were facing more than 2000 RPA soldiers. We were good, but not that good. The numbers were heavily in their favour. I was worried but I wasn't scared. All I had where questions. How the hell had a medical mercy mission ended in such a horrific tragedy? How had it been allowed to even get to this? Why were we not allowed to fire our weapons, to defend these poor refugees? God, I thought, I hope we live through this day. And if we do, I tell you what, won't I have a story to tell."

Terry Pickard

On the 22nd of April 1995 more than 4,000 Rwandans were massacred and thousands more injured in a place called Kibeho. Terry Pickard, a seasoned soldier and medic, was one of a 32-strong force of Australian UN peacekeepers in Kibeho on that terrible Saturday. While the United Nations' presence prevented the death toll from being even worse than it was, the massacre continues to haunt him.

The rules of engagement that stopped him from intervening in the senseless slaughter and the life and death decisions he was forced to make when dealing with the injured condemned him to more than a decade of recurring nightmares and debilitating flashbacks.

The horror and unimaginable tragedy of the Kibeho Massacre still looms large in the lives of Rwandans and the people sent to help the African country. No one who walked away from that day was ever the same again.

Combat Medic is a personal account of one Australian soldier who found himself at the centre of events that shocked the world, and the personal toll that he paid.

Terry Pickard's army career spanned nearly 20 years. More than 15 years after Rwanda he continues to struggle with post traumatic stress triggered by his experiences.

Available at all good bookstores or purchase online at www.bigskypublishing.com.au
Postage within Australia is free. PO Box 303, Newport NSW 2106 Australia Ph: +61 2 9918 2168 Fx: +61 2 9918 2396

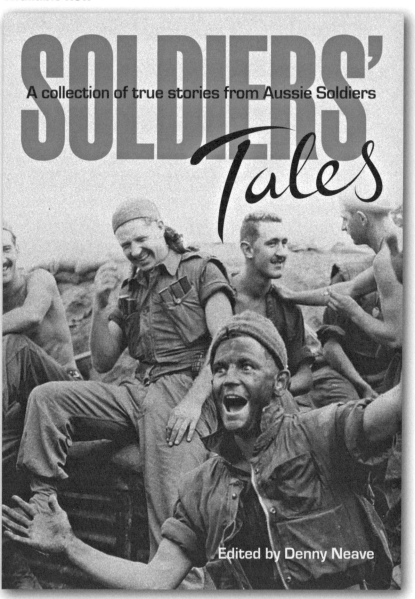

" Plodding through mud up to the knees for days on end with a 25lb pack plus weapons and ammunition made me curse the war in no uncertain terms. Then one day I heard a soldier behind me praying, 'Dear God, help me pick up me feet, I'll put the bastards down."

Captain Glenn Davidson, New Guinea, WWII

A collection of stories that are entertaining, emotional and humorous, *Soldiers' Tales* is a wonderful tribute to the Aussie Digger.

From World War One to the modern day conflict, Australian soldiers share their stories and anecdotes usually saved for Anzac Day or a catch-up with mates over a cup of tea or an icy cold beer.

In their own words they provide a fascinating glimpse of the many funny and touching moments that our Diggers often hold tight to their chest. The collection of stories featured in *Soldiers' Tales* vividly provides a taste of what a soldier's life is like in both war and peace.

From the pyramids of Egypt where a pint-sized Captain used lateral thinking to gain respect, Anzac day on the porch with Banjo Patterson or a scorpion in the pants in Vietnam, their stories showcase the laconic sense of humour of the Aussie digger – that wonderful ability to get the job done with a sense of fun and a helping hand for a mate.

Soldiers' Tales is a collection of yarns to warm the heart and bring a smile to your face or a tear to the eye. A wonderful collection of stories that will delight readers of all ages and linger on well after the book has been put aside.

Available at all good bookstores or purchase online at www.bigskypublishing.com.au
Postage within Australia is free. PO Box 303, Newport NSW 2106 Australia Ph: +61 2 9918 2168 Fx: +61 2 9918 2396

Available September 2009

PURE
massacre

Aussie soldiers reflect on
the Rwandan Genocide

Kevin O'Halloran

BIG SKY PUBLISHING

"To be actually there, seeing piles of dead kids and babies lying there next to their mothers, and not being able to stop it is what really got to me. After seeing all the wounded and dead, my opinion of the UN changed. I thought we were sent here to help these people not to sit back and let them get slaughtered."

Private P.V. Commerford

Rwanda is no stranger to violence. In 1994, an orgy of killing swept across the tiny land-locked nation and genocide, the size and magnitude unseen since the Hitler horrors of WWII, erupted. Around one million men, women and children were mercilessly shot, hacked to death or burnt alive.

To alleviate the suffering and restore order to shattered lives, a group of Australian UN peacekeepers, made up of soldiers and army medical personnel, was sent to Rwanda under a United Nations mandate. These Australians would be exposed to a lack of humanity they were not prepared for and found hard to fathom.

On 22nd April 1995, the daily horror and tragedy they had witnessed escalated out of control. At a displaced persons' camp in Kibeho, in full view of the Australian soldiers, over 4,000 unarmed men, women and children died in a hail of bullets, grenades and machete blades at the hands of the Rwandan Patriotic Army. Constrained by the UN peacekeeping Rules of Engagement, these Australians could only watch helplessly and try to assist the wounded under the gaze of the trigger-happy killers.

Pure Massacre is a record of what happened during this peacekeeping mission. Kevin "Irish" O'Halloran, a Platoon Sergeant at the time, stresses the weaknesses of the UN charter and what happens when "good men do nothing". He pulls together the perspectives of those Australian soldiers who served in Rwanda at this time. *Pure Massacre* gives a new and personal voice to the Kibeho Massacre.

It takes a special type of bravery, discipline and compassion to do what these soldiers did. Little did they know, when the second tour of Rwanda was over, that they would be the highest decorated UN peacekeeping contingent since the Korean War. For many, their service in Rwanda would come with a personal toll. No Australians died during and immediately after the massacre at Kibeho, but as *Pure Massacre* testifies, the suffering and tragedy is embedded in their memories.

Available at all good bookstores or purchase online at www.bigskypublishing.com.au
Postage within Australia is free. PO Box 303, Newport NSW 2106 Australia Ph: +61 2 9918 2168 Fx: +61 2 9918 2396

Aussie SOLDIER

HELP WITH OUR NEXT BOOKS

Aussie Soldier – Iraq and Afghanistan
Aussie Soldier – Peacekeepers

Are you interested in participating in the next *Aussie Soldier* book?

If you have served in either Iraq or Afghanistan, or on a peacekeeping mission and are interested in sharing your own experiences in the next *Aussie Soldier* book we would like to hear from you.

Register by email to **military@bigskypublishing.com.au** or by post.

Simply include your name, contact details, unit, year of deployment and a brief statement in relation to your contribution.

All contributions welcome so have your say.

General Submissions
If you believe you can help with the above projects or have a manuscript or contributions that you are interested in publishing please contact us or visit our website for information regarding submission guidelines.

Big Sky Publishing
PO Box 303
Newport NSW 2106

Email:
General   **info@bigskypublishing.com.au**
Military   **military@bigskypublishing.com.au**

Visit **www.bigskypublishing.com.au** for further information including other projects and books.